EAVESDROPPING IN THE NOVEL FROM AUSTEN TO PROUST

Eavesdropping in the Novel from Austen to Proust investigates human curiosity and its representation in eavesdropping scenes in nineteenth-century English and French novels. Ann Gaylin argues that eavesdropping dramatizes a primal human urge to know and offers a paradigm of narrative transmission and reception of information among characters, narrators, and readers. Gaylin sheds light on the social and psychological effects of the nineteenth-century rise of information technology and accelerated flow of information, as manifested in the anxieties about – and delight in – displays of private life and its secrets. Analyzing eavesdropping in Austen, Balzac, Dickens, Collins, and Proust, she demonstrates the flexibility of the scene to produce narrative complication or resolution, to foreground questions of gender and narrative agency, and to place the debates of privacy and publicity within the literal and metaphoric spaces of the nineteenth-century novel. This innovative study will be of interest to scholars of nineteenth-century English and European literature.

ANN GAYLIN is Associate Professor of Comparative Literature at Yale University. She has published articles on Wilkie Collins and Marcel Proust. Her articles have appeared in *Texas Studies in Literature and Language* and the *Cincinnati Romance Review*.

CAMBRIDGE STUDIES IN NINETEENTH-CENTURY
LITERATURE AND CULTURE

General editor
Gillian Beer, *University of Cambridge*

Editorial board
Isobel Armstrong, *Birkbeck College, London*
Leonore Davidoff, *University of Essex*
Terry Eagleton, *University of Manchester*
Catherine Gallagher, *University of California, Berkeley*
D. A. Miller, *Columbia University*
J. Hillis Miller, *University of California, Irvine*
Mary Poovey, *New York University*
Elaine Showalter, *Princeton University*

Nineteenth-century British literature and culture have been rich fields for interdisciplinary studies. Since the turn of the twentieth century, scholars and critics have tracked the intersections and tensions between Victorian literature and the visual arts, politics, social organisation, economic life, technical innovations, scientific thought – in short, culture in its broadest sense. In recent years, theoretical challenges and historiographical shifts have unsettled the assumptions of previous scholarly synthesis and called into question the terms of older debates. Whereas the tendency in much past literary critical interpretation was to use the metaphor of culture as "background," feminist, Foucauldian, and other analyses have employed more dynamic models that raise questions of power and of circulation. Such developments have reanimated the field.

This series aims to accommodate and promote the most interesting work being undertaken on the frontiers of the field of nineteenth-century literary studies: work that intersects fruitfully with other fields of study such as history, or literary theory, or the history of science. Comparative as well as interdisciplinary approaches are welcomed.

A complete list of titles published will be found at the end of the book.

EAVESDROPPING IN THE NOVEL FROM AUSTEN TO PROUST

ANN GAYLIN

CAMBRIDGE UNIVERSITY PRESS

PUBLISHED BY THE PRESS SYNDICATE OF THE UNIVERSITY OF CAMBRIDGE
The Pitt Building, Trumpington Street, Cambridge, United Kingdom

CAMBRIDGE UNIVERSITY PRESS
The Edinburgh Building, Cambridge CB2 2RU, UK
40 West 20th Street, New York, NY 10011-4211, USA
477 Williamstown Road, Port Melbourne, VIC 3207, Australia
Ruiz de Alarcón 13, 28014 Madrid, Spain
Dock House, The Waterfront, Cape Town 8001, South Africa

http://www.cambridge.org

© Ann Gaylin 2002

This book is in copyright. Subject to statutory exception
and to the provisions of relevant collective licensing agreements,
no reproduction of any part may take place without
the written permission of Cambridge University Press.

First published 2002

Printed in the United Kingdom at the University Press, Cambridge

Typeface Baskerville Monotype 11/12.5 pt.   *System* LaTeX 2ε   [TB]

A catalogue record for this book is available from the British Library

Library of Congress cataloguing in publication data
Gaylin, Ann Elizabeth.
Eavesdropping in the novel from Austen to Proust / Ann Gaylin.
p.   cm.
Cambridge studies in nineteenth-century literature and culture; 37
Includes bibliographical references and index.
ISBN 0 521 81585 1
1. English fiction–19th century – History and criticism.   2. Eavesdropping in literature.
3. Austen, Jane, 1775–1817 – Views on eavesdropping.   4. Collins, Wilkie, 1824–1889 – Views on eavesdropping.   5. Balzac, Honorâ de, 1799–1850 – Views on eavesdropping.   6. Proust, Marcel, 1871–1922 – Views on eavesdropping.   7. Literature, Comparative – English and French.   8. Literature, Comparative – French and English.   9. French fiction – History and Criticism.
I. Title.   II. Series.
PR868.E25 G39   2002
823′.809353–dc21   2002025656

ISBN 0 521 81585 1 hardback

For my parents

Contents

Acknowledgments		*page* x
	Introduction	1
1.	I'm all ears: *Pride and Prejudice*, or the story behind the story	26
2.	Eavesdropping and the gentle art of *Persuasion*	42
3.	Household words: Balzac's and Dickens's domestic spaces	58
4.	The madwoman outside the attic: eavesdropping and narrative agency in *The Woman in White*	113
5.	*La double entente*: eavesdropping and identity in *A la recherche du temps perdu*	139
	Conclusion: covert listeners and secret agents	167
Notes		179
Select bibliography		222
Index		237

Acknowledgments

This book owes its existence to a diverse body of architects, those numerous official and unofficial planners who helped conceptualize and construct its eventual stories and wings. They helped fashion the public, intellectual chambers of this edifice as well as its private spaces, and the countless corridors and back hallways connecting them all. My collaboration with these individuals forms the vital if less obvious story behind this project, a tale I can only begin to tell in the space available here.

It is difficult to express the extent to which Maria DiBattista's knowledge, guidance, and friendship have shaped my work. I cannot adequately account for her generous gifts of time, energy, and intellectual attention to this project. Her reading of innumerable drafts, unfailing support, broad understanding of both the English and French literary traditions, and sensitivity to the narrative and moral concerns of the book have made her my ideal reader and my role model in this endeavor.

I am grateful to those who helped my thinking and writing in their early stages, including Thomas Pavel, U. C. Knoepflmacher, and A. Walton Litz. I would like to express my deep appreciation to colleagues at Yale who offered careful readings of the manuscript and made invaluable suggestions for improvement, particularly Peter Brooks, Shoshana Felman, Michael Holquist, Annabel Patterson, and David Quint. I give special thanks to other scholars who provided intellectual dialogue and helpful criticism: David Trotter, Laurie Langbauer, and the anonymous readers at Cambridge University Press. I am indebted to Princeton University, the Whiting Foundation, and Yale University for supporting the research and writing of this book in the form of graduate student, dissertation, and Morse Junior Faculty fellowships. I wish to thank everyone at Cambridge University Press who helped turn the idea of a book into a concrete reality. They include Gillian Beer, who supported the book's inclusion in the Cambridge series, and my editors, Linda Bree and Rachel DeWachter, who shepherded me and the project through all stages of its production.

Acknowledgments

I owe a special debt to those without formal roles in this project, who willingly gave of their private time and attention. Among these friends, Allan Hepburn holds a unique place. His unflagging support, generous sharing of knowledge, and canny editing assisted me at every stage in this long process. I am grateful to others who offered encouragement and an ever-ready ear: Thomas and Tiffany Arnold, Christos Cabolis, Tracy Chevalier, Margit Dementi, Maria Georgopoulou, Sarah Hardy, Derek Kreuger, Catherine Labio, Sara Laimon, Pericles Lewis, Niki Parisier, Kathy Rowe, Nancy Selleck, Susan Weiner, Paul Wapner, Nancy Worman, Wendy Zierler, and to many others whose contributions are too numerous to list. Finally, this book could not have been completed without the loving support of my family, especially my parents, who have always encouraged me to satisfy my intellectual curiosity and my fascination with other people's stories.

An earlier version of Chapter 4 appeared in *Texas Studies in Literature and Language* 43:3, pp. 303–33, and is printed in revised form by permission of the University of Texas Press. A preliminary version of the material in Chapter 5 appeared in the *Cincinnati Romance Review*, published by the University of Cincinnati. I thank Sotheby's Picture Library, London and the Tate Gallery, London/Art Resource, New York for permission to reproduce works in their collections.

Introduction

PROLEGOMENA

We all do it, although we deny it. We eavesdrop. Sometimes we listen in on others deliberately, more often inadvertently. Once hooked, we have trouble resisting the urge to listen, particularly if the conversation is interesting. Will she leave her husband? Will he take over the company? Whom does she really love? We try to make sense of what we have heard: we imagine, we plot, we interpret. We continue to eavesdrop.

This book aims to make sense of an activity to which we rarely admit, about which we hardly speculate, yet which has long been represented in fiction. Eavesdropping has existed in the novel as long as the novel has existed. Trained to think, to articulate, and to represent our ideas in visual terms, we tend to ignore the significance of hearing, and overhearing, in narrative.[1] It has been largely overlooked, or, if you will, underheard.[2] Appearing intermittently, eavesdropping dramatizes some of the fundamental issues that inform our hermeneutic and epistemological efforts. A nonconsensual, deceptive activity, it introduces intriguing moral questions about human interaction and subjectivity, since eavesdropping always depends on discovering connections among other people. A secret witness deliberately or unintentionally acquires information about others that may be used to villainous ends or may be kept benignly private. Overhearing affords ample opportunity for private information to become public or for secrets to fall into the wrong hands. Eavesdropping raises issues of privacy, publicity, and their spatial and psychological relations; it represents a process of acquiring secret knowledge about self and other. This study comprises not just a thematics of eavesdropping in the nineteenth-century novel, but an examination of a structural dynamic that underlies the motivation and reception of narrative in Austen, Balzac, Dickens, Collins, and Proust.

My point is not that eavesdropping is unique to the nineteenth-century novel, nor to narrative. Rather, I wish to dwell on the scene's paradigmatic status in the novel, to demonstrate how it crystallizes those particular aspects of individual narratives that seem most significant and, at the same time, reveals some of the basic impulses that motivate novelistic representation. Illicit listening in the novel stages the manner in which stories are generated and resolved. Such moments tend to expose the central issues around which specific narratives turn. Hence my approach to eavesdropping modulates according to the particular novel under consideration. My related argument about such topics as publicity and privacy and their relevance to novelistic representation is not meant to be prescriptive to the nineteenth century, but to demonstrate how such concerns acquire particular urgency in that era.

The word "eavesdropping" implies placement of a listener in space. "To eavesdrop" originally meant to stand within the "eavesdrop," or the space under the eaves of a building likely to receive rainwater from the roof. The word contains within it the concept of being near a private space (a house) and its secrets, and suggests a punishment for being so positioned; a person in the "eavesdrop" is likely to get wet. From this spatially oriented locution, which places an individual next to but not within an enclosed, protected space, eavesdropping comes to mean to listen secretly to the private conversation of others. The evolving meaning of the word changes from a physical encroachment on tangible private property to a metaphoric intrusion on psychological and discursive space. Eavesdropping suggests a particular sense of space: one that indicates boundaries of public and private areas, and transgressions of the former into the latter. It represents liminality: not being fully a part of the private world, but somewhat protected, while still part of the natural and public world. In its very demarcation, this border state presupposes the trespass of another individual's sense of private space. Such transgressive activity usually carries with it the threat of danger or physical injury to the trespasser. Illicit acts usually do not go unpunished.

In other languages, the locutions for eavesdropping also register the idea of location vis-à-vis privacy or domestic space, although in a less precise manner than in English. The German *lauschen*, meaning "to listen, strain one's ears, prick up one's ears, eavesdrop," offers an adjectival form *lauschenig*, which means "snug, cozy, idyllic; hidden, tucked away," and intimates a listening in on a space that is apart from a public area. The Russian *pod slushivanye* (literally, "underlistening") etymologically positions the eavesdropper in a hidden space close to the speakers.

Polish contains two locutions to express overhearing: *podsłuchiwanie* and *przysłuchiwanie*, where the former implies a transgression of privacy (being underneath the private conversation) and the latter a less morally weighted and less clandestine listening, usually in a semipublic place (the preposition *przy* meaning "next to" or "beside"). The French and Italian expressions for and prohibitions against eavesdropping, while not stressing a domestic environment, often indicate a proximity to walls or doors, structures that separate one space from another or regulate the passage from one to the next. These expressions include "les murs ont des oreilles;" "écouter aux portes;" "origliare alla porta;" "i muri hanno orecchie." Other locutions are even less spatially precise and articulate overhearing as "surprendre une conversation," "être aux écoutes," or "ascoltare di nascosto," "udire per caso, di nascosto." In Spanish, the expression emphasizes the quality of being hidden: "escuchar a escondidas."

The configuration of individuals and flow of information presented in eavesdropping are not exclusive to the novel. Indeed, eavesdropping plays a central role in drama from classical Greek tragedies through Shakespeare and eighteenth-century French and British comedies. As the pun in its title suggests, Shakespeare's *Much Ado About Nothing* (1598) is constructed almost entirely around scenes of deliberate and inadvertent overhearing or "noting." Indispensable moments of eavesdropping in *Hamlet* reveal the protagonist's melancholia and the machinations of the Danish court. We recall the beginning of Polonius's parting words to Laertes, although we may not remember equally well his warning to "give every man thy ear but few thy voice" (I, iii, 68). But no one forgets his secret listening behind the arras, or how deadly such plotting becomes for him. An elaborate scene in Sheridan's *School for Scandal* (1777) combines intentional and inadvertent acts of overhearing to resolve questions about people's characters and motives (IV, iii). Through eavesdropping, an atmosphere of scandal and scheming — one that multiplies false stories and narrative complication — gives way to one of sincerity and understanding. Eavesdropping is also rife in the French dramatic tradition. Covert listening is thematized in Molière's *Tartuffe* and several Marivaux and Beaumarchais plays. Even the convention of the "fourth wall" articulated by Diderot but not fully implemented in theater until the nineteenth century demonstrates a consistent attraction to such scenes. Given its prominence in drama, eavesdropping might be a theatrical device imported into the novel, the genre that Mikhail Bakhtin, among others, has characterized as constantly appropriating elements from other genres without manifesting "well-defined generic contours" of its own.[3] My interest in this admittedly theatrical, even melodramatic, moment resides in the way the novel seizes upon eavesdropping to motivate and resolve its plots and to comment on how and why novels work and work on us.[4]

Bakhtin perceives the centrality of eavesdropping to the genre of the novel and bases this recognition on the paradoxical correlation between its subject matter (private life) and a narrative transgression of privacy and private spaces.[5] He asserts, "The literature of private life is essentially a literature of snooping about, of overhearing 'how others live' ... What matters are the everyday secrets of private life that lay bare human nature – that is, everything that can be only spied and eavesdropped upon."[6] A wide variety of novelists from the English and French literary traditions represent narrative activity in a manner that confirms Bakhtin's statement. Samuel Richardson has been disparaged for his "keyhole view of life," by which he discloses to his readers the intimate aspects of his heroines' individual experiences.[7] Frances Burney uses eavesdropping scenes to provide narrative complication or resolution. In Tobias Smollett's *Peregrine Pickle* (1751), the Englishman Cadwallader pretends he is deaf so that other characters will not fear divulging private matters in his presence. In a similar vein, André Gide asserts that every true novelist is an eavesdropper.[8] From the beginnings of the modern Western novel until now, writers have turned to eavesdropping to figure and figure out why we wish to know "how others live."

In the nineteenth century, the eavesdropping scene comes into its own as the flow of information – in novels and other media – accelerated. During this period, social, technological, and economic structures developed that fostered communication and produced a transfer of news from one body – individual, social, political, or economic – to another.[9] Such changes transformed the experience of daily life in the nineteenth century. By making information more available to a larger public, institutions such as the penny post, the telegraph, and newspapers transformed local events into potentially national knowledge. Although the division of public and private spheres of activity emerged earlier, it is in this era that the desire to distinguish between the two became keenly felt, in part because "the rise of publicity ... changed the significance of privacy and created a real or imagined need for secrecy."[10] The creation of an information society brought with it an anxiety about public opinion and placed an increased value on the notion of "discretion."[11] Moreover, in a period that witnessed vast migrations to cities, social experience itself changed. People were in closer proximity to unknown others. Physical propinquity coincided with psychological mystery, producing both curiosity and opportunity to learn about others, as well as desire to shelter one's own private life from them.[12] Social mobility in general increases publicity, which in turn produces the greater desire for and value of privacy. Those who could afford to do so tried to protect private life through either the organization of living space or retreat to the suburbs or the country.

Narratives of the nineteenth century, the era considered the "golden age of private life," represent this yearning for a private space free from inquisitive eyes and ears.[13] At the same time, they represent the successful marketing of stories about other people's private lives and darkest domestic secrets; they constitute evidence of the achievements of information technology, including the publishing industry and lending libraries. Eavesdropping offers an aural correlative to "the spectacle of intimacy," the Victorian compulsion to publicize private life and its secrets in order to celebrate the virtues of domestic ideology or to provide cautionary tales about families who fail to separate public and private spaces and activities.[14] Like the "intimate sphere" that was believed separate from the public sphere of business but that was "profoundly caught up in the requirements of the market,"[15] literary representations of privacy depended, paradoxically, upon publicity and its technologies for their existence. Concomitantly, authors depended on the reading public's desire to know secrets and buy books about such intrusions into private life in order to support their own private lives. Representations of eavesdropping figure this concern about the potential infiltration of private space and the dissemination of its secrets into the larger community that produces public opinion. Covert listening stages the problems of demarcating public and private spaces and the passing of information between these areas, spheres that, in this period, become more ideologically weighted, and anxieties about them, more complex. Eavesdropping assumes a *double entente*, a double hearing or understanding. It acts out both the urge to know and the fear of others knowing, both the compulsion to display domestic bliss, and, beneath this obsession, the voices of skepticism, resentment, and defiance that deny middle-class assumptions about separate spheres and gendered identities.

Examples from Thackeray, Dickens, and Balzac demonstrate a variety of configurations in which characters, narrators, or readers can eavesdrop. Thackeray's *Vanity Fair* (1847–48) embodies the transmission of secret, often compromising, information from private places to larger, public ones in the figure of the informant, Tom Eaves, who brings private information to public attention. Tom always "happen[s] to be passing" by when anything concerning the great families of London occurs; he knows all their secret "stories and mysteries."[16] Mr. Eaves represents the teller of tales, the lucky narrator always privy to the stories that everyone wants to know. His name suggests the physical proximity that encourages secret listening; from eaves to eavesdrop is but one short step. Thackeray's own illustrations for the novel portray Becky Sharp and other characters behind a curtain or door, listening to private conversations, and running the risk that reciprocal acts will be committed against them. In Dickens's *Oliver Twist*, Nancy secretly listens to Fagin's plotting with Monks, yet despite her precautions, cannot prevent Noah Claypole from overhearing her own private conversation with Rose Maylie and Mr. Brownlow. In figuring characters or narrators as eavesdroppers, writers stress how this covert activity reveals what Thackeray calls the "many secret griefs" and "mysteries" of individuals and their "secret reasons" or motivations.[17] At the same time, by representing "oral discourse" in a disparaged form in texts that exist as "written discourse," novelists in effect make room for their own project.[18] They establish themselves as professionals with loftier aims than curiosity, even as they draw upon that aspect of narrative desire that eavesdropping figures in order to entice readers to their stories.

Balzac, for example, in *La Maison Nucingen* (1838), uses the premise of a conversation overheard in a restaurant as the frame story to a narrative revealing one of the central mysteries of *La comédie humaine*: What is the secret source of Rastignac's wealth?[19] The novella's unidentified first-person narrator confesses that he acquired this knowledge through eavesdropping on a conversation in the adjoining booth. He makes the reader complicitous in secret-sharing by admitting that he was accompanied by a woman whose reputation would be compromised if he revealed her name. Forbidden erotic interest and narrative interest coincide to make the reader an accomplice – an eavesdropper – after the fact. The story satisfies the reader's desire to know about one of the central figures of *La comédie humaine*, but reminds him or her that such knowledge springs from multiple illicit activities. The frame story's linkage of covert acts with the satisfaction of two kinds of desire parallels the association within the embedded tale of adultery and ill-gotten wealth: Nucingen has used his wife's lover Rastignac as the front-man for an elaborate business swindle and has paid him for his services. One illegitimate turn, it would seem, deserves another. Eavesdropping gives concrete form to readerly desire.

Within the nineteenth-century novel, eavesdropping appears in two guises: as intentional or inadvertent. As a premeditated activity, hidden listening involves the deliberate invasion of a private space in order to obtain information from others without their knowledge, so as to use it for one's own ends. Servants and other individuals lacking social, economic, or political power often eavesdrop to acquire knowledge about their employers or social "betters," to prevent danger to themselves, or to pass on such information to another person. In the second scenario, the eavesdropper often represents a "moral" authority; his or her accidental acquisition of knowledge, and with it, narrative agency, can result in the restoration of stability, order, or narrative closure. In Dickens's fiction, for instance, listening is often morally valenced: evil characters deliberately eavesdrop, whereas good characters happen to overhear information that frustrates villains' plots. The exemplary characters enact a moral recuperation of the transgressive energy that covert listening represents; reprehensible behavior is transformed into a force confirming social order.[20]

Dombey and Son offers examples of both forms of eavesdropping. The invidious Mr. Carker positions himself or his spies in places where they can secretly acquire information about Dombey's private life. In contrast, another Dombey employee, Mr. Morfin, represents authorially sanctioned eavesdropping. Inadvertently overhearing Carker's plots, he uses what he learns to bring the novel to a happy resolution. Morfin is blessed with aural inviolability; his landlady (the ideal candidate for domestic spying) is deaf, and thus cannot eavesdrop on his personal affairs. Morfin's listening, significantly, is disinterested: he does not personally benefit from the information he gleans but uses it to prevent crime. The fact that such eavesdropping is coded as inadvertent allows transgression and its vital energies to be appropriated into acceptable forms of behavior that insure the stability of the social order; middle-class overhearing thus regulates criminal eavesdropping.

A THEORY OF EAVESDROPPING

Eavesdroppers suffer from curiosity; they always want to know more. Scenes of illicit listening in novels indirectly address the central question "why do we wish to read about other people's – *imaginary* people's – private lives?" What purpose does this reading serve? We read because we are curious. Eavesdropping dramatizes a primal human curiosity to know, and to know those aspects of others' lives that we are not supposed to know, those that they wish to keep hidden from us.[21] This desire to know is linked to pleasure, although specific instances of eavesdropping, while inducing pleasure for some, create pain for others. In *A la recherche du temps perdu*, the way Marcel idly participates in the sexual encounter between Jupien and Charlus by eavesdropping on them suggests that overhearing two people having sex gives him vicarious pleasure. The episode also suggests a primal scene of curiosity. Marcel cannot prevent himself from desiring to know. He needs to pursue his curiosity to its natural end – suspecting Charlus of more hearty sexual escapades, following Robert de Saint-Loup into a brothel, peeking at Charlus chained to a bed and being whipped – to fulfill his desire to know. As such, eavesdropping represents a version of narrative's origin, a point where curiosity takes hold and from which storytelling springs.

Readers read because they are curious. Vicarious experience of other lives enables them to learn and grow, to transfer the experiences of fiction to the world of their everyday reality.[22] As Marcel Proust suggests, "Nous ne connaissons jamais que les passions des autres, et... ce que nous arrivons à savoir des nôtres, ce n'est que d'eux que nous avons pu l'apprendre." ("It is only with the passions of others that we are ever really familiar, and what we come to discover about our own can only be learned from them.")[23] The secret listener's position as an outsider, an interloper, helps him or her to understand a situation more clearly because he or she is not directly implicated in it. This aspect of eavesdropping has significant ramifications for the reader of the novel, whom the writer, in constructing eavesdropping scenes for our pleasure, implicates as "an almost conspiratorial consciousness."[24] As eavesdroppers set up to listen to a story, readers can indulge their yearning to discover secrets. The illicit listener figures readerly pleasure: secretly engaged in socially suspect activities (learning others' secrets, close to yet not fully a part of intimate spaces and their stories), yet safe from being caught. But just as eavesdropping implies an eradication of the boundary between one space and another and suggests the passage of a story from one community to a larger, more public one, so, too, does it seem infectious: once we eavesdrop, we are implicated in the story we have acquired. Once it becomes part of our repertory of stories, it also becomes part of ourselves. In its transformation of listeners into participants, eavesdropping draws us into situations and reminds us of our acts of speaking, listening, and hermeneusis that occur outside the narrative we are reading.[25] Fictional representations of overhearing remind us that our stories are vulnerable to similar acts of appropriation. Contrary to critical clichés about the individual subject reading in a secluded room, the scene of eavesdropping suggests the inevitability of readers' involvement in the social world.

Eavesdroppers intercept information *as it changes hands*. A secret is by nature unstable, a temporary phenomenon, like eavesdropping; "a secret known by two is no longer a secret."[26] Covert listening represents the volatility of the secret and secret information, the moment when a secret is exposed, when communities and individuals change in their relation to each other. Just as an individual may eavesdrop on a conversation, his own words may be overheard. In the process of interception, information and its significance change as well.

Eavesdropping is an act of interpretation. It dramatizes our sense-making urge: the human craving for meaning. As discrete, unrelated facts, information must be assimilated into knowledge. Understanding implies the integration of data into a context in which events, people, and things are meaningful. This interpretative context assumes narrative form. Yet Jürgen Habermas notes how the "absence of ambiguity... [is] rather the exception in the communicative practice of everyday life."[27] Ambiguity becomes even more pronounced when one hears only part of a conversation and must deduce the rest. Hence eavesdropping requires a greater hermeneutic effort than ordinary communication because clandestine listeners must usually form their conclusions from incomplete or inaccurate information. In studies of controlled eavesdropping, the linguist Graham McGregor has shown how a hidden listener to an exchange between two individuals extrapolates from the conversation to draw broader conclusions about the situation and its participants.[28] He has found that eavesdroppers form stories to account for the information overheard.[29]

Thus, eavesdroppers process discrete facts into narrative. Eavesdropping provokes narrative; listening to one story begets additional telling and retelling. McGregor's research reveals that interpretive responses are often flawed because they are based upon incomplete information.[30] McGregor's and Habermas's observations offer wide implications for examining literary representations of eavesdropping. In the novel, the use of a scene that catalyzes narrative situations and encourages the proliferation of stories is particularly resonant, for it figures this human propensity to tell stories and hence to shape information into knowledge. Moreover, in the novel, eavesdropping figures the everyday experience of knowledge acquisition: partial, incomplete, imperfect. It represents our urge to make sense of the information and stories with which we are presented. As Michel Butor explains, narrative "extends considerably beyond the scope of literature; it is one of the essential constituents of our understanding of reality."[31] Eavesdropping's constructive aspect – the way it stimulates production of a story to account for the partial information overheard – exemplifies storytelling's accounting of and for experience. In its telling, a narrative constructs and reflects reality. Studying eavesdropping, then, like the study of narrative in general, helps us understand how we make sense of the world.

Eavesdropping produces narrative complication. It figures not only the desire for secret knowledge but the multiple uses to which information may be put, and the many stories generated, from an originary moment of overhearing. Episodes of secret listening mobilize or redirect narrative energies. They engender situations such as misunderstandings, partial hearings, or incorrect scenarios that require narrative to explain or account for them.[32] A character often overhears only part of a conversation and makes erroneous assumptions about the situation and the individuals it concerns. This causes a misunderstanding that may require the length of the narrative to resolve. Even if overheard information is accurate, its secret appropriation almost always alters the course of the story and encourages narrative dilation. Alternatively, by providing information otherwise unavailable to characters and thus correcting misunderstandings or solving mysteries, eavesdropping can produce narrative closure.[33]

Acts of eavesdropping can fashion identity, both for listeners and for speakers. Listening covertly can also undo a sense of self. Eavesdroppers draw conclusions about those whom they listen to and the stories they tell; they may also discover that their perceptions of themselves are vastly different from other people's. Eavesdropping opens up a range of psychological positions that depend on whether the party listens or is listened to. Those being overheard may know that their conversation is being monitored and therefore adapt their statements to baffle the auditor, as Beatrice's friends do in *Much Ado About Nothing* in an attempt to make Beatrice fall in love with Benedick. Sometimes auditors hear information that pertains to them; the airing, or blaring, in public of that information may create consternation or embarrassment for them. Such is the case in *Wuthering Heights* when Heathcliff overhears Catherine say that it would "degrade" her to marry her unruly foster-brother.[34] Heathcliff imagines that class stands between them; the information he comes to possess humiliates him. He leaves Wuthering Heights and makes his fortune in order to rectify the perceived social imbalance between him and Catherine. Yet his entire formation of identity is premised on a false assumption. What he overhears is only a partial truth, one that nevertheless injures him deeply. Eavesdropping thus produces affective positions of embarrassment, dependency, gullibility, doubt, curiosity, pride, vanity, ridicule, absurdity, and so forth. In this manner, eavesdropping induces anxieties. This study examines the way identity is created by an individual's appearance in public, either as the subject of discussion or as an auditor in a conversation. Identity is at stake in eavesdropping, for identity is formed at the point where private matters enter public discussion. The making of identity is about the controlled or out-of-control leakage of information into other people's hands.

In this sense, I would emend the Foucauldian notion that power articulates every relation, whether in the public or private sphere. The Foucauldian concentration on power dynamics that has recently dominated nineteenth-century studies focuses on technologies of discipline and the forces of repression – those mechanisms that produce conformity with dominant ideology.[35] Yet in situations of oppression, power also produces variants on subject formation. I would stress the productive, often transformative, energy of anxiety, the complement to the disciplinary forces that have been the main focus of recent critical investigation. If anxiety creates a sense of self – we are nothing without our neuroses, tics, fears, fantasies – then eavesdropping dramatizes, through its tableaux of private worries breaking into public cognizance, the making of a self founded on a split between two versions of identity. Part of the anxiety about eavesdropping or being eavesdropped upon is a relation of passivity to power. We cannot control what others think about us in such situations; a "reality" of identity is created that has nothing to do, necessarily, with what we feel is the reality about ourselves. Eavesdropping leads to revelations about character that emphasize the limitations of self-conceived identity and the plurality of means by which identities are constructed – deliberately and inadvertently. It also emphasizes the volatility of such constructions: the fact that identity is neither fixed nor consistent.

Eavesdropping scenes therefore dramatize the ways in which identity is shaped by forces of rumor, innuendo, suggestion, and discussion. It literalizes the concept of distance between self and other – between others' position and place of cognition and our own – and reminds us that our conception of ourselves is dependent on our specific place in a physical and psychological world.[36] What is left of ourselves once we have become the subject of intimate conversations? What is left of others once we discuss their personalities? What remains of our self-conceptions when we discover how discrepant our sense of self is from the social versions of our identities, bandied about, praised or blamed as they may be?[37] Conversely, how do we transform situations of apparent powerlessness into those that trick others into thinking they know more about us than they really do? A set-up eavesdropping scene – where we know someone is secretly listening and pitch our conversation accordingly – enables us to fashion a version of identity that passes as authentic yet is as fictitious as the novels in which such scenes appear.[38] Fabricated eavesdropping scenes stress the factitiousness of identity and the narratives that help produce it. Although such contrived moments of overhearing occur rarely in life, the fact that they occur with relative frequency in fiction suggests they represent moments of narrative self-consciousness – when narratives stage and comment on their own constructive processes.

Eavesdropping often reveals those secrets about ourselves that we may not wish to know or to acknowledge. As Walter Benjamin notes, in the nineteenth century, domestic space offers an illusion about the bourgeois citizen's ability to construct an intimate, private self; interior space provides a "casing" to contain "the phantasmagorias of the interior."[39] Identity has a secret component. The paradox of this intimate self is that it must sometimes be secret even to the self. Eavesdropping can reveal such secrets and secret selves, despite our attempts *not* to know. In *Dombey and Son*, for instance, Florence Dombey inadvertently hears a conversation about herself between an orphan and her guardian aunt. Florence's eavesdropping compels her to recognize what she has long denied: her plight is worse than that of the orphan, bereft of a parent's love, for Florence has a father who deems her unworthy of love. After overhearing her own story told to the conventional object of Victorian pity, Florence acknowledges her misfortune and judges her father as "cruel and unnatural" – though she quickly suppresses such thoughts.[40] In Victorian fiction, secret selves may be discovered, although they may not be allowed a place by the hearth.[41]

We can use eavesdropping scenes to make more precise narratological models of voice and situatedness. Such scenes call attention to the two principal narrative voices of nineteenth-century fiction: the first-person singular and the third-person omniscient, including variations on the two, such as narratives comprised of successive or imbedded first-person narratives (*The Moonstone* or *Wuthering Heights*, for instance), or one intertwining them, like Dickens's *Bleak House*. Each narrative voice evokes different aspects of the eavesdropping situation to establish a particular relation between narrator and narratee that produces different assumptions about the location of authority and knowledge.

Unlike the third-person omniscient voice, which assumes a position of authority vis-à-vis the reader, a first-person narrative like *Jane Eyre* fosters an intimacy with its reader, addressing him or her numerous times throughout the story to reinforce a degree of closeness, and suggesting that the oral and written exchanges taking place within the novel are replicated in the interaction between Jane and her reader.[42] Creating a character-narrator evokes a situation of personal speaking and listening and establishes a rapport between narrator and narratee. This assumed contract is often couched in terms of orality.[43] When a character-narrator is an eavesdropper, she brings the reader closer to the story she relates by aligning the reader's activity with hers and hence increasing the identification we have with her physical and psychological situation. But unlike the direct address of the "dear reader," eavesdropping emphasizes how reading can be an appropriation of stories by listeners for whom they may not be intended, and for ends not immediately apparent. In *Wuthering Heights*, the series of imbedded first-person narratives (Lockwood's, Nelly's, Cathy's) bring us closer to each storyteller and make us sympathize with them even as we recognize their shortcomings. However, we never hear Heathcliff's story directly from him; his words are filtered through the narrative voice of others. In its series of embedded narratives each with its own agenda, *Wuthering Heights* cannily does not allow the gypsy waif, the outsider, a voice of his own. Although he may listen secretly to other characters' stories, such positioning never fully translates for him into the narrative authority that they each hold in turn. His narrative marginalization duplicates his social ostracism; for Heathcliff, acquisition of wealth never converts into social acceptance.

In contrast, the impersonal, omniscient narrator of nineteenth-century fiction represents a different kind of covert listener: the sanctioned eavesdropper, the figure who is nowhere yet everywhere, able to see and hear everything. No conversation, no deed, is hidden from his observation. Alain Lesage's 1707 novel *Le diable boiteux* resorts to the figure of the lame devil Asmodée with supernatural powers to remove the roofs of houses and thus expose the secrets of private life. Dickens invokes this novel and its prying genie in *Dombey and Son*, but hopes for "a more potent and benignant hand than the lame demon in the tale, [to] show a Christian people what dark shapes issue from amidst their homes."[44] In other words, Dickens wishes to transform the magical trickster figure (similar to Hermes, the "god of boundaries and messenger between worlds" in Greek mythology)[45] into the abstract, omniscient third-person narrator of realist[46] fiction. In novels of the nineteenth-century, an era in which improved technologies of information make private stories available to an ever-expanding, anonymous public, the supernatural agents assume less fantastic, more impersonal form. Although individual characters eavesdrop, the third-person omniscient voice represents a snooping that occults and naturalizes the covert activity necessary to produce stories of private individuals for public consumption. As authorial eavesdropping is recast in benign terms, the respectability of the writer increases, so that novel-writing becomes a profitable, even reputable, profession. Such snooping also confirms the prestige of those whose secrets are stolen; nineteenth-century fictional eavesdropping presumes that middle-class life and its private stories are worth knowing.[47]

The third-person voice presumes to enlighten or educate the reader; its eavesdropping, then, is morally sanctioned. In *Middlemarch*, for example, Eliot concludes the episode in which Bulstrode offers Ladislaw money to atone for his mistreatment of Will's mother with the following assertion: "No third person listening could have thoroughly understood the impetuosity of Will's repulse or the bitterness of his words."[48] Yet the representation of the encounter assumes that the narrator – that "third person listening" – will not only understand but also help others to comprehend the complexity and depth of both men's emotions. The intrusion of the third-person narrative voice exposes an "exemplary private truth outside the reach of public knowledge," yet justifies its own perceptiveness and moral scope in doing so.[49] In both first- and third-person narratives, the singularity of the voice suggests either personal or objective authority; both assert the psychological or social truth of what they tell. But the positioning of a narrator as an eavesdropper also reveals the fabricated nature of such narrative conventions (and by implication, the fictions in which they appear) and indicates the slippage between the truth we seek and its telling.

More generally, eavesdropping complicates spatial models of narrative. Since illicit listening is an activity that requires and constructs at least two different spaces, and that presents stories crossing the boundary between the two, an investigation of eavesdropping helps develop a multidimensional paradigm of narrative, one considering psychological dimensions of space as well as of time. Previous theories have discussed narrative as a chain of events, an intersection of the syntagmatic and paradigmatic, or a group of "actants" – analyses offering planar configurations for an activity that is more than two-dimensional.[50] Gérard Genette's analysis of multiple levels of diegesis inaugurates a spatial conception of narrative.[51] Eavesdropping expands such a paradigm to represent the full temporal and psychological dimensions of fiction. We often consider narrative elements (plot, characters, narrators, readers) in terms of spatial metaphors: distance, proximity, interiority, exteriority.[52] Eavesdropping presents the intricate, shifting relations of these factors spatially. It figures both their functioning within a space, and the kinds of psychological, epistemological, and narrative communities that their interactions construct.[53]

Unlike voyeurism, which leaves characters at a comfortable distance from the activities they witness, clandestine listening takes place nearer to the overheard exchange.[54] It implicates snoops more closely in the conversations they overhear. At the same time, eavesdropping figures the fantasy position that the act of reading creates. As readers, we are privileged eavesdroppers: unlike the secret listeners within a narrative, we run no risk of being overheard by the characters to whose story we are privy. Yet eavesdropping within the novel reminds us of our own vulnerability to other people's appropriation of our conversations. Although while reading we may identify with the omniscient narrator and assume a position of superiority and security, the implicit alignment of specific characters with such omniscience, as in Balzac's *Les parents pauvres*, often calls attention to the very fictitiousness of the third-person voice, and the position of invulnerability that it represents. If the omniscient narrator of realist fiction is impervious to retaliatory eavesdropping, in reality we are not.

Acts of eavesdropping assume spatial specificity: someone who is hidden, but proximate, overhears private conversation. The spatial resonances of eavesdropping become crucial in discussing novels of the nineteenth century, an era obsessed by the desire to separate public and private zones of activity, yet one whose political, economic, cultural, and social formations are built upon the imbrication of public and private spheres. Its domestic ideology reflects a sense of the private self that began to emerge in the early modern period but achieves its fullest expression only in this era. This private subject conceives itself within a physical and psychological space protected from intrusions by the public world and its pressures; in this intimate space, one can be completely at ease. Covert listening in the nineteenth-century novel figures the desire for such distinctly separate zones at the same time that it demonstrates how the semipermeable boundaries between them constantly shift, making the marking and policing of such boundaries impossible. Eavesdropping plays the double agent: it repeatedly establishes the illusion of a separation of public and private spheres and spaces so dear to the Victorians, only to reveal the tenuousness of the false binary.

Covert listening situates characters and narrators within specific locations at a particular and for a limited time. Bakhtin uses the term "chronotope" to designate the intertwining of space and time, the primary categories of perceiving reality in its most specific immediacy. In the nineteenth century, the chronotopes of the parlor and the threshold become particularly significant as the places "where the major spatial and temporal sequences of the novel intersect."[55] In both sites, public and private spheres and activities converge; boundaries are fluid. The threshold characterizes the narrative flow of information in general. Another kind of threshold, the parlor is the household space where the public has controlled access to family information. Unlike conversation, eavesdropping represents unlawful intervention and transmission. Its hidden individual or individuals form a silent, invisible community, in contrast to the legitimate and semipublic community of the parlor. Eavesdropping thus complicates the chronotope of the threshold and establishes a metaphoric liminality within the parlor. Indeed, eavesdropping stages the notion of chronotope, for it stresses the particular confluence of space and time in a very specific manner: in its trespass of demarcations of space, privacy, and the secrets they hold, it reminds us of their specificity. In other words, it reminds us of the importance of boundaries in the very moment and act of their being defied.

Eavesdropping occurs in particular places but is not, finally, limited to a specific location. Rather, it is situational: its site is defined by the activity that takes place within it. As such, covert listening represents where "the real sites ... that can be found within culture, are simultaneously represented, contested, and inverted."[56] Conceived of in this manner, eavesdropping stages transgression, which is "always a boundary phenomenon" – an activity that takes place on the edges of a culture's discursive constructs and that questions their validity.[57] Eavesdropping renders transgression in concrete terms. It challenges notions of private and public space, and dramatizes the cultural assumptions about people and events that take place in such areas.

The sociologist Erving Goffman defines "public places" as "any regions in a community freely accessible to members of that community," while "private places" are "*soundproof* regions where only members or invitees gather – the traditional concern for public order beginning only at the point where a private gathering begins to obtrude upon the neighbors."[58] Goffman points out that:

Theoretically, it is possible for boundaries like thick walls to close the region off physically from outside communication; almost always, however, some communication across the boundary is physically possible. Social arrangements are therefore recognized that restrict such communication to a special part of the boundary, such as doors, and that lead persons inside and outside the region to act *as if* the barrier had cut off more communication than it does. The work walls do, they do in part because they are honored or socially recognized as communication barriers, giving rise, among properly conducted members of the community, to the possibility of "conventional situational closure," in the absence of actual physical closure.[59]

Goffman notes how walls establish the necessary fiction of privacy; in reality, private space is less impervious to others' penetration than one might wish. Civility constructs the illusion of fully private places. Polite people do not allow themselves to listen to the intimate conversations taking place near them in a restaurant; they erect an invisible wall between themselves and the diners at the next table. Eavesdropping dramatizes the artificiality of such wishful constructs. No wonder both French and English expressions caution that "les murs ont des oreilles" ("the walls have ears"). A contrived scene, secret listening reveals a natural human urge to know about others. It also exposes the factitiousness of barriers we erect *not* to know about them and ourselves.

More generally, eavesdropping represents a form of what Donna Haraway terms "situated knowledge," in which the listener has access to a limited amount of information from a specific location. Such locations make us "answerable for what we learn how to see" and hear. Haraway contends that such "situated and embodied knowledges" are more responsible than "unlocatable knowledge claims" based on the "illusion" of "infinite vision."[60] Haraway's "situated knowledge" recalls Mikhail Bakhtin's emphasis of "situatedness" in the novel: the condition in which every utterance is located in a specific chronotope where particular interlocutors engage in multiple and simultaneous "languages" (or discourses).[61] Michael Holquist dwells on Bakhtin's "emphasis on *particularity* and *situatedness*, the degree to which [his project] insists that apparently abstract questions about selfhood are pursuable only when treated as specific questions about *location*."[62] Both Bakhtin and Haraway stress location in the formation of and limits to knowledge. Eavesdropping stages situated knowledge: it dramatizes a specific location in space, and a relational aspect between people and between people and stories. Eavesdropping helps us theorize how such sites of "situated and embodied knowledges" might be represented in the novel, since scenes of overhearing emphasize both the specific situation of a listener in a particular space and the limits to knowledge that such positioning produces.

Eavesdropping stresses the experience of physical, epistemological, and psychological difference. Moments of secret listening insist upon the importance of others in the construction and understanding of the self. Other peoples' conversations play formative roles in the elaboration of how we understand them and ourselves. Eavesdropping offers in miniature a representation of the repeated efforts by which we try to process these other stories; it dramatizes how we need other people and their stories to create meaning and meaningful identities. In its representation of the particularity of individual acts of perception and their location in specific places and times – in social, physical, and historical context – eavesdropping focuses critical attention on the kinds of perception, the acts of knowing, that the novels of a certain period reveal and shape. As a border activity, dwelling on yet transgressing the boundaries between one space and another, overhearing is a *translatio* – a carrying across – from one social situation into another; such aural trespass emphasizes the transformation – of both utterance and listener – that occurs in the act of transmission.

DOMESTIC INTELLIGENCE: INDIVIDUAL READINGS

I have concentrated on eavesdropping in situations of domestic spying rather than on the political and professional espionage that acquires prominence by the end of the century. Limiting the kinds of eavesdropping scenes under discussion enables me to focus on concepts of domesticity, the ideology of the home, and constructions of gender central to the nineteenth-century novel. It also exposes the paradox of representing the ideology of separate spheres, in that the portrayal of private space requires the narrative violation of that area supposedly impervious to intrusion. Representations of covert listening stage the publicity of the private either to extol its virtues or to point out its failings. Finally, by keeping my discussion focused on nonprofessional snoops and their overhearing, I stress that the urge to know is not confined to the modern figure of the detective or the spy but, rather, is universal to human experience. Some of us may wish to be detectives, but we are all readers.

My first two chapters concentrate on how eavesdropping in Jane Austen's novels affects the stories that characters construct about each other within her fictions, as well as the larger narratives themselves. Although her novels offer abundant examples of how eavesdropping provokes or resolves narrative situations, I limit my discussion to *Pride and Prejudice* (1813) in Chapter 1 and *Persuasion* (1818) in Chapter 2. The novelist of manners *par excellence*, Austen uses an episode of exemplary bad manners to mobilize or suspend narrative possibilities and educate her readers in the codes of civility. In Austen's fictional world, eavesdropping represents the coincidence of narrative stratagem and the thematics of miscommunication. Clandestine listening foregrounds one of Austen's central concerns: communication. Her novels sometimes demonstrate how eavesdropping can enable individuals to overcome their isolation from each other and provide narrative resolution, as in *Persuasion*, where a scene of contrived overhearing helps the heroine speak obliquely of her constancy to the man she loves. More frequently, however, it becomes divisive, creating misunderstanding among individuals, and fostering narrative complication and distention. Such is the case in *Pride and Prejudice*, where an initial episode of inadvertent secret listening produces Elizabeth Bennet's prejudiced understanding of Darcy's character. Austen's texts contrast two models for transmission of information: eavesdropping, which is transgressive and narratively productive; and conversation, a counter-narrative paradigm weighted toward discovery of information and narrative closure.

Eavesdropping in Austen and throughout the nineteenth century reveals marked differences in gendered agency. Particularly in *Persuasion*, episodes of overhearing dramatize the social constraints on women's verbal and physical activity. Conversely, a set-up eavesdropping scene in *Persuasion* also suggests how, through "strategies of indirection," women may act powerfully but still maintain "proper" ladylike behavior.[63] The story of lovers' reconciliation foregrounds the intimate interaction of the public and private communities that form Austenian society. For Austen, public and private represent interconnected zones of activity, rather than spheres that must be kept separate. Hence the importance, in her novels, of the parlor. As its derivation from *parler*, "to speak," implies, the parlor represents the space of conversation for inhabitants of a house and for privileged others within a community who gain access to this interactive and intermediate social area of a dwelling.

In contrast to Austen's novels, the works of mid-nineteenth-century writers demonstrate an increasing anxiety about not just the transgression of boundaries that eavesdropping represents but also the "monstrous" narrators whose secret listening enables their own storytelling to occur.[64] To a greater degree than Austen, later writers explore the psychological barriers violated in the act of eavesdropping, and the fears and pleasures that such violations produce. These narratives reflect the increased complexity of the social worlds they represent: rather than the small country town, the novels of the 1830s through the 1860s that I discuss explore the more intricate – and vexed – social, political, and economic formations of two capital cities, Paris and London. Austen's last completed novel raises issues of the limited perspective of an individual telling a story. Later nineteenth-century writers examine characters as narrators and present anxieties about the power and agency that a character can assume because of his or her position as storyteller. They also attend to the vast array of literal and social spaces available to the nineteenth-century reading public, and to the porous boundaries between public and private sites, activities, and identities.

My third chapter turns from narrative problems to social concerns and their representation through eavesdropping in texts from the 1830s and 1840s. The chapter weds an attention to architectural spaces to a discussion of the nineteenth-century ideology of separate spheres. To contextualize these literary works, I briefly trace developments in domestic architecture in England and France in the eighteenth and the nineteenth centuries. Innovations such as the introduction of the corridor and the individualization of rooms demonstrate how architects incorporated notions of privacy and domestic ideology into the design of houses. The changing architecture of the home and its representation in nineteenth-century fiction register increasing fears about keeping private information and space secure from appropriation and penetration. I investigate these issues in the novels of Balzac and Dickens. Both writers' fiction demonstrates a thorough understanding of their era's physical and psychological construction of space. Their portrayal of domestic spaces at various socio-economic levels indicates the extent to which domestic ideology, originally a middle-class ideal, had infiltrated all levels of society by the time both novelists were writing. The representation of eavesdropping in these novels, however, also exposes the constructed nature of domestic ideology; these narratives hint at the futility of erecting barriers between public and private zones and stories. Moreover, the need to display privacy and to convince readers of the attractions of bourgeois life suggests a more ambivalent attitude toward the domestic ideal than convention would admit. Eavesdropping reveals this contradictory attitude toward privacy and its fictional representation. In its dramatization of the fluctuations of private space and its secrets, covert listening reminds us of how space functions as both social product and social agent. Domesticity is an affective as well as spatial concept. In Balzac and Dickens, the walls between public and private spaces and activities take precise literal and figurative forms; their domestic fictions remind us that these constructs are both artificial and porous.

My discussion of Balzac and Dickens centers on four texts: Balzac's *Le Père Goriot* (1835), *La Cousine Bette* (1846), and *Le Cousin Pons* (1847), and Dickens's *Dombey and Son* (1846–48). I examine specific acts of covert listening in precise locations and analyze how these eavesdropping scenes home in on concerns central to each text in which they appear. All four novels closely link eavesdropping and cultural concerns about privacy, family secrets, and social position. In their eavesdropping scenes, these novels attend to the physical and affective dimensions of private space. In Balzac's *Le Père Goriot*, the *pension de famille*, or boarding-house, offers a departure point for an investigation of nineteenth-century attitudes toward public and private zones. Eavesdropping scenes represent in miniature the uneasy interpenetration of public and private spheres on which the boarding-house depends. In his "domestic dramas" comprising the diptych of *La Cousine Bette* and *Le Cousin Pons*, Balzac contrasts Bette and Pons as characters whose relative ability to capitalize on overheard information determines their positions within their extended families and the success of their projects. Whereas Bette parlays her knowledge of private information and secret relations into plotting her "beloved" family's destruction, Pons's inadvertent eavesdropping only confirms his marginalization. Instead, his building's concierge represents the successful eavesdropper who exploits her position as official regulator of public access to private life to amass invaluable information and material possessions. A guardian of the threshold, the *portière* determines the people and information that enter and leave the apartment complex. In *La Cousine Bette* and *Le Cousin Pons*, the spaces of private life – family mansion, secret love-nest, or humble garret apartment – are subject to unrelenting aural surveillance, their inhabitants and their secrets constantly exposed to a larger public. The ideology of separate spheres functions effectively only when the secrets of private life have no value on the open market.

The concept of being "at home" or "*chez soi*" acquires its greatest literary representation in nineteenth-century fiction. Eavesdropping in Dickens's *Dombey and Son* marks the subtle distinctions between the concepts of "house" and "home." It shows the danger that inhabitants of public and private worlds incur when they are not able to distinguish between business firm and family home and the secrets and attitudes appropriate to each of these spaces; it thus educates its readers to be proper Victorians. I examine the different ideological associations of the private home versus the "public house," the sanctity of the home versus the perils of the "house of ill-repute," a phrase implying an establishment unable to keep its secrets from the public domain. In contrast to the private home, the "public house" is open to all; it brings together a diverse community through domestic secrets spread to the public at large. *Dombey and Son* expands the definition of eavesdropping to include all domestic spying. Such taxonomy emphasizes the situational and psychological aspects of curiosity and its obverse, paranoia; we dwell in material, social, and affective locations. Although Balzac's novels demonstrate a greater cynicism toward the possibility of creating ideal private spaces than do Dickens's, the texts of both reveal a longing for domestic spaces that are safe, free from the intrusive public's purview. At the same time, their novels suggest that such secure spaces may, in fact, exist only in fiction.

Balzac's and Dickens's novels are symptomatic of a general mid-nineteenth-century attitude toward privacy and its representation. Eavesdropping in their fiction reminds us that privacy and private subjects are unstable constructions of intimate and public forces. Lived space is social space. In Balzac's and Dickens's novels, people constantly change homes and social identities. Such social mobility produces anxiety as well as anticipation. Eavesdropping figures placement and displacement in social structures – literal and metaphoric – and the affective energies accompanying them.

My fourth chapter concentrates the issues of the first three chapters in precise locations: physically, in the English country house, and structurally, in the figure of the female narrator. A complicated tale of multiple narrators and narrative thefts, Wilkie Collins's *The Woman in White* (1860) makes us conscious of the transmission of stories within the novel, among characters and, more generally, between narrator and readers. Collins's novel dramatizes acts of aural appropriation and the changes to narrative agency and gendered identity that such thefts produce. *The Woman in White* takes up issues of gender, knowledge, and agency explored in *Persuasion* and *La comédie humaine*, but embodies them in the female narrator, not just female characters. Her eavesdropping represents a double transgression: she oversteps the boundaries of proper ladylike behavior in her illicit listening and in assuming narrative agency – power over other people's stories and identities.

The Woman in White also draws the reader into a hermeneutic enterprise of uncovering characters' hidden motives and his or her own motivations for reading. Peter Brooks notes how both narrator and reader are implicated in narrative's "seductive" if transgressive – or seductive *because* transgressive – activity. He writes, "To read a novel – and to write one – means to be caught up in the seductive coils of a deviance: to seduce, of course, is to lead from the straight path, to create deviance and transgression."[65] In *The Woman in White*, eavesdropping figures narrative desire; it associates the trespassing of literal and metaphoric boundaries with erotic interest. In Collins's novel, the most transgressive characters are the most attractive ones to the reader and to each other. These rebellious characters flout conventional expectations about gendered appearance and behavior. *The Woman in White* insists upon the pleasures as well as the dangers of secret listening, reading, and writing. It exposes a correspondence between sexual and textual bodies and the pleasures that each offers. At the same time, the novel signals the difference between our acts of covert listening and those of characters and narrators. Although its conclusion confirms normative gender roles, the narrative itself thrives on challenges to assumptions about gender, law, and privacy – challenges presented, time and again, through eavesdropping.

Toward the end of the century, eavesdropping in any number of novels offers ample proof of the fault lines in the gendered binary of public and private spaces. Although I do not devote a chapter to *Pot-Bouille* (1881–82), Zola's novel provides a prime example of how the apartment-house represents the breakdown of all such distinctions. Adulterous wives who slip from one private space to another and defy the bonds and bounds of matrimony; unmaidenly, pregnant housemaids who shout their employers' secrets to each other through the central airshaft of the building; an unnamed novelist who pilfers his neighbors' secrets to earn a living and a coveted position on the second floor: all contest the ideology of separate spheres that assumes an ability to keep private stories and bodies from public circulation.[66] In each scenario, eavesdroppers are the rule, not the exception, in the practice of everyday life. *Pot-Bouille* represents the culmination of a century of rampant eavesdropping. Twentieth-century narratives suggest a very different attitude toward secret listening and its implications.

I end my discussion of eavesdropping in the nineteenth-century novel with Proust. *A la recherche du temps perdu* (1913–27) extends the space of eavesdropping from the backstairs to the psyche. In this early twentieth-century novelist's work, the boundaries between self and other, between private and public personae, and between intimate and public activities, are even less easily demarcated than they were in the nineteenth century. Here, the making up and the making over of the self are attempts both to define an evolving subject and to elude definition by the other. Proust takes as his topic a primal human desire to know, and to know the self, by examining one's own and other people's experiences. *A la recherche* represents hidden listening as paradigmatic of this instinctive curiosity. The young protagonist eavesdrops upon other people's conversations and apprehends life (and love) through the mediation of other people's affairs. In its exploration of the relation between self and other and the communicative acts that occur between them, *A la recherche* expands its analysis of the suggestive relations between reader and narrator that earlier texts such as *The Woman in White* flirt with exposing. Both texts use eavesdropping scenes to explore readerly desire and the ways in which the implied or figured author or narrator capitalizes on the reader's yen to know secrets. In both novels, the self-conscious, melodramatic eavesdropping scene reminds us of our own acts of transgressive curiosity, their pleasures and perils. Covert listening stages the proximity of desire and danger, pleasure and fear. If *The Woman in White* incarcerates its seductive, deviant eavesdroppers, Proust's narrative suggests how to make such transgression creatively productive.

My investigation of clandestine listening dwells on three crucial moments in *A la recherche*: the lesbian encounter at Montjouvain in *Du côté de chez Swann*, the *pas de deux* between Charlus and Jupien that opens *Sodome et Gomorrhe*, and the narrator's discovery of the male brothel in *Le temps retrouvé*. These episodes of secret listening to secret pleasures treat explicitly the subject that nineteenth-century narratives represent obliquely: sexual identity and desire. They relate erotic and epistemological yearnings in a manner that eradicates the conceptual borders of two seemingly different projects.[67] In its representation of "perverse" sexual proclivities, *A la recherche* intimates that our urges to transgress boundaries of the known or conventional assume many forms, and are always part of a larger epistemophilic quest. By presenting his young protagonist covertly listening to other people's affairs before representing the hero's own amorous exploits, Proust seduces his reader into a position of analogous, if set-up, eavesdropping. To know the self, *A la recherche* intimates, one must start by listening – secretly and overtly – to others' queer, wonderful stories. Only through such listening can one come to read the self in all its contradictions and fluctuations.

Proust represents the culmination of nineteenth-century attitudes toward the construction of public and private spaces and selves. The larger implications of eavesdropping in twentieth-century narrative are beyond the scope of this project. Twentieth-century technological innovations make eavesdropping an omnipresent reality, in which private spaces and information are available to an all too unidentifiable public of individuals as well as to the police; such new technologies, and the spying and eavesdropping they facilitate, catapult the conception of public and private spaces and identities into an entirely new dimension. One would think that the consciousness of being subject to an almost inescapable surveillance would be paralyzing. Yet far from limiting our behavior, the awareness of new, subtle means of infiltrating private space seems only to whet our appetite for more diverse forms of hidden listening and more spectacular displays of intimacy.

Eavesdropping is a narrative episode that acknowledges – even encourages – readerly identification with and implication in transgressions that reveal the secrets of private life. Nineteenth-century novels represent the covert acquisition and dissemination of information about various interior spaces: literal, psychological, libidinal, and narrative. The paradigmatic eavesdropping scene registers historically specific concerns in the nineteenth-century novel while presenting aspects of the novel and the novelistic community that endure. Moments of illicit listening make us rethink the ways in which narratives work and work on us, enticing us in, asking us to ask questions, motivating our own stories about them and about ourselves. In raising such issues I wish to create a space for "double entendre," about the nature of narrative and about questions of human identity, agency, and curiosity.

CHAPTER I

I'm all ears: Pride and Prejudice, *or the story behind the story*

> La double entente déborde largement le cas limité du jeu de mots ou de l'équivoque et imprègne au fond, sous des formes et des densités diverses, toute l'écriture classique... Le lecteur est complice, non de tel ou tel personnage, mais du discours lui-même en ce qu'il joue la division de l'écoute, l'impureté de la communication.[1]
>
> Barthes, *S/Z*

> Words learn'd by rote a parrot may rehearse,
> But talking is not always to converse.
>
> Cowper, "Conversation"

Almost everyone who has read Emily Brontë's *Wuthering Heights* or seen William Wyler's 1939 film version remembers the dramatic scene in which Catherine, unaware of Heathcliff's presence on the other side of the kitchen wall, confides her feelings for him to Nelly. Heathcliff stays only long enough to overhear Catherine say, "it would degrade me to marry Heathcliff now." Thus, he never learns of Catherine's love for him, and her complete identification with him ("he's more myself than I am... Nelly, I *am* Heathcliff").[2] This eavesdropping scene is crucial to the very existence of the narrative, a story based primarily on the miscommunication between and resulting separation of the two central characters. If Heathcliff had not overheard this conversation, or if he had stayed to hear it in its entirety, *Wuthering Heights* as we know it would not exist; the story set in motion by this partial acquisition of information (or misinformation) would not unfold because there would be nothing to tell.

This essential scene, in which what is not overheard is as important as what is, demonstrates both Roland Barthes's theory of narrative as being the presentation of an enigma and the deliberate postponement of its solution,[3] and D. A. Miller's related theory of "the narratable": the condition of lack, "the instances of disequilibrium, suspense, and general insufficiency from which a given narrative appears to rise."[4] The ensuing narrative attempts to overcome this "insufficiency" or solve the "enigma" that confronts either characters, the reader, or both. Paradoxically, the story's existence presupposes the delay of the very condition that it presumes to overcome. Eavesdropping scenes often figure moments of narrative beginning, for they represent how narrative lack is created.[5] Such scenes operate simultaneously on a metafictional level, involving the snares that a writer has left to trap the reader, and internally, exploring gaps in characters' understanding – usually in the form of erroneous or incomplete information – that cause them to act in ways that forestall narrative closure.[6] Conversely, eavesdropping, by providing necessary information that would otherwise be unavailable to characters, can also provide narrative closure and entrance into the "nonnarratable," where supposedly "every mystery has been solved, every major lack liquidated and rift made good."[7] Eavesdropping is thus a Janus-faced narrative element, both creating and erasing opportunities for story.

As noted earlier, the linguist Graham McGregor has demonstrated how, in situations of controlled eavesdropping, an individual listening to a conversation between two others makes inferences about both the conversation and its participants.[8] McGregor points out that interpretive activity constitutes more than three-quarters of listeners' responses to overhearing. Significantly, most interpretive responses consist of *creating* stories to explain the overheard conversation.[9] Thus, eavesdropping begets additional storytelling; such listening is not passive, for it generates new narrations (acts of telling) as well as retellings. McGregor's research also reveals that such interpretive responses to listening are often flawed or inaccurate, based as they are upon partial information.[10] His studies have important implications for examining literary representations of such overhearing. In the novel, a scene that proliferates stories is significant, for it dramatizes the act of hermeneusis that underlies storytelling and signals narrative's origin in the attempt to understand (a situation, an event, another person, oneself, a relationship, etc.) and convey that understanding to others.

Eavesdropping is aptly suited to narratives replete with dramatic scenes, as *Wuthering Heights* is, abounding in episodes – or as Emily Brontë's sister Charlotte would say, filled with "story." A great deal happens in Emily Brontë's novel precisely because this eavesdropping scene occurs. But an analysis of eavesdropping and its relation to the creation and resolution of narrative situations can also be applied to Jane Austen, a writer whose novels the elder Brontë censured for not having "story enough for me."[11] In his classic 1917 essay on Austen, the novelist and playwright Reginald Farrer modifies Brontë's pronouncement. He traces a progression in Austen's novels from *Pride and Prejudice* (1813), which he considers "a story pure and simple," to her final novel *Persuasion* (1818), which he characterizes as being "entirely devoid of any 'story' at all."[12] Yet in both these books, Austen uses an eavesdropping scene either to initiate or to resolve her narrative, the "story" that Brontë misses. The fact that two vastly different novelists – one representing Regency, the other coming out of the English Romantic tradition – both employ eavesdropping scenes at crucial, emotionally charged moments in their narratives suggests the overall importance of eavesdropping as a narrative mechanism and structural dynamic. Overhearing provides "a constantly recurring device in Jane Austen's novels."[13] They offer a logical starting point for a discussion of eavesdropping in the nineteenth-century novel.

In Austen's fiction, eavesdropping represents the coincidence of narrative stratagem and the thematics of miscommunication.[14] Barthes terms "idyllic" the "communication which unites two partners sheltered from any 'noise' (in the cybernetic sense of the word)" and he contrasts this interaction with "narrative communication" where "lines of destination [of information] are multiple" and potentially misdirected.[15] Eavesdropping presents an incomplete or faulty relay of information that leads to erroneous conclusions – conclusions that frustrate the "idyllic" communication of characters and the nonnarratable, and thus engender misunderstanding and the delay of narrative closure. Austen's novels often demonstrate how eavesdropping can be enabling, allowing individuals to overcome their isolation from each other. More frequently, however, it is divisive, creating gaps of understanding among individuals, as breaks in the actual words overheard mar the content and, hence, the message of an overheard conversation. In *Pride and Prejudice*, such a device not only provokes "narratability;" it also underscores one of the novel's central considerations: that of an individual's judgment of others, and the range of accuracy that this evaluation can present.

First Impressions, Austen's initial title for *Pride and Prejudice*, signals a concern about an individual's ability to evaluate others. The novel reveals that conclusions about people's character based upon superficial "first impressions" are often false because they are founded on partial information. Tony Tanner suggests that "the 'activity' which is recorded by Jane Austen is largely an activity of seeing and saying, thinking and feeling, wondering and assessing, hoping and fearing, conjecturing and interpreting. The movements are predominantly movements of the mind and heart,"[16] movements largely internal, hidden, and thus appropriate to novels concerned with the representation of the early nineteenth-century woman's limited range of social and political action.[17] Eavesdropping, an event that involves less physical movement than the cerebral acts of perception, inference, and cognition, figures this "activity." It represents a surreptitious appropriation of the information in other people's conversations and an evaluation of their characters. Illicit listening, far more than overt participation in a conversation, is prone to result in errors in judgment; partial or inaccurate information yields similarly flawed conclusions.

This may strike us as a counterintuitive proposition. At first, eavesdropping would seem to be a shortcut that reveals another individual's "true" character or intentions and that obviates the prolonged process of becoming acquainted. In early nineteenth-century England, getting to know someone of the opposite sex was often frustrated by the difficulty of finding opportunities for private interaction. Information gleaned by eavesdropping would initially appear to be all the more "authentic" for having been obtained secretly, without the speaker's knowledge: it would represent an involuntary revelation of character or events. However, this shorter epistemological path, rather than leading to a more rapidly formed and reliable judgment, in fact often leads to misunderstandings, misinformation, and, consequently, erroneous conclusions similar to those that first impressions produce. Eavesdropping becomes less a shortcut than a shortcircuit of information – one that, by its creation of enigmas, engenders the possibility for narrative.

Austen's works appeal to and transform a tradition of eavesdropping in the English novel. Specifically, her novels reveal a debt to Frances Burney's, which Austen read and which contain similar scenes of eavesdropping. Several critics have perceived that Austen drew heavily upon Burney's *Cecilia* for the title of *Pride and Prejudice* as well as the social and emotional configuration of its protagonists: a proud, socially elevated hero and a worthy but socially inferior heroine.[18] However, no one has explored the parallel between the initial eavesdropping scene in Burney's first novel *Evelina* and the corresponding episode in *Pride and Prejudice*.[19] In *Evelina*, the heroine's friend overhears a conversation between Lord Orville and Sir Clement Willoughby. Although Lord Orville admires Evelina's beauty, he calls her "a poor weak girl" who is "ignorant or mischievous."[20] In *Pride and Prejudice*, Elizabeth Bennet overhears a conversation between Darcy and Bingley in which Darcy, assessing the people at the Meryton ball, makes disparaging comments about her beauty and reveals his snobbish pride. Thus both novels present scenes in which the heroine learns how unfavorably she has impressed the hero in their first encounter. In both novels, the result is the same: a misunderstanding between the protagonists that takes the length of the narrative to overcome. However, in *Evelina* the heroine learns of this indirectly, through a friend. She is much more a heroine in the Richardsonian tradition, whose merit consists less in what she does than what she does not do: she does not listen to other people's conversations; her virtue resides in saying "no." In contrast, Elizabeth Bennet directly overhears the unfavorable comments about herself. Instead of bemoaning Darcy's negative impression of her, Austen's heroine acts. She creates a humorous story out of a mortifying incident and tells it "with great spirit among her friends; for she had a lively, playful disposition, which delighted in any thing ridiculous" (59).[21] Evelina is criticized for her apparent want of intelligence and education; Elizabeth merely for not being as conventionally pretty as she might be and, later, for her undesirable connections, not because she lacks mental acuity.

The two novels also differ considerably in the consequences and eventual correction of this "first impression." Burney's book concludes happily through another eavesdropping scene that does not implicate the heroine; instead, a friend overhears how Lord Orville loves Evelina and respects her "natural love of virtue" and her "mind that might adorn *any* situation" (346). In this second conversation, Lord Orville refutes, one by one, the objectionable remarks he had made earlier about Evelina. Burney stages the vindication of her heroine using the same device she had employed to denigrate her: an episode of overhearing. Moreover, Burney returns to eavesdropping in the final pages of the novel by relating an event that, before the novel's beginning, generated the larger narrative. In it, Dame Green confesses how she eavesdropped upon the conversation between Evelina's dying mother and her guardian, Mr. Villars, and thus acquired the knowledge that enabled her to substitute her own baby daughter for Evelina in the home and heart of her father. Through the revelation of such secrets, the solving of all enigmas, Evelina regains her birthright – her name and dowry – and can therefore marry Lord Orville. She acquires her father, her history, and her future. Evelina's situation is no longer one of mystery and misunderstanding, of surrogacy and substitution, but one of comprehension and reunion, of reinstatement and reward.

Although similarly created, the misunderstanding in *Pride and Prejudice* plays out in a completely different manner and indicates less a concern for the heroine's social status and a testing of her virtue than a presentation of her *Bildung*, the development of her intellectual and moral understanding, within an increasingly complex and changing social world.[22] Eavesdropping in *Pride and Prejudice* dramatizes the danger of miscommunication through appropriation of information not intended for a hidden listener. It also proliferates points of view and stories, and complicates our sense of the people who tell them and the characters of the individuals they concern. Darcy and Elizabeth (as well as the reader) must learn to distinguish the "true" story and not to anticipate how the story will end – not to "jump to conclusions." In a novel that begins with an ironic assurance of "a truth universally acknowledged," Austen examines the validity of such assumptions, and of an individual's quick judgments about others (51).

A concern for the truth and true stories resonates throughout the book. Forms of the word "true" recur in moments of storytelling or of verifying an individual's character. In his letter to Elizabeth, Darcy asserts, "of the *truth* of what I shall relate, I can summon more than one witness of undoubted veracity" (229, emphasis added), and thus presents his story as the "true" one. Lydia's exclamation to Sir William when he announces his daughter's engagement to Mr. Collins displays the ease with which people confuse the true and the false, and links such errors of judgment to narrative: "how can you tell such a story?" (167). The reader of *Pride and Prejudice*, "a studier of character" like Elizabeth Bennet (88), could equally declare about many of the characters, "I hear such different accounts of you as puzzle me exceedingly" (136). The reader, too, finds himself or herself in the position of making judgments about characters and situation, and of trying to anticipate marriages and endings.

Conversation comprises a direct, unmediated form of communication between two individuals. In contrast, eavesdropping is an oblique means of acquiring information about another. It offers not an understanding gained through openness and willingness to listen to another person, but rather, information about him or her gleaned in a way that contradicts rules of "proper" behavior and that can demonstrate a lack of respect for that person.[23] In *The Way of the World*, Franco Moretti characterizes *Pride and Prejudice* as a novel that opposes suspicion and willingness to listen.[24] However, suspicious people are actually eager listeners; they wish to hear anything that will confirm their unfavorable opinions of others. Elizabeth, contrary to Moretti's assertion, is thus both suspicious of Darcy, ready to believe ill of him, and eager to have her early impressions confirmed by others' stories about him; she is an all too avid listener.

Elizabeth believes she knows "the whole story" about Darcy, when in fact she possesses only part of it. Her conversation with Wickham confirms Elizabeth's premature judgment. She is the misled reader whom Barthes constructs in his reading of *Sarrasine*: the one who falls into all the traps, or "snares," erected for him or her, in the same way that the artist in Balzac's tale misjudges characters and situations. A crafty storyteller, Wickham corroborates her false narrative about Darcy by not telling "the *whole* story," creating narrative delay and obfuscation through what Barthes calls "equivocation."[25] Wickham's narration extends the partial transmission of information and resulting incorrect narrative that Elizabeth's eavesdropping began.

Eavesdropping in *Pride and Prejudice* not only prolongs the story of Elizabeth and Darcy; it also triggers other stories and narrative complications. Hence, in the discussion after the ball, Charlotte Lucas complacently relates how she eavesdropped, and how her "overhearings were more to the purpose than" Elizabeth's (66). Her secret listening, by providing "proof" of Bingley's high opinion of Jane, authenticates the partiality that everyone has been suspecting. However, Elizabeth's eavesdropping is "more to the purpose" of our narrative, for in providing only a partial truth, it creates the misunderstanding around which the central story revolves. Darcy's most consequential eavesdropping, on Mrs. Bennet's conversation, makes him aware of the danger Bingley is courting in wooing Jane and compels him to remove his friend from Netherfield, thus delaying the resolution of this marriage plot (141). His "overhear[ing]" compels Darcy's "judgment;" it provokes him "to decide on the propriety of his friend's inclination . . . upon his own judgment alone, he was to determine and direct in what manner that friend was to be happy" (141, 218).

In contrast, Mrs. Bennet is a gossip rather than an eavesdropper: one who relays information she has heard, rather than actively seeking it out and drawing conclusions for herself. She functions as the voice of hearsay: the person most prone to believe other people's stories and to relay them as absolute fact. Quick to disparage Darcy, she eagerly relates how "every body says that he is ate up with pride" (66). She encourages stories about Jane and Bingley's engagement to circulate; her concern throughout the novel is with what "every body" will think, rather than with any attempt to evaluate the situation and form her own opinion. If her daughter represents an intelligent, if flawed, example of what

Bakhtin calls a "living hermenuetics," then Mrs. Bennet stands for the uninformed or overinformed weight of public opinion in understanding and interpreting other people's words and actions.[26] *Pride and Prejudice* cautions its readers to evaluate people and situations carefully, to rely neither on the hearsay of uninformed busybodies nor on the partial understanding that eavesdropping or snap judgments offer.

Although not a gossip, Elizabeth, like the reader, proves an eager listener to these first- and secondhand stories. While staying at Netherfield in order to nurse her sister, Elizabeth at first tries to read, but she is "so much caught by what passed [in conversation among the others], as to leave her very little attention for her book; and soon laying it wholly aside, she drew near the card-table, and stationed herself between Mr. Bingley and his eldest sister, to observe the game" (84). The story unfolding around her – which she is learning through primarily aural means – is more engrossing than the tale she is reading. A few pages later Elizabeth amuses herself by pretending to do some needlework, but really by "attending to what passed between Darcy and his companion [Miss Bingley]" (92). Austen continually presents Elizabeth as a recipient and evaluator of stories, and as a creator of her own. She listens to first Wickham's and then Darcy's version of the Pemberley story: Wickham's failed attempt to elope with Georgiana. Predisposed to dislike Darcy, Elizabeth initially believes Wickham's version; her eavesdropping has supposedly afforded her insight into his character, so that she thinks she knows the "real" Darcy, when it has actually conditioned her to regard him adversely. Eager as she is to have her negative impression confirmed, Wickham's story does not fall on deaf ears. In addition, when Miss Bingley warns Elizabeth about Wickham, she merely assumes that the "malice of Mr. Darcy" has prompted the "interference" (137), although the only damaging "interference" here is Elizabeth's preformed opinion that makes the true story inaudible. Because of this particular narrator's questionable motive, the "true" story is not fully heard or heeded, but instead appears, as Darcy's letter does at first, as "the grossest falsehood" (233).

Even the sensible Charlotte Lucas allows herself to listen to other people's conversations. Presented, like Elizabeth, at the beginning of the novel as an admitted eavesdropper, Charlotte continues to listen to the conversations of others when it is in her best interest, and ceases when it proves otherwise; she has very pragmatic, selective hearing. "[P]retending not to hear" the conversation between Mr. Collins and Mrs. Bennet in which he admits defeat in courting Elizabeth, Charlotte thus learns she may woo Mr. Collins for herself (154). Her subsequent sympathetic listening to his woes, which Elizabeth believes Charlotte endures out of friendship for her, later proves to be motivated by self-interest (162). Only when she has secured Mr. Collins for herself does Charlotte "wisely... not hear" her husband's pontificating (192). Charlotte has learnt not to listen.

No wonder, then, that in this very small world of Longbourn and Meryton, people are consumed by fear of being overheard by others. The hypocritical Miss Bingley is afraid that she and Darcy have "been overheard" as she has been criticizing Elizabeth to him (97); such a disclosure would irrefutably reveal her true stance toward the Bennets. Her anxiety about information being put into circulation is justified, for, as Darcy's cousin Fitzwilliam remarks to Elizabeth, when he unwittingly reveals that Darcy has been discouraging Bingley from pursuing Jane, "if it were to get round to the lady's family, it would be an unpleasant thing" (217). Yet as much as everyone fears, with reason, the revelation of his or her private knowledge that can create this "unpleasant thing," everyone is also filled with curiosity about other people's stories and conversations. Indeed, this unpleasantness among characters actually provides the reader's source of pleasure, for the misunderstanding between Elizabeth and Darcy, with its verbal sparring, constitutes and prolongs the narrative. When Elizabeth witnesses the silent, antagonistic exchange between Darcy and Wickham, she wonders, "What could be the meaning of it? – It was impossible to imagine; it was impossible not *to long to know*" (116, e.m.). Eavesdropping dramatizes this longing to know – the urge to possess not just secret information, but the larger stories that make such information meaningful. Such larger stories turn information into knowledge.

Characters in *Pride and Prejudice* constantly weigh the advisability of telling versus withholding stories. Often, bearing news can confer upon an individual greater status than he or she would normally have; the urge to tell is motivated more by egotism than concern for others or for communication. Alternatively, a character may decide not to divulge stories, either for self-protection or to shield others Thus, while Maria Lucas gleefully declares with self-importance, "How much I shall have to tell!" of her visit to the Collinses, Elizabeth privately adds, "And how much I shall have to conceal," even though her very next thought is, "To know that she had the power of revealing what would so exceedingly astonish Jane... was such a temptation to openness" (245). Everyone has stories to tell, and the temptation to tell them is great. But just as stories are continually being told, they are also covered up, as well as imperfectly heard. Consequently, the desire to listen to stories is tempered by knowledge that of certain tales, it is best not to "believe a word" (66).

In novels that embody a theory of "more talk, less action," an individual's manner of speaking and the language he or she uses, even in conversations not overheard, offer critical revelations of character.[27] Besides people's appearance and associates, their conversation is one of the few means to judge their character: not only what they say, but how they say it, and to whom. Scholars have long recognized the crucial role that dialogue plays in Austen's texts in the assessment and understanding of others.[28] The novel "always includes in itself the activity of coming to know another's word, a coming to knowledge whose process is represented in the novel."[29] Appearing to be a shortcut, eavesdropping is revealed eventually as a detour in this fundamental process of "coming to knowledge."[30] Elizabeth Bennet, who prides herself on her powers of discernment and who possesses a "quickness" (52) and a "lively, sportive, manner of talking" (395), is particularly responsive to others who display similar abilities. Wickham attracts her initially through his engaging manners and "happy readiness of conversation" (116). When they meet for the second time, Austen plays with readers who have assumed that Wickham is the intended partner for Elizabeth. Through the use of the word "happy" to refer to both Wickham and Elizabeth in the same sentence, the narrator suggests a future union between them (120).[31] The narrator sets up readers as acknowledged eavesdroppers and entices us to make this association between verbal and emotional affinity – and to draw false conclusions. As a result, we undergo the same learning process as other stories' recipients: by the narrative's end, we, like the characters, have been disabused of our initial judgments of character and story.

In *Pride and Prejudice*, characters' skill or ineptitude as talkers and listeners often discloses their moral or intellectual acumen. More perceptive characters listen more attentively, and hence are more open to other people's ideas and more willing to delay forming opinions. Conversely, those who too readily talk rather than listen lack an awareness of others and possess an inflated sense of their own significance. In this second category, Lady Catherine monopolizes conversations (198), speaks in "so authoritative a tone, as mark[s] her self-importance" (197), and insists on knowing the substance of everyone else's conversations (206). The impetuous Lydia "seldom listen[s] to any body for more than half a minute" (249), but only prattles, like her mother. Pompous

Mr. Collins's discourse is filled with trite expressions appreciated only by the equally pedantic Mary (108). Whereas Elizabeth derives great amusement from listening to other people's conversations (84, 92), Miss Bingley quickly "tire[s] of a conversation in which she ha[s] no share" (103).

Gifted individuals not only "catch on" more quickly; they also "catch" more than others, so that "part of [Mr. Denny's] intelligence, though unheard by Lydia, [is] caught by Elizabeth" (132). Elizabeth and Darcy, both as eager eavesdroppers and as acknowledged participants in conversation, learn in the course of the novel to postpone making judgments until they have heard "the whole story." Characters like Jane, "a willing listener" (253), accept other people's views and often refrain from passing judgment upon them (128). The Gardiners are talented listeners and speakers, so that Elizabeth feels proud to have her uncle converse with Darcy (276). Unlike Wickham, who "smile[s], look[s] handsome, and sa[ys] many pretty things," but who is as empty as his words (341), Darcy only speaks to the purpose; "he does not rattle away like other young men" (271), and indeed, admits to difficulty in "conversing easily with those [he] ha[s] never seen before" (209). During the course of the novel, the reader, like Elizabeth and Darcy, finds she has "a very different story to hear" than the one that eavesdropping produces (60). Our willingness to hear this other story indicates an ability to change for the better, to enter into a conversation with another, rather than insist on telling the story from our own point of view. Elizabeth's response to Wickham's inquiry about whether Darcy has improved registers this alteration: "When I said that he improved on acquaintance, I did not mean that either his mind or manners were in a state of improvement, but that from knowing him better, his disposition was better understood" (260–61). It is less Darcy than Elizabeth's *understanding* of him that has changed.

By the end of the novel, both she and Darcy have learnt the necessity for a different kind of listening: an unmediated and open listening that allows the other a chance to tell his or her story directly without prior "pre-judice," which Moretti defines as "to emit a verdict before having had time to think." Such listening requires both time and patience – qualities that, by definition, "first impressions" preclude.[32] When Elizabeth and Darcy jettison prejudice (a predisposition to judge, and unfavorably judge, other people) and pride (an overconfidence in oneself and one's abilities to judge), they reach an understanding about each other based upon tolerance and compromise. Their relationship is built less on a complete coincidence of thought, disposition, and character (as is the case with Jane and Bingley) than on a premise of the need to communicate continually: to listen with an open ear to the ideas of another person and not to judge until the other has spoken, told her or "his story."

Consequently, Elizabeth and Darcy finally reach their "good understanding" through a direct conversation in which both parties are, in turn, listeners and talkers (375). Because their interaction has been so mediated and distorted by prior information – through eavesdropping or other people's stories – direct communication becomes essential in surmounting misunderstanding. For this to occur, they must be willing to enter into a conversation with an other who is of both a different class and different sex.[33] Thus Elizabeth longs to talk to Darcy when he returns to Longbourn, so that she is "in no humour for conversation with any one but himself; and to him she ha[s] hardly courage to speak" (346). Instead of the polite, perfunctory, and utterly public forms of communication that group interaction has afforded them, she desires "to enter into something more of conversation, than the mere ceremonious salutation attending his entrance" (350). Only when they leave the busy parlor and walk alone outside is there opportunity for this private conversation, one that helps them come to an understanding because it does away with all enigmas, snares, and red herrings.

In his "Doctrine and Discipline of Divorce," John Milton states that "a meet and happy conversation is the chiefest and noblest end of marriage, for we find here no expression so necessary implying carnal knowledge as this prevention of loneliness to the mind and spirit of man."[34] Stanley Cavell explains how Milton's definition of conversation is broader than our contemporary use of the word: it encompasses relating to and living with others and is "something more like our concept of intercourse."[35] Indeed, both words have a sexual significance. Although we rarely associate "conversation" with sexual intercourse, English legal terminology until 1970 used the phrase "criminal conversation" to refer to the "action by a husband for damages against the seducer of his wife, the seduction being described as a 'criminal conversation.' "[36] Particularly to an eighteenth-century public, but under the English legal system at least until the mid-nineteenth century, adultery was considered a form of trespass, since a woman was deemed her husband's property and had no separate legal identity from his.[37] Such an illicit "conversation" transgresses social norms in thought and in deed, and like eavesdropping – another trespass whose etymology is bound up with legal history – involves the appropriation of something private.[38] This meaning rests upon an earlier, more comprehensive conception of "conversation," as "the action of consorting or having dealings with others; living together; commerce, intercourse, society, intimacy,"[39] a significance implicit in Milton's assertion that God's "end" in creating marriage was "the apt and cheerful conversation of man with woman, to comfort and refresh him against the evil of solitary life, not mentioning the purpose of generation till afterwards" (703). Milton also speaks of the soul's "desire of joining to itself in conjugal fellowship a fit conversing soul" (709), so that conversation comprises not just sexual but intellectual and spiritual intercourse.

The more comprehensive meaning of "conversation" resonates throughout Austen's novels, and explains why creating situations where characters can enter into conversation with each other is of vital importance.[40] Discussing comedies of marriage, Cavell points out that "talking together is fully and plainly being together, a mode of association, a form of life... [in which] the central pair are learning to speak the same language," or at least languages that can be mutually understood.[41] The same holds true in *Pride and Prejudice*. Thus, Bingley's offhand compliment that "[Darcy] can be a conversible companion if he thinks it worth his while" (125) becomes, on second hearing, a necessary attribute for our hero. And Elizabeth's desire to keep Darcy "to herself, and to those of her family with whom he might converse without mortification" becomes more understandable (391). This conversation involves the exchange of ideas, emotions, and attitudes with an other; it comprehends an association and familiarity with that other. The reserved Darcy shrinks from "conversing" with strangers. He must grasp that only by determining to "give himself the trouble," by entering into conversation with an other, can the strange become the familiar – a lesson he learns by talking with, rather than about Elizabeth (209).

As Cavell writes, "Comic resolutions depend upon an acquisition in time of self-knowledge... this is a matter of learning who you are" (56). In *Pride and Prejudice*, self-knowledge is spurred as much by interaction with another as it is by introspection, so that, after reading Darcy's letter, Elizabeth declares, "Till this moment, I never knew myself" (237). Learning about the other provokes an understanding of the self; those who never bother to understand anything outside themselves – the Lady Catherines, the Mr. Collinses, the Lydia Bennets – will never truly know themselves. Austen sees "man [*sic*] ... not as a solitary being completed in himself, but only as completed in society."[42]

By the end of the novel, Darcy and Elizabeth possess all the ingredients for "an union that must have been to the advantage of both" (325), based upon mutual "[r]espect, esteem, and confidence" (262). The last of these, with its double valence of "trust in" and "confiding in" is particularly significant in considering the protagonists' conversation as a relational mode as well as a verbal exchange. The word "confidence" recurs repeatedly after they have traded stories of their sisters' meditated and actual elopements. Their reciprocal "confidence" comprehends information that could be compromising, and yet whose telling to this particular person assumes that a secret will be kept. This confidence depends upon not only a trust in the other, but also a confidence in language to communicate. In contrast, Lydia's marriage, like her mother's, will rest on none of these foundations. In her first encounter with her family as a married woman, Lydia reveals a secret: Darcy was present at the ceremony, and in fact helped arrange it. She unconcernedly responds to Elizabeth's amazement at his presence, "I quite forgot! I ought not to have said a word about it. I promised them so faithfully!... It was to be such a secret!" (332). The justice of this betrayal at the level of plot seems evident. Elizabeth's refusal to betray Darcy's confidence leads Lydia to elope with Wickham; in contrast, Lydia's unwitting revelation of Darcy's goodness helps reconcile him to Elizabeth. Elizabeth and Darcy's "conversation" will remain private and profound, whereas that of Lydia and Wickham will be ever subject to a public audience and its disapproval.

Public performance and private conversation offer two models of social relationship in *Pride and Prejudice*; these social models have narrative implications as well. Darcy recognizes a similarity between himself and Elizabeth, and tells her, "We neither of us perform to strangers" (209). Barthes explains how:

Idyllic communication denies all theater, it refuses any presence *in front of which* the destination can be achieved... Narrative communication is the opposite: each destination is at one moment or another a spectacle for the other participants in the game... of which the reader is the ultimate beneficiary... the various listeners (here we ought to be able to say *écouteur* as we say *voyeur*) seem to be located at every corner of utterance.[43]

Barthes stresses the oral nature of narrative communication, in which the reader is the final eavesdropper, the last participant in a chain of aural reception in a world of "distinct cacography" (132). The Wickhams are constant exhibitionists, and their life together will be one long performance.

Their narratable "conversation" will always be overheard, and in fact, requires an eavesdropper to instill value in it, for it exists less as an inherently meaningful interaction than as a spectacle, an activity for the benefit of an outsider, upon whom it depends. The Darcys do not perform; they converse. Their "idyllic" conversation will never be subject to novelistic eavesdropping; their marriage removes them and *Pride and Prejudice* from the realm of the narratable.[44]

* * *

Another illicit activity is often required to resolve the narrative situation that eavesdropping unleashes. In *Pride and Prejudice*, this second transgression facilitates Darcy's and Elizabeth's reconciliation. As in *Evelina*, the protagonists achieve direct communication through the workings of intermediaries: Lady De Bourgh and Mrs. Gardiner. Austen writes that Elizabeth "soon learnt that they were indebted for their present good understanding to the efforts of his aunt, who *did* call on him in her return through London and there relate ... the substance of her conversation with Elizabeth" (375). Through Lady De Bourgh's unconsciously revelatory narrative, Darcy learns to hope that Elizabeth returns his affection. In *Pride and Prejudice*, Elizabeth is more active than Burney's Evelina, whose friend eavesdrops for her. Consequently, Austen resorts to a form of narrative transgression in which all participants are directly engaged: the betrayal of the secret that Darcy has paid Wickham to marry Lydia. Elizabeth compels her aunt to reveal Darcy's covert role in Lydia's marriage. As Elizabeth abashedly notes later, their "comfort springs from a breach of promise" (389).

This transgression is part of an almost complete revelation of information necessary to conclude the narrative. The only information not revealed is that which would dispose Jane not to like Darcy: his dissuading Bingley from pursuing Jane, based on his opinion that Miss Bennet did not really care for Bingley. This last narrative thread is never completely tied up. As Elizabeth recognizes, "Here was knowledge in which no one could partake; and she was sensible that nothing less than a perfect understanding between the parties could justify her in throwing off this last incumbrance of mystery" (253–54). Yet, in the narrative we are given, this "mystery" is never revealed to the characters, despite the fact that Jane and Bingley do reach "a perfect understanding." "'Closure' is not to be equated with full 'disclosure.'"[45]

Although the conclusions to Austen's novels present situations of communication and "closure," rarely do they admit total "disclosure." There is always some information that is not revealed, as Austen herself acknowledges in *Emma*: "seldom... does complete truth belong to any human disclosure; seldom can it happen that something is not a little disguised, or a little mistaken."[46] That residue contains the potential for other narratives. Narrative closure is, in essence, the author's point of discretion, the point where she declines to give us more information or to present to us any more mysteries. The potential still remains, but fictional closure covers it up with the appearance of full disclosure. Narrative resolution comes in *Pride and Prejudice* when characters and the narrator are content to converse and not to eavesdrop.

Austen's *Persuasion* resorts to eavesdropping to resolve a narrative produced by the interference of a well-intentioned maternal surrogate. *Persuasion*'s primary story revolves around the elements of the secondary plots in *Pride and Prejudice*: persuasion – wielding oratorical powers to convince someone else to act (or refuse to act) – and discretion – determining when to speak and when to remain silent. The novel dramatizes the power of language, particularly its oral manifestations. Whereas Lady Catherine fails in her efforts to prevent the union of Darcy and Elizabeth, Lady Russell initially succeeds in convincing Anne not to marry Wentworth. Thus *Persuasion* is a book about a "second chance," a second story; it begins where most books would end, or more precisely, at the point where it has "thwarted" the more typical Austen ending.[47] A novel preoccupied by endings, *Persuasion* uses eavesdropping to achieve its fictional resolution.

CHAPTER 2

Eavesdropping and the gentle art of Persuasion

> Your tale, sir, would cure deafness.
> Shakespeare, *The Tempest*

> In ages of imagination this firm persuasion removed mountains; but many are not capable of a firm persuasion of anything.
> Blake, *The Marriage of Heaven and Hell*

A novel that Austen herself criticized as being "too light, and bright, and sparkling," *Pride and Prejudice* ends optimistically, with its principal characters wed on linguistic and narrative levels.[1] In a text whose last two words are "uniting them" (396), Elizabeth and Darcy have overcome the obstacles to a happy marriage and thus, in Austen's imagined world, to happy lives.[2] Instead of a "truth universally acknowledged," Elizabeth and Darcy have learned the truth about each other and themselves. Rather than listening to proliferating stories, they finally get the story "right," by listening to each other. The conclusion implies that their subsequent tale, in its almost perfect completeness, need not be told. Narrative plenitude replaces narrative lack; in Barthes's words, narrative (dis)closure replaces narrative "'reticence,' the rhetorical figure which interrupts the sentence, suspends it, turns it aside."[3]

Austen's final novel presents a much less ebullient ending, and, in its more complex and pervasive use of eavesdropping, offers a more qualified sense of individuals' ability to communicate, and the possibilities for complete disclosure. Rather than attempting to relate the "true" story, *Persuasion* (1818) explores the subjective nature of storytelling. Individuals leave the imprint of their imagination on the stories they tell.[4] Through its representation of speakers and listeners, the novel offers Austen's most overt discussion of the disparity between men's and women's positions in society, and the differences in their means for physical or verbal agency.

Eavesdropping, like narrative, often operates as a transgression of the very situation it ultimately seeks to establish. Covert listening violates the kind of direct communication that it occasionally produces, just as narrative presumes the existence of secrets, yet its activity is the eventual revelation of such secrets, the replacement of lack with plenitude, of reticence with utterance. Paradoxically, such extraordinary deviations from open conversation are sometimes the only means to effect unmediated communication. In *Persuasion*, episodes of overhearing occur at critical moments of the narrative; they signal the conditions of narratability yet work to enact its eventual replacement with the non-narratable. More overtly than in *Pride and Prejudice*, Austen links concerns of gender and speech through their representation in acts of eavesdropping.

An eavesdropping scene resolves the narrative of *Persuasion*. It replaces narrative uncertainty with certainty and completeness, enabling Wentworth and Anne to reach a mutual understanding. Austen places the scene in the penultimate chapter of her novel, and situates this event at the White Hart Inn, in the Musgroves' suite. In this semipublic space, Captain Wentworth overhears Anne Elliot's impassioned defense of woman's constancy, which she delivers to Captain Harville. The outburst is Anne's longest and most vehement speech in *Persuasion*; the specific conditions of its occurrence, its content, and its listeners are crucial to the novel's structural, thematic, and ideological concerns.

From as early as 1821, critics have noted the importance of the novel's final eavesdropping scene, although none has emphasized secret listening itself in exploring these concerns.[5] Barbara Hardy, in her discussion of listening and narrating, and Stuart Tave, in his examination of listening and "moral awareness," are the only scholars to have used the term "eavesdropping" in their analyses of *Persuasion*.[6] Tony Tanner characterizes the protagonists and their society as being in a state of "in-betweenness," although he never specifically considers how eavesdropping represents this liminal position structurally and figuratively.[7] At the beginning of the novel, Anne is "in between" homes, social circles, and marital status.[8] The narrative is set at a transitional moment, when the values of the landed aristocracy are giving way to those of the commercially based middle class. *Persuasion* replicates the "in-betweenness" of society on a linguistic level. Communication is not direct but mediated. The eavesdropping scene figures the transitional state of society, the indeterminate status of the heroine, and the difficulty of direct communication among characters. An act that polite society would censure, overhearing nevertheless provides the solution to this state of "in-betweenness." Eavesdropping emphasizes the social and psychological problems of being in such a position, yet it also provides the means of resolving the unsettled state of the narrative and of reconciling its characters and the social worlds they represent.

Overhearing is particularly resonant in a novel whose heroine is continually placed in the position of listener, and whose "central, unifying action... is the act, both literal and metaphoric, of hearing."[9] If Elizabeth Bennet can be faulted for her readiness to write of, or write off, the characters of individuals, and to tell them so unhesitatingly, Anne Elliot is a character whose presumed failings are a reticence toward speaking, and an inclination toward listening rather than telling. She is "a heroine who has great difficulty in making herself heard."[10] These two heroines represent the tendency of Austen's protagonists to be either "imaginist[s],"[11] eager creators of stories, like Elizabeth, Emma Woodhouse, and Catherine Morland, or more reserved, quiet listeners to stories, such as Anne, Elinor Dashwood, and Fanny Price.[12]

In *Persuasion*, Austen associates speaking with authority and power; the heroine's muteness reflects a corresponding lack of agency. The narrator describes how Anne has "never since the loss of her dear mother, known the happiness of being listened to, or encouraged;" she can "do little more than listen patiently."[13] Neither her word nor her person is accorded any status in her family, except by Lady Russell, the surrogate mother whose own persuasiveness had convinced Anne to break off her engagement to her "perfect listener eight years before the novel's story began."[14] Anne hardly embraces the status quo,[15] but she recognizes the futility of offering advice: "her word had no weight; her convenience was always to give way – she was only Anne" (11).

The narration itself enforces Anne's muteness.[16] Most of the dialogue in the novel is between characters other than Anne. Although, through free indirect discourse, readers have more complete access to Anne's thoughts than to any other Austen heroine's, seldom do we hear her speak directly.[17] Overhearing her thoughts does little to lessen her inaudibility at an intradiegetic level. Anne rarely addresses another character directly; such utterances usually indicate a critical moment in the narrative, like the final eavesdropping scene at the inn. Instead, the narrative style conspires with the fact that Anne has no listener or confidante except herself (and the reader); most of her conversations are internal, and indicate the strength of her inner voice and conscience. The narration presents direct conversations between Anne and other characters only when the latter begin to listen to her in the second half of the novel.

Persuasion dwells on relations between social and verbal power. The final eavesdropping scene represents the culmination of several significant episodes that indicate the nature of Anne's and Wentworth's relationship to each other and to other characters. Such scenes display individuals' degree of narrative agency by the position each occupies within a particular eavesdropping episode. Most often, women must gather information indirectly by overhearing others, or must express themselves by strategies of "indirection."[18] A woman writer presenting the difficulties of female utterance, Austen repeatedly uses moments of eavesdropping to figure this kind of mediated or oblique communication.

One of the first eavesdropping scenes in *Persuasion* presents Anne and Wentworth in separate conversations in the Uppercross drawing room, just after Wentworth's return to the neighborhood. The chapter opens with a statement of their physical proximity to but emotional and verbal distance from each other; they encounter each other only in public, and interact directly only in the most superficial manner. Although they are "repeatedly in the same circle," they "had no conversation together, no intercourse but what the commonest civility required... There *had* been a time, when of all the large party now filling the drawing-room at Uppercross, they would have found it most difficult, to cease to speak to one another" (63). Anne and Wentworth are close enough that the primarily silent, "listening and thinking" Anne can hear "the same voice" (64) she heard when conversing with Wentworth herself eight years ago. Wentworth dominates the conversation, partly because of his position as new arrival, and partly because "his profession qualified him, his disposition led him, to talk" (63). Whereas Anne pays more attention to Wentworth's conversation with others than she appears to give her own, as in many encounters in the first half of the novel, Wentworth not only does not listen to Anne but avoids talking to her and tries not to hear her when she speaks.[19]

In this scene, Anne's overhearing painfully reminds her of the affinity between her and her estranged lover. In separate discussions with Mrs. Musgrove over her son's death, Anne and Wentworth register similar reactions to the mother's sorrow: "Anne suppressed a smile, and listened kindly, while Mrs. Musgrove relieved her heart a little more; and for a few minutes, therefore, could not keep pace with the conversation of the others" (64). In an analogous manner:

There was a momentary expression in Captain Wentworth's face at [Mrs. Musgrove's] speech, a certain glance of his bright eye, and curl of his handsome mouth, which convinced Anne that instead of sharing in Mrs. Musgrove's kind wishes, as to her son, he had probably been at some pains to get rid of him; but . . . in another moment he was perfectly collected and serious; and almost instantly afterwards coming up to the sofa, on which she and Mrs. Musgrove were sitting, took a place by the latter, and entered into conversation with her, in a low voice, about her son, doing it with so much sympathy and natural grace as showed the kindest consideration for all that was real and unabsurd in the parent's feelings. (67)

Their thoughts coincide, but Mrs. Musgrove physically separates them on the sofa. Through this exchange, Anne realizes that, although a frustrating harmony still exists between them in other matters, their emotional estrangement, like Mrs. Musgrove's form, is "no insignificant barrier indeed" to reconciliation or even civil intercourse (67).[20] Here Anne's covert listening confirms affinity but denies her the possibility of acting upon such knowledge. In addition, Mrs. Musgrove's public sorrow over the loss of her "very troublesome, hopeless son" forms an important contrast to Anne's private, silent anguish for a lost love, a grief rendered more poignant by Wentworth's presence and coldness toward her (52). Whereas the mourning parent can take comfort in conversation with others about her loss, the sorrowing lover has no such solace.

Austen places another eavesdropping scene in the middle of the narrative, where Anne overhears Wentworth explain to Louisa Musgrove the kind of woman he admires. Occurring in Chapter 10 of Part I, this episode anticipates some of the thematic and structural concerns of the final eavesdropping scene, located in the penultimate chapter of the book, in what was initially Chapter 10 of Part II. This second episode of overhearing further establishes Anne as the passive listener to other people's conversations. As Anne walks with her sister and brother-in-law, she tries to distract herself with "musings and quotations" – other people's words – but Wentworth's conversation with the nubile Misses Musgrove intrudes upon her consciousness (82). Anne attempts to join the conversation, "but nobody heard, or, at least, nobody answered her" (83). When the party disperses, she finds herself sitting behind the hedgerow where Wentworth and Louisa are discussing the merits of woman's firmness over pliancy. In other words, they discuss persuasion. Austen contrasts Anne's inability to speak or be heard with Louisa's "eager speech" and her determination not to be "easily persuaded" (84, 85), a pointed allusion to Anne's having been induced to break off her engagement with Wentworth. His praise of Louisa's attitude ("let those who would be happy be firm") confirms Wentworth's belief that Anne demonstrated "too yielding and indecisive a character" (85). The former lovers are now even more divided, physically, by the hedgerow, and emotionally, by Wentworth's growing attraction to Louisa. Rather than provide her with knowledge that would enable Anne to win back Wentworth, eavesdropping here corroborates misunderstanding and provides narrative dilation.

Persuasion is suffused with scenes of not merely conspicuous but also covert overhearing, scenes in which eavesdropping is committed but unacknowledged. The most discreet of these occurs in Molland's sweet shop in Bath, where Anne and Wentworth meet again for the first time after Louisa's fall in Lyme.[21] After an "embarrassed" encounter with Anne at the confectioner's, Wentworth loses the opportunity to talk to her when Mr. Elliot arrives to escort her home (167). After their departure, the narrator omits to inform the reader that Wentworth remains in the shop while his female companions discuss the probability of the cousins' marriage. Wentworth becomes a silent "nobody," disregarded by the narrative and the speakers, yet just as pained by their speculations as Anne has been by rumors of his matrimonial plans (11). The importance of this conversation becomes clear only after Anne and Wentworth are reconciled, when he informs Anne that, although he knew when he reached Bath how much he loved her, "jealousy of Mr. Elliot had been the retarding weight, the doubt, the torment. That had begun to operate in the very hour of first meeting her in Bath" (229). This hidden eavesdropping scene prolongs their misunderstanding. More importantly, it situates Wentworth in Anne's usual place: silent, overlooked, passive, hurt. In this covert episode of overhearing, he undergoes the "penance" of experiencing the typical feminine position; it reeducates him about Anne's character and awakens him to the difficulties of her situation as a nineteenth-century woman of the gentry.[22]

The event also creates a secret in the narration, one that is revealed later in the lovers' explanatory conversation. Thus, unavowed eavesdropping scenes create enigmas for both characters and readers that are dispelled only through direct communication and extended narrative.[23] Withholding information, Austen discloses it only when such knowledge serves to highlight the disparity between the current moment of plenitude and the former moment of misunderstanding. The retrospective narration of miscommunication is "made up of exquisite moments" (232), for they represent unspeakable happiness through contrast with its narratable opposite.

A final eavesdropping scene near the end of *Persuasion* reiterates concerns about the difficulty of communication and the problems of women's verbal and social agency.[24] The episode emphasizes the fact that direct communication between Anne and Wentworth has been almost nonexistent until this point; they learn about each other largely through conversations with other people and through acts of inadvertent overhearing. Like gossip, such mediated stories almost never provide accurate information; instead, their interactions have produced only "inadvertencies and misconstructions of the most mischievous kind" (211).

The scene replaces a shorter, more contrived conclusion in an earlier draft. In the revised ending, Austen dropped most of the original Chapter 10 of Part II and inserted a new Chapter 11, so that the original final Chapter 11 became Chapter 12. Overhearing features in both conclusions, but changes to the initial configuration of characters within the eavesdropping triangle have tremendous implications for the larger narrative. The first version involves an awkward use of Admiral Croft, who enables the lovers to reach an understanding.[25] Anne overhears the Admiral say to Wentworth:

"As I am going to leave you together, it is but fair I should give you something to talk of – and so, if you please –" Here the door was very firmly closed; she could guess by which of the two; and she lost entirely what immediately followed; but it was impossible for her not to distinguish parts of the rest, for the Adml on the strength of the Door's being shut was speaking without any management of the voice, tho' she cd hear his companion trying to check him.[26]

During their discussion, Anne hears the senior officer virtually command his brother-in-law to ascertain whether Anne is engaged to Mr. Elliot (10). This ending presents Anne eavesdropping on men's conversation and perpetuates her characterization as a passive listener waiting for others to initiate change.[27] As a bystander in the scene that largely determines her fate, all Anne can do is "liste[n], as if her Life depended on the issue of his Speech" (13). Her only action here has been acquiescence: she complies with the Admiral's request that she visit his wife and remains in the parlor despite discovering that the Captain is also there. Anne cannot begin the simplest conversation with Wentworth: "She longed to be able to speak of the weather or the Concert – but could only compass the releif [sic] of taking a Newspaper in her hand" (11). Despite overhearing how Admiral Croft and Wentworth are misinformed about her marriage plans, she takes no direct action to undeceive them but simply reacts to their actions and words. After Wentworth explains his mission, she replies unintelligibly (14). Wentworth must again solicit a response from her, which he formulates for her: "Pronounce only the words, *he may*. – I shall immediately follow him with your message" (14). Anne responds in a reply marked by fragmentation, sudden stops, and hesitations:

"No, Sir" – said Anne – "There is no message. – You are misin – the Adml is misinformed. I do justice to the kindness of his Intentions, but he is quite mistaken. There is no Truth in any such report." (15)

In this exchange, the supposed need to inform the Admiral still obtrudes upon their conversation, even though it makes possible their own communication.[28] This first direct and sustained interaction between Anne and Wentworth is less verbal than ocular, a conversation that precludes both verbal communication and its narration. Despite her inactivity, Anne and Wentworth enter a realm of plenitude where the only "lack" is the absence of that which makes narrative possible: "Suspense and Indecision" (16).[29]

The revised conclusion of *Persuasion* involves the protagonists more directly in representing miscommunication and the barriers to understanding that must be transgressed through eavesdropping.[30] The later version foregrounds problems of women's activity, speech, and reticence. In the eavesdropping scene, both lovers engage in ostensible and actual conversations; both their exchanges include an overt and a hidden *destinataire*. While Anne converses with Harville, she deliberately addresses Wentworth, just as the Captain, "while supposed to be writing only to Captain Benwick, . . . had been also addressing her" (225). Austen places the new scene after the lovers' first direct but frustrated interaction at the concert, when Anne discerns that Wentworth still cares for her but cannot make known her love for him.[31] As a woman, Anne's opportunities for open conversation with Wentworth are limited. She cannot pay him a visit, nor send him a letter; their recent social encounters have led to additional "misconstructions." Hence, only an extraordinary means of communication – one that violates the conduct-book code of behavior and temporarily destroys the reticence characterizing both Anne and the narrative style – can induce Anne and Wentworth to converse. The new eavesdropping scene, with its doubly mediated flow of information – first Wentworth overhears Anne pleading women's greater constancy to Harville, then he writes a letter to her expressing his feelings – stresses the impediments to direct communication. This second ending's emphasis on mediated communication continues that initiated at the concert, when Wentworth speaks to Anne but indicates the constancy of his love *indirectly*, by referring to his friend's devotion to the memory of his dead beloved (175).

Moreover, the second ending involves the lovers more actively and decreases the importance of the third person in the eavesdropping triad. In the draft, Wentworth stresses that Anne must consider him "as speaking only for another" (12), that he is merely the mediator in a scenario devised by an older, paternal figure. In the final version, Anne speaks for herself, and Harville becomes merely the ostensible recipient of Anne's speech. Positioning the heroine as the most active character in the eavesdropping triangle represents a radical change, not only from the first version, but also from Austen's resolution to *Pride and Prejudice*, where Elizabeth provokes the breaching of a confidence but does not provide information herself. In *Persuasion*, it is not a benevolent Mrs. Gardiner or a meddling Lady Catherine who helps reconcile the protagonists, but the heroine herself who woos her lover back.[32]

The revision reverses the roles that Anne and Wentworth have played in the novel, respectively, as (passive) listener and (active) speaker.[33] Here, Anne speaks and Wentworth overhears; she avows, albeit in an indirect fashion, the constancy of her love, while Wentworth is "restricted to the feminine position of helpless onlooker and overhearer."[34] The reversal simultaneously underscores and initially subverts the gendered positions that Anne and Captain Harville are discussing. Anne declares that women feel more and remain more faithful than men do because:

> "We live at home, quiet, confined, and our feelings prey upon us. You are forced on exertion. You have always a profession, pursuits, business of some sort or other, to take you back into the world immediately, and continual occupation and change soon weaken impressions." (221)

Women are "quiet, confined," whereas men have activity to occupy and divert them. This distinction recalls Wentworth's earlier admission that the Navy distracted him from his disappointment over their broken engagement; he confesses his great need "at that time, to be at sea ... I wanted to be *doing* something" (65, e.m.).

In contrast to the variety of occupations available to men in early nineteenth-century England, one of middle-class women's few occupations was conversation, although some topics remained off-limits for them; propriety restricted women's activity. Unlike men's distinct professions and hobbies – the Navy, law, business, the Church, or hunting, fishing, riding – the "work" women continually bring forth to occupy their hands, if not their minds, is rarely specified in novels as needlework, tatting, embroidery, knitting, etc., but is dismissed as merely "work."[35] Even in this later scene, Wentworth's eavesdropping is not inadvertent, but deliberate. He is "striving to catch sounds, which yet she did not think he could have caught" (222). Indeed, he is not a patient listener, for his overhearing provokes an outburst of writing in which he declares, "I can listen no longer in silence. I must speak to you by such means are within my reach" (225). But he is listening, and listening to Anne, whose words now carry an urgent appeal.

Wentworth's eavesdropping, so all-consuming that he drops his pen, signals a change to male possession of the oral and textual word. Anne relates how in the past, "Men have had every advantage of us in telling their own story. Education has been theirs in so much higher a degree; the pen has been in their hands" (223).[36] Her speech marks the moment when the pen "fall[s] down" (222). In her defense of women's greater constancy, Anne speaks persuasively on behalf of her sex and her love. Her speech tries to reclaim history, or at least the history of love, from male hands; at the oral level, she succeeds. Wentworth admits in his note to her, "I am every instant hearing something which overpowers me" (226).[37] In this changed ending, Anne temporarily possesses narrative agency; Admiral Croft, a symbol of benevolent paternal authority, is no longer in control. Although at the novel's end Sir Walter still "prepare[s] his pen with a very good grace" to inscribe his daughter's marriage in that ultimate record of patriarchy and male history, *The Baronetage*, this book is read only by effete fathers and their dissolute heirs (237). Its narrative may be ending, particularly if Mr. Elliot continues to elude Mrs. Clay's matrimonial clutches.

But *Persuasion* does not conclude on a note of female triumph. Instead, the eavesdropping scene stands as an expression of Anne's position both as individual, steadfast lover, and as woman articulating but accepting her limited sphere of action. The gender debate concludes in a draw on literal and metaphoric levels. Neither argument prevails; Anne fails to convince Captain Harville that women's love is stronger and longer lasting. Both debaters find themselves at a loss for words. Yet Austen inscribes a gender difference in this silence: Anne "could not immediately have uttered another sentence; her heart was too full, her breath too much oppressed," whereas Harville declares, "There is no quarrelling with you. – And when I think of Benwick, my tongue is tied" (224). Anne's emotions silence her, so that she cannot speak.[38] Harville's do as well, but he articulates this silencing; he does have the last word, even if it is about the inability to speak.

Critics attempt to place Austen in various politically charged categories, often at opposite extremes: Austen as conservative writer[39] or Austen as revolutionary feminist with an agenda of social reform.[40] Austen's novels in fact constitute less an apology for the situation of middle-class women in her society or an exhortation to revolt against it than a staging of the polemic.[41] In using a set-up scene of listening to dramatize the difficulties confronting women and women writers, Austen invites the other sanctioned eavesdropper, the reader, to enter the debate about gender politics.

Consequently, once she has delineated gendered differences in linguistic and narrative agency, Austen turns to the resolution of her story. Using similar vocabulary to describe the lovers' reactions to each other, the text intimates that the discord of ideas and emotions is being replaced by a concord of feeling and language. Just as Wentworth's note confesses how he is "every instant hearing something which overpowers me," the receipt of this letter, with its emotional urgency, evokes in Anne "overpowering happiness" (226). In the note Wentworth asks for "a word, a look" (226); Anne worries that she will "lose the possibility of speaking two words" to him (227). Both long for direct dialogue rather than indirect or visual communication.[42]

As direct conversation and harmony of ideas replace misinformation and mediated communication, Anne and Wentworth walk "towards the comparatively quiet and retired gravel-walk, where the power of conversation ... make[s] the present hour a blessing indeed" (228). In this relatively secluded space, the lovers reunite in language as in emotion. By telling each other about their past "years of division and estrangement," they close the gap that has existed between them. Their histories and their understanding converge, just as their future is held in common (229). This reconciliation reworks much of the material from the original version of Chapter 10, but with important changes. Specifically, the revision replaces Wentworth's choppy, emotionally charged half-utterances and indirect discourse with a smoother, more harmonious conversation, in which much of Wentworth's story unfolds in direct discourse, a voice emphasizing that communication is no longer mediated.[43]

When the lovers reach the Elliots' house, the narrative conveys their emotional attachment in terms of domestic, intimate space:

At last Anne was at home again, and happier than any one in that house could have conceived. All the surprise and suspense, and every other painful part of the morning dissipated by this conversation, she re-entered the house so happy as to be obliged to find an alloy in some momentary apprehensions of its being impossible to last. (233)

Anne's feeling "at home" is produced less by being "in that house" than by being with Wentworth; they have established an emotional dwelling space, a "homely" (*heimlich*: familiar, private) place whose existence does not depend upon landed estate or physical abode, but upon continuous conversation in the larger sense.[44] In *Persuasion*, home is indeed where the heart is. Stanley Cavell explains how:

> We think of marriage ... as the entering simultaneously into a new public and a new private connection, the creation at once of new spaces of communality and of exclusiveness, of a new outside and inside to life, spaces expressible by the private ownership of a house, literally an apartment, a place that is part of and apart within a larger habitation.[45]

This "private connection" requires physical, emotional, and narrative separation from the public world – in essence, secrecy.[46] Hence Anne recognizes "the absolute necessity of *seeming* like herself" and of leaving "with no feeling of gratitude *apparent*" (226, 228, e.m.). Similarly, Charles's request that Wentworth accompany Anne home produces on the Captain's part "a most obliging compliance *for public* view; and smiles reined in and spirits dancing *in private* rapture" (e.m.).[47] Once the couple have reached a private understanding, they must keep it concealed from public view and knowledge. Paradoxically, Anne and Wentworth have created such intimacy through a means that intrudes on private spaces and conversations – through eavesdropping.

Eavesdropping implies proximity. It entails contiguity between public and private spheres. In similar fashion, the lovers' newly created private space is closely linked to a larger, public world.[48] Austen's description places them upon the "*comparatively* quiet and retired gravel path," yet amid the "sauntering politicians, bustling housekeepers, flirting girls, ... nursery maids and children" (228, 229, e.m.). It acknowledges the interrelation of the two zones. Just as its many conversations involve clearly identified speakers and listeners as well as secret or acknowledged eavesdroppers, *Persuasion* operates on the tension created between the novel's public plots and private stories – the narrative of societal interactions among the Elliots, Musgroves, Harvilles, and Dalrymples, and that of love between Anne and Wentworth.[49]

Austen's novels stress the paramount importance of conversation as an initiator and index of all human interaction and community, both in society and in private. Society for Austen is not the "vast external framework, like the 'social system' alluded to in Dickens's *Dombey and Son*," but a much more intimate "subjective structure" that rests upon interactions among individuals in small groups.[50] Within this context, public and private do not represent the spheres of political and economic influence that Jürgen Habermas describes. Rather, all significant action in Austen's novels takes place in the greater Habermasian private sphere – a selective one consisting of what Raymond Williams calls the "knowable community" of the upper middle class and gentry.[51] But this sphere does affect the larger political and economic activities that enter only obliquely into her narratives. The paragraph immediately following the lovers' reunion describes the Elliots' evening party, and indicates Anne's relationship with each character in terms of the conversation she has with each of them. Anne enjoys:

> [w]ith the Musgroves... the happy chat of perfect ease; with Captain Harville, the kind-hearted intercourse of brother and sister; with Lady Russell, attempts at conversation, which a delicious consciousness cut short; with Admiral and Mrs. Croft, everything of peculiar cordiality and fervent interest, which the same consciousness sought to conceal – and with Captain Wentworth, some moments of communication continually occurring, and always the hope of more, and always the knowledge of his being there! (233)

Both the catalogue of relations and the final dialogue of the scene close with conversation between Anne and Wentworth. Both passages imply that their story will never end, that "there is no humanly envisionable conclusion to the conversation of marriage."[52] This infinite conversation obtains at the same time that the repeated "perfection" and "fixity" of the lovers' reconciliation signals an awareness of the narrative's need to conclude (229, 230). Conversation in Austen's novels registers the distinction between the ideal conclusions of fiction and the often untidy endings in life.[53]

* * *

Despite its imperfections, language is "indispensable in making any society possible."[54] *Persuasion* acknowledges not only the limitations inherent in language, but also an individual's self-imposed restrictions on divulging information to others. In her debate with Captain Harville, Anne suggests that the facts supporting her argument "may be precisely such as cannot be brought forward without betraying a confidence, or in some respect saying what should not be said" (223). Tact is central to ethical behavior. The passage affirms the periodic reticence that heroines such as Elizabeth Bennet or Emma Woodhouse learn,[55] or, like Fanny Price or Anne Elliot, already demonstrate. *Mansfield Park*'s Mary Crawford, and Emma Woodhouse, two of Austen's most outspoken female characters, are each censured for a "particular brand of impropriety – her audacious speech," which can "deteriorat[e] into selfishness."[56] Chronologically, these heroines progress neither from speech to silence, nor from being reserved to being witty and articulate.[57] Rather, they represent a necessary fluctuation between free expression and linguistic reserve.

The marriage of Anne and Wentworth unites the best of both old and new worlds, characterized by verbal tendencies, respectively, of restraint and frankness.[58] Austen does not privilege "judicious reserve" over openness;[59] indeed, as Mr. Elliot demonstrates, carefully chosen speech, or a lack of candor, may signal an artificial mask rather than a genuine delicacy of behavior (153). Instead, Anne's tact complements the candor of the Musgroves and the naval officers. Anne educates Wentworth in the value of listening. Though accepting her position of limited verbal and physical agency, she has learned the imperative of female utterance.

Persuasion suggests a changed attitude toward storytelling in general. Instead of presenting two sides to every story, as does *Pride and Prejudice*, the narrative of *Persuasion* acknowledges the subjective basis of any storytelling. Every story is "prejudiced," for it emerges from a subjective consciousness. This understanding also resides in the recognition that a story changes from one telling to the next even when told by the same person, as indicated in Wentworth's appraisal of Anne, first just after his return, and later, once the two have reunited. Initially, through a doubly mediated exchange, Anne learns that the Captain finds her "so altered he should not have known [her] again" (61). Yet, once the lovers are reconciled, he tells her, "To my eye, you could never alter" (231). Rather than confront him with the inconsistency of his judgment, Anne merely "smile[s], and let[s] it pass" (231). A veteran listener, she recognizes the subjectivity inherent in any version of the "truth." Both stories are "true" from Wentworth's standpoint, but that perspective has altered. The value of the Captain's account resides less in what he says, than in the feelings it conveys.

Persuasion stresses our need to "[tell] the whole story [our] own way" with the hope of having a sympathetic listener (200). Wentworth's second statement represents his desire to erase past misunderstanding. Anne's decision not to challenge this accommodation of truth acknowledges the boundaries determining absolute truth. Austen affirms not only the limits to what can be told, but also how it can be told.[60] *Persuasion* presents an epistemological relativism, a "situatedness" in the stories that the characters tell and in the manner in which the narrative unfolds, at the same time that it invests this position with the possibility for insight and responsibility.[61] Eavesdropping figures that relativism in terms of space; it reminds us that, in our interactions with others, we always listen and speak from a specific – and limited – place.

Like Captain Harville, Austen "turn[s] the actual space to the best possible account," and works within the confines of being a nineteenth-century woman and a woman writer (95).[62] She delineates the limits to woman's possibilities for action, as she demonstrates an ability to work within them in a forceful, effective manner.[63] *Persuasion*, in its focus on the small spaces and the limitations of human existence – the Harvilles' cozy lodgings, the psychological or moral inadequacies of characters, the inability of language to overcome differences in subjective human experience, or the restricted opportunities for female activity – offers the possibility of creating a strong and lasting society within its compass.[64]

Austen's fiction charts the physical and emotional geography of human interaction. It reminds us of the complicity between public and private acts and accounts. The primary scene of social intercourse in Austen, the parlor or drawing room – at once social and intimate – spatially represents "a disinclination to separate the public and private."[65] Her heroines "grow as moral actors, not because they are protected from exposure to public life, ... but because they are at home in a place which can accommodate both public and private action."[66] The distinction between public and private here signifies less the separation of a public, "masculine" world of business from a private realm presided over by the feminine "angel of the house" than that between an individual's private thoughts and public utterances, between intimate conversation and social intercourse, and the interaction between them necessary to create a responsible society.[67]

Social experience in Austen takes place within a "knowable community." Interactions are both "face-to-face" and "very precisely selective," occurring within the relatively limited social range from prosperous farmers (*Emma*'s Robert Martin) to lesser aristocracy (*Persuasion*'s Lady Dalrymple); most individuals fall within the upper-middle class or gentry.[68] Divisions of spaces, people, and activities become more elaborate and concrete as the nineteenth century progresses, and its fiction displays the more complicated array of social experiences and attitudes in metropolitan cities. In the city, opportunities and motivations for eavesdropping increase. Walls between people are not hedgerows and mourning mothers, but doors, corridors, and stairways that materially separate business from home, employees from employers, kitchen from parlor, maid from mistress. Such physical spaces and their limits symbolize the broader differences of class and gender that present themselves in Balzac's and Dickens's novels. Eavesdropping dramatizes an evolving attitude toward public and private spaces and spheres in Victorian fiction. British and French novels of the 1830s and 1840s expand upon *Persuasion*'s distinction between living in a particular "house" and feeling "at home," and the kinds of people and activities proper to the home. Covert listeners are not just couples creating or overcoming misunderstandings, but also baronesses, disgruntled workers, prosperous businessmen, curious neighbors, concierges, old maids, bachelors, prostitutes, and thieves – individuals with motives as varied as their social positions and aspirations. As attempts to relegate "undesirables" to specific spaces and activities intensify, so, too, do the subversive efforts to violate such limits. In the ensuing decades, eavesdropping scenes stage the affective, social, and ideological dimensions of private space.

CHAPTER 3

Household words: Balzac's and Dickens's domestic spaces

> Un tour de clé ou un verrou poussé, et la vie intime de famille doit pouvoir être inviolable dans sa citadelle, qui est la chambre et ses dépendances.
> Julien Guadet

> L'architecture est l'expression des moeurs.
> Balzac, *La Fausse Maîtresse*

> A Paris, où les pavés ont des oreilles, où les portes ont une langue, où les barreaux des fenêtres ont des yeux, rien n'est plus dangereux que de causer devant les portes cochères. Les derniers mots qu'on se dit là, et qui sont à la conversation ce qu'un post-scriptum est à une lettre, contiennent des indiscrétions aussi dangereuses pour ceux qui les laissent écouter que pour ceux qui les recueillent.
> Balzac, *Le Cousin Pons*[1]

The nineteenth century has been called the "golden age of private life, a time when the vocabulary and reality of private life took shape."[2] As Jürgen Habermas and Richard Sennett, among others, have pointed out, the emergence of the bourgeois public sphere at the end of the eighteenth century in England and France produced its intimate, interconnected opposite, the private sphere, a necessary corollary to the concept of a civil society distinct from the state and its institutions.[3] Concomitant with the concepts of the individual and of privacy, the middle classes formed a sense of the family as the center of private life, a life seemingly removed and a solace from the public world of politics, business, and its pressures.

During the next century, the private realm became conceived as a haven from the cares and "contamination" of the larger public world, and the home idealized as the "sanctum sanctorum" of private life. Domestic spaces – in everyday life and in their literary representation – acquired a new psychological intensity. In the fiction of Balzac and Dickens, characters long for secure private spaces yet fear that they cannot be kept safe from prying eyes and ears. The manner in which these writers, working on opposite sides of the Channel, depicted domestic spaces reflects the incipient changes to domestic architecture that occurred during this period and the increased psychological and ideological weight that people attached to such dwellings and the idea of home. A new sense of self and privacy initiated during the Renaissance, finding public and political form in the late eighteenth century, and reaching its apogee in the nineteenth century, finds a correlative in the kinds of spaces the individual imagines and occupies. "Comfort" becomes a term used to evaluate domestic space in the nineteenth century. Being "at home" or "*chez soi*" assumes an unprecedented prominence in the conception of the self.[4]

In this context, eavesdropping assumes a uniquely resonant position as an activity that threatens this idealized space, its inhabitants, and their secrets. The occurrence of such clandestine activity within the space supposedly impervious to "all terror, doubt, and division" renders suspect the ideology of separate spheres, even as it provides a generative concept for fictional representation.[5] Eavesdropping provides an apt device for analyzing the tension in nineteenth-century England and France between the desire to assure privacy and the "naturalness" of the ideology of separate spheres, and the urge to stage or publicize private life in order to affirm its virtues. However, the repeated, obsessive, enactment of this dramatization renders suspect the degree to which even its most devoted adherents espoused the possibility of complete privacy at a time when technologies of publicity were increasing on an unprecedented scale.

This ambivalent attitude toward privacy and technology offers clues for understanding our own vexed relations toward the same issues, even if our response takes quite different forms. If the Victorians present a simultaneous desire for privacy and its spectacle, we seem to revel in a culture of confession and self-display yet to demonstrate a paranoia about intrusions on our privacy. By looking closely at nineteenth-century texts, we can trace our culture of publicity and its obverse to the earlier century's complicated attitude toward exposure and concealment of private lives.

This chapter is more expository than the others in my study, in part because of the sheer expanse of territory that it covers, encompassing the increasing compartmentalization of private space in nineteenth-century domestic architecture, its diverse representation in Balzac's and Dickens's fiction, and the many ways that eavesdropping stages the publicity of the private that such segregation of spaces and activities attempts to frustrate. Covert listening reminds us not only of the manner in which space "embodies social relationships" but also how space is at once social product and social agent. Representations of space "intervene in and modify spatial *textures* which are informed by effective knowledge and ideology."⁶ In the nineteenth century, domesticity was "as much a spatial as an affective obsession."⁷ In many of Dickens's texts, such as *Dombey and Son* or *Little Dorrit*, living space acquires such importance that buildings themselves acquire human characteristics and become London's "most evident inhabitants;" similarly, Balzac's apartments "respir[ent] l'honnêteté" (breathe, radiate respectability) or present "[des] façade[s] menaçante[s]" (menacing façades).⁸

In their recent study, *The Spectacle of Intimacy*, Karen Chase and Michael Levenson perceive how although the nineteenth century did not "invent the family or the thrill of opening its secret doors... the conditions of mid-nineteenth-century English life – the sheer extent of the home fetish, the maturing apparatus of information (newspapers, journals, the telegraph), the campaign for legal reform of the family, . . . the self-consciousness of modernity – gave it special claim on its own attention."⁹ An era obsessed with the ideology of separate spheres paradoxically witnessed the publicizing – in novels, pamphlets, how-to manuals, poems, plays, essays, journals, etc. – of that part of life that was to be kept away from the public.¹⁰ In nineteenth-century Britain and France, the "spectacle of intimacy" assumed vast proportions; the multivolume or serialized novel is only one of the many cultural forms publicly reiterating the pleasures and value of privacy and domestic life.¹¹ Bourgeois France adopted middle-class domestic ideology somewhat later than Britain, due in part to the waves of political unrest that washed over the country from 1789 to 1850. Balzac's fiction demonstrates a more ironic attitude toward the idealization of domesticity than Dickens's novels of the 1840s yet is equally concerned with the affective and social implications of private space and transgressions of it.

As the title of Chase and Levenson's book suggests, most of the critical attention generated by the publicity of privacy that informed much of nineteenth-century British and French culture has focused on the *visual* aspects of the revelation of private life and its spaces. The past ten years in particular have generated a number of interdisciplinary studies or collections of essays that examine the intersection of literature, the visual arts, and architecture and that characterize nineteenth-century culture as one based on imagined or actual looking. Christopher Prendergast points out that "realism invites us above all to *look* at the world."¹² Chase and Levenson observe "the extent to which domestic life itself was impelled toward acts of exposure and display" in a "celebration of the triumphs of privacy" and the domestic ideal it represented, as well as its spectacular failures.[13] Sharon Marcus's *Apartment Stories* analyzes in detail the manner in which the reading public's familiarity with the illustrated compendia of social types known as *tableaux* and *physiologies* most popular in the 1830s influenced Balzac's own encyclopedic effort and prepared his readers for his translation of such projects into narrative form.[14] Marcus also notes how Parisian apartment-house façades of the Restoration period aspired to an ideal of visual transparency – achieved through the increased use of windows and simplified ornamentation of the structural masses of apartment buildings in the capital.[15] Philippe Hamon's study of literature and architecture in nineteenth-century France examines how they structure human experience, how literature often relies on the metaphors of architecture, and how architecture helps organize human strategies of desire or repulsion.[16] Notably, recent scholars have explored visual aspects of the representation of private life and space in Balzac.[17]

All such studies emphasize the occular nature of the display of intimacy forming the obverse to the principle of privacy and domestic isolation that the separation of spheres advocated. By focusing on the visual aspects of the publicity of the private, this scholarship acknowledges the vast technological changes that were altering the experience of everyday life in England and France; the inventions that transformed quotidian experience often relied on sight to apprehend and process information.[18] But such investigations also replicate how physical barriers to private life are essentially visual. Walls work by preventing families from seeing what their neighbors are doing. Except in the most prosperous homes, walls rarely block out all aural cues about whatever is happening on the other side of the screen, the partition, or the door.

In contrast, eavesdropping emphasizes the psychological aspect of nineteenth-century domestic architecture. Its secret listeners expose physical barriers' limited ability to prevent snooping. In this manner, covert listening reminds readers that complete privacy is a myth. Private space depends upon our ignoring the reminders of what exists beyond the bedroom wall or the green baize door. Despite the nineteenth-century obsessive division of space into smaller and smaller units, with discrete functions assigned to each, walls, particularly in the subdivided former *hôtels privés* of Restoration Paris, provide visual isolation; they seldom block out noise completely. Instead, people learn to disregard the coughs, shouts, or moans on the other side of the wall. We *will* ourselves not to hear, or pretend not to hear, what goes on next door.

Eavesdropping scenes in novels remind us of this necessary fiction; they point out those aspects of contiguous existence that we would like to forget. Moments of covert listening remind us of how easy it is to erase the aural wall of privacy that separates families or individuals within families, since such barriers are less physical than psychological.[19] Eavesdropping functions as the obverse of efforts to repress indications of other lives and ways of life other than those deemed respectable, since it often implicates servants or those wishing to gain power, wealth, or status in learning the secrets of people economically or socially above them. Scenes of covert listening remind the comfortable bourgeois of the proximity of the working classes just below him, from whose ranks he may have just extricated himself. If one does not share a wall with neighbors, even the most stately private homes – like Dombey's, the Dedlocks', the Nucingens', the Restauds' – have servants and backstaircases.

Admittedly, the works of either Balzac or Dickens could easily be the subject of a full-length study on this topic; numerous critical works have already compared the two authors productively.[20] By treating the two in a single chapter, I wish to suggest how eavesdropping in their novels represents at once an idealized construction of home and a publicizing of its delights and dangers that is symptomatic of a general mid-nineteenth-century attitude. These novels draw upon the myth of absolute privacy and domestic bliss even as they suggest its limitations. The dramatization of other individuals' private lives and secrets tentatively confirms the safety of its bourgeois readers and feeds a mania for public knowledge about private matters. I focus my discussion on Balzac's *Le Père Goriot* (1834 –35) and *Les parents pauvres* (1847), and on Dickens's *Dombey and Son* (1847–48), with periodic excursions into other texts. In each of these novels, the issues of domestic space, family secrets, and individual privacy are worked out somewhat differently and indicate the different attitudes in a comparative *histoire de mentalités* that the two authors represent. In these realist novels, where details of dress, manner, and environment become essential in describing the character of an individual, domestic space indexes more than someone's social position. In their characters' attitude toward this space and their attempts to maintain it as a *lieu sûr* (safe haven), novelists reveal their degree of cynicism toward, acceptance of, or anxieties about, an ideology of domestic space.

The urban novels by Balzac and Dickens that I examine suggest the difficulty of establishing an ideal about privacy and private space based upon the English country house, with its physical isolation from neighboring dwellings. The tremendous rise in publicity and urbanization that occurred in England and France during the nineteenth century might lead us to conclude that anxieties about transgressions of private space and information are particularly urban, and hence, that representations of eavesdropping as a narrative symptom of such concerns will consequently appear most frequently in novels set in cities. In fact, what might seem predominantly a problem found in urban representation is actually quite widespread in nineteenth-century fiction, as my earlier discussion of eavesdropping in Austen demonstrates, and as I will show in my next chapter on Collins's *The Woman in White* (1860). Moreover, early novels by Dickens and Balzac, such as *Oliver Twist* (1837–38) and *Eugénie Grandet* (published in 1833, set in the 1810s), suggest that the opposition of the city as site of corruption and surveillance and the country as refuge from such infiltration of private space is a nostalgic dream rather than a reality, just as the separation of spheres represents ideal rather than actuality.

Dickens's novel inverts the relation between fantasy and reality when, as Oliver falls asleep in his snug room in the Maylies' country house, he dreams of Fagin and Monks spying on him. The nightmare so terrifies him that he wakes, to discover that his dream is real, although later efforts to trace the men or to find tangible evidence of their having been at the window fail. George Cruikshank's drawing for the scene emphasizes the intimacy of Oliver's room and its country setting: a vase of flowers stands on the windowsill, leaves frame the opening through which Monks and Fagin peer.[21] A private home is a natural one, the narrative and its illustration intimate. Yet the fact that the felons are able to infiltrate Oliver's dream suggests that no space, even the idyllic country community with which the narrative concludes, is safe from the eavesdropping and spying that occur in more obviously dangerous sites in London, such as the bridge where Noah Claypole overhears Nancy's conversation with Rose Maylie and Mr. Brownlow, or the thieves' den where Nancy eavesdrops on Monks and Fagin's plotting.[22] In the country, even in sleep, one must be vigilant.

Eugénie Grandet, in the section of *La comédie humaine* titled "Scènes de la vie de province" ("Scenes of Provincial Life") presents numerous examples of aural as well as visual snooping and of intricate plots combining economic and romantic interests. The novel's primary action takes place within the four walls of the Grandet house and adjoining garden. Despite its focus on the domestic sphere and country life, *Eugénie Grandet* is filled with acts of aural and visual surveillance; if the community is smaller, the spying is more intense.

Published in 1871–72 but set in 1829–32, George Eliot's *Middlemarch*, subtitled *A Study of Provincial Life*, reveals how, even in the country, one's secrets are never safe. Raffles's sudden appearance in Middlemarch threatens to expose the shady financial and ethical foundations upon which Bulstrode's respectable reputation rests. Hence the banker sits "in an agony of fear lest Raffles should be overheard in his loud and plain references to past events – lest Mrs. Bulstrode should be even tempted to listen at the door."[23] Eliot's fictional community has a greater heterogeneity of social classes than Austen's more compact social world of the country gentry, but overhearing secrets and producing and circulating stories are, in both, cause for intradiagetic anxiety and misunderstanding as well as extradiagetic pleasure and education. As social mobility and technologies of information increase, so do transgressions of privacy and secrets – and with them, anxieties about such perils. Servants are no longer those whom you grew up with and whose families you know, but workers whose past is known only through their "characters" – written testimonials to their reliability and discretion. The characters they bring with them become important guarantees that they will not exchange "the family's" secrets for profit. Within a village or country town, one is almost certain to be seen or overheard and become the subject of gossip; we refer to the village or town gossip, a single, identifiable figure, whose motives and movements one can gauge. In the city, curiosity remains, but the opportunities and individuals for covert listening multiply. Moreover, the city offers the potential for eavesdroppers one does not know, is not aware of, whose motives and movements are uncertain. Thus, although fictional eavesdropping is not a predominantly urban phenomenon, examples of it proliferate and assume more varied forms in the city.

The vast amount of material I cover in this chapter generates individual readings that resonate with each other rather than a totalizing argument. After a brief history of domestic architecture, I consider four novels by Balzac and Dickens as different textual tableaux that dwell on specific aspects of anxieties about eavesdropping, privacy, private space, and secrets. In doing so I emulate Balzac's use of the term "scene" in his divisions of *La comédie humaine*.[24] Although we can read each text of *The Human Comedy* individually, recurring characters and his division of the work into "scènes" encourage us to think of each tale as a room in a vast house or apartment building whose front has been cut away to reveal the various activities in each, with connections among them. Each narrative space remains isolated and complete only if we do not know of the others' existence; once we see and hear connections, we are attuned to the reverberations of stories from room to room. The French popular press of the time included illustrated cross-sections of apartment buildings that exposed varied interior spaces, their inhabitants, and their activities to the reader. Dioramas, in which the observer peeked at elaborate staged scenes through a small aperture, constituted one of the most popular entertainments of the 1820s and 1830s.[25] Balzac's oeuvre thus represents in extended narrative form what Frédéric Soulié's tableaux text "Les drames invisibles" chronicles. His illustrated account of the heterogeneous inhabitants of a single apartment house encompasses all of Paris society.[26] My aim in this chapter is to remind us of the aural component of such "spectacle[s] of intimacy."

The structure of *La comédie humaine* replicates the relation of its characters to privacy and private space. Within each narrative all appears unified and secure, yet allusions to other texts remind readers, if not characters, that the individual "scenes" are part of a larger human drama. The intimate spaces in Balzac's fiction are almost always less isolated than they initially appear, with echoes of other fictional spaces and private lives. With their numerous plots and subplots, set in a variety of locations within a single novel, Dicken's narratives depict such diverse domestic establishments. Both Balzac's and Dickens's fascination with the theater and theatrical devices encourages a division of this chapter into aural scenes. Indeed, eavesdropping's theatrical – even melodramatic – tendencies support this organizational strategy.

SETTING THE SCENE: A BRIEF HISTORY OF PRIVATE SPACE

Various architectural and social historians have traced the development, from the Renaissance on, of a new sense of the self, and with it an increased desire for privacy, reflected in the kinds of spaces the increasingly private subject wishes to inhabit.[27] From designing houses on a straight axis, where one can see directly through each room into the next, and in which family, visitors, and servants had to pass through a succession of connecting rooms to reach a particular room, architects implemented the corridor in the late seventeenth and early eighteenth centuries to afford the individual a measure of privacy and safety from unwanted intrusion. Throughout this period, when houses were constructed with a combination of corridors and enfiladed main apartments, the inclusion of a passage deliberately inscribed a difference in the access of various social classes. It provided a more direct access to family for family members and privileged guests through the interconnecting rooms, while insuring the servants' discreet circulation through a carefully regulated space.

The eighteenth century's increasing dependence on the "closet" (or *cabinet*) – a small room used for private purposes, such as reading, letter-writing, and religious contemplation – indicates an intensified desire to create a space of one's own, which could afford time alone. It designated a private space within a larger architecture of enfiladed or thoroughfare rooms designed "to introduce Convenience, Proportion, and Regularity."[28] The eighteenth-century epistolary novel, with its emphasis on interiority, on private writing about "an internalized, highly personalized drama" and on the "survival of the psychic self" within confined and confining spaces, matches literary vehicle (the personalized space of the letter) with a psychologically charged spatial correlative, even if the novel is concerned with opening up these spaces to public view.[29]

Witold Rybczynski notes how, in contrast to the centralization of French social life in Versailles and Paris, the more independent English aristocracy's wealth and pride resided in their rural properties, insuring the emergence of the English country house as the locus for social life.[30] As one American observed at the time, scarcely anyone of importance "live[s] in London. They have *houses* in London, in which they stay while Parliament sits, and occasionally visit at other seasons; but their *homes* are in the country."[31] The English townhouse was usually part of a row. Its arrangement had been standardized by the end of the seventeenth century and changed little over the next 150 years. However, the organization and design of the English country home was the focus of tremendous attention during the eighteenth and nineteenth centuries. Through its location in rural areas, the country home encouraged a relation with nature that urban dwelling prohibited. Consequently, the large, public rooms of the English country house were usually on the ground floor, which enabled easy access to the gardens and parks. In contrast, the French urban *hôtel* tended to locate the public areas on the first floor (American second floor), or *piano nobile*. Already, however, the placement of the *hôtel privé*'s more private rooms toward the back of the building, with the rear façade opening out on to a pleasure garden, indicated a separation, both physical and psychological, from events that took place in the more public front courtyard. In the eighteenth-century English country home, the numerous and diverse public rooms were used for multiple functions, despite the names by which they were designated.[32] Not until the following century was the differentiation of rooms by function consistently maintained.

In the nineteenth century, the ubiquity of the closet or cabinet as a private space in both urban and rural upper-middle-class and aristocratic homes gave way to a more regular division of space into smaller, independent rooms with individualized purposes, and access to private spaces became more systematized.[33] From constructing rooms with multiple doors, architects began to design rooms with only one entrance, a feature that became prevalent in the nineteenth-century English house, although rooms on the Continent continued to have more than one door until the middle of the century.[34] Whereas eighteenth-century architecture designated a single enclosed place within the house, such as the closet, as a space of retreat, the nineteenth-century disposition of space treated the whole domestic edifice as a place of privacy, emphasizing the family's separation from the outside world. The bedroom came to be considered an exclusively private space, in contrast to the usage as late as the eighteenth century, where the *chambre* functioned as both reception room and sleeping quarters. As a result, the elaborate drapery of the bed, the curtains that had afforded its occupants a measure of privacy from other persons in the room, gradually disappeared during the nineteenth century.

During the eighteenth century, the concept of interior decoration began to receive serious attention for the first time. The emergence of this discipline reflects the growing consideration given to the interior of the house, its arrangement and adornment. As one contemporary planner stated, "On habite une maison à l'intérieur et non à l'extérieur" ("One dwells in the interior, not the exterior, of a house").[35] Balzac's *La Cousine Bette*, with its lavish descriptions of every character's apartment – its individual rooms and the manner in which they are decorated – not only indicates the author's obsession with domestic interiors at the time, but illustrates the degree to which attention to interiors spread through all levels of society. Thus, although the disposition of many of the apartments and homes that Balzac describes reflects a late eighteenth-century sensibility and an attachment to separate chambers for husband and wife, his presentation of characters' interaction with these spaces and each other suggests a more thoroughly nineteenth-century domestic ideology.

As part of conceiving the family as the center of private life, a sanctuary from a dangerous outside world, the middle- and upper-class family developed a sense of its members' being limited to those connected by blood or marriage. Servants, who throughout the early modern era were considered part of a larger family structure, by the eighteenth century began to be viewed as potential spies who might divulge family secrets to a larger community. Consequently, the wish to control the access of these necessary "intruders" to the family and its secrets intensified. As the upper and upper-middle classes claimed private spaces of their own, they began to regulate the spaces of their servants and their interaction with their employers. In contrast to having servants work, eat, and sleep with their masters, the innovation of the bell-rope followed by the bell-pull system in mid- to late eighteenth-century English and early nineteenth-century French dwellings provided means of communication with the servants that removed the need for them to remain in the hall (the large, central public room), or, at bedtime, in rooms adjacent to their masters.[36] The invention of the dumbwaiter, also in the eighteenth century, enabled masters to keep their servants at a distance, and, as its name implies, to forestall attempts to gather or transmit information about the family.[37] Instead, until the early nineteenth century, the affluent lodged their servants in a single dormitory for both male and female servants, away from the family (usually in the attic, or, in country homes, in a separate, often northern, wing).[38] The rich began to segregate their employees by sex; eventually, men and women slept separately, usually with one or two servants per room.[39]

The organization of the mid-nineteenth-century English country home renders concrete the anxiety about the promiscuity of servants and the desire to regulate their interactions with the family. By the time the architect Robert Kerr produced *The Gentleman's House* in 1864, the servants were lodged behind the green baize door, with the butler presiding over the male servants' zone and the housekeeper governing the behavior of the female servants in her own realm. Each area had its own staircase to a separate set of bedrooms, with the servants' hall and the steward's room providing the neutral ground between them.[40] Kerr states that "it becomes the foremost of all maxims... that the Servants' Department shall be separated from the main house, so that what passes on either side of the boundary shall be both invisible and inaudible to the other."[41] Once this conception of privacy was accepted by the upper classes, it could be applied to more modest homes as well. The Victorian ideal of privacy and morality had reached its fullest architectural expression.[42]

Urban architecture developed somewhat differently, but also reflected an increasing desire to segregate different socio-economic classes and ensure the privacy of the family and its secrets. In France, the eighteenth century witnessed a boom in the construction of the freestanding *hôtel particulier*, "the French urban dwelling in its most representative form."[43]

The *hôtel* provided separate apartments for husband and wife, including "the *antichambre* or waiting room; the *chambre* or bedsitting room, used both for sleeping and reception; the *cabinet*, the least public place, to which only the most important visitors were admitted; and the *garde-robe*, serving as dressing room and closet." The rest of the family had more modest accommodations. A few common rooms (the *salles* or *salons*) offered space for large gatherings and concerts. An examination of the architectural evolution of the *hôtel* also reveals a progressive specialization of rooms for a particular function, as well as an increased attention to the means of circulation through space, by the introduction of corridors, in the eighteenth century. François Mansart's layout of the urban mansion, with its "longitudinal axis running from the courtyard through a paired vestibule-salon configuration into the garden," became standard in the eighteenth century.[44] His plan placed the servants in a separate wing tangent to the central *corps de logis*. Separate, smaller service stairs insured that the major stairs would lead the visitor, undistracted by domestic traffic, up to the grand suite of reception and private chambers.

Until the end of the eighteenth century, the imperatives of group interaction overrode the rights of the individual; not until the final years of the century did a private space of family intimacy begin to serve as a model and spread through different socio-economic levels. Already, however, the development of the "boudoir" in the eighteenth century signaled the increasing importance of spaces less public than the salon and the association of space with gender. One contemporary definition of the boudoir described it as "une pièce intime féminine, fermée et sombre, attenante à la chambre à coucher et au cabinet de toilette, très bien décorée" (an intimate, feminine room, enclosed and dark, very well decorated, which adjoins the bedroom and the dressing room). The boudoir, that retreat sanctioning luxury and sensuality, disappears in the nineteenth century, when the conception of "female nature" begins to change from highly sexualized to an ideal stressing woman's maternal instincts and innate morality.[45] The boudoirs of Balzac's high society women of the Restoration and July Monarchy vanish by the end of the century, except in the apartments of those women whose profession associated them with sexuality. Zola's Nana, for example, has her "protectors" establish her in a luxurious apartment whose decor and furnishings exude, if not "calme," certainly "luxe" and "volupté."

In France, the changes to the distribution of space in domestic interiors accompanied an altered conception of the family and gender roles in the first third of the nineteenth century. As in England, women were considered primarily responsible for the creation of "un nid douillet" (cosy nest) at home;[46] the separation of spheres was accepted at about the same time on both sides of the Channel. In France, the idea that a correspondence existed between family life and a kind of space reserved for familial intimacy became fully established around 1830, with the establishment of Louis-Philippe's bourgeois monarchy. The king set himself up as a model husband and father to distance himself from the Bourbon monarchy's presumed immorality and decadence. His attitude represents an ascendancy of bourgeois values similar to the ideological shift in England. In this period, the individually designated rooms for socializing were distinctly male: the smoking room, the billiard room, and the *cabinet* or study, the room for a man's exclusive use. The space designated as woman's was at first the bedroom, but as that increasingly came to be considered an inviolably private space, the salon remained as the primary place where a woman would receive visitors. The disappearance of the boudoir except in the most privileged households indicates the gradual prioritizing of the roles of mother and wife over that of the individual woman and her need for privacy in the nineteenth century. The salon becomes not just the place for receiving visitors, but, with the dining room, the heart of the domestic establishment.

In bourgeois families, the decor and furniture of this *salon de famille* stressed less luxury than comfort, the place where one could be fully *chez soi*. In less privileged homes, the dining room (often called the *salle commune*) took over both functions of sociability and alimentation.[47] Separate apartments for husband and wife characteristic of the aristocracy gave way during the nineteenth century (albeit more slowly in France than in England) to the conjugal bedchamber, emphasizing marital unity and concord.[48] The term *appartement* itself, used for the first half of the century to designate this suite of rooms within a larger living space, by 1850 came to denote an entire residence.[49]

In contrast to the increasing sense of intimacy and privacy within the home, the outside world and its less privileged inhabitants were viewed with suspicion, even hostility. Increasingly in both capitals, through urban planning and market forces, the poor were removed from the dwellings of the rich; only those in domestic service remained. English urban architecture by the middle of the nineteenth century reflected the segregation of classes by neighborhood, not merely by floor within apartment building. During the first quarter of the century, the most opulent private homes were merely a street away from abject hovels, in which a family of seven or eight lived in one room. However, with the large-scale construction of the railway lines in the 1830s and 1840s and the greater expansion of the city, entire slums disappeared and were replaced with company housing and middle-class private homes. In *Dombey and Son*, Dickens records such a demolition of slums in Camden Town to make way for the railways. In London, the 1847 construction of New Oxford Street through the rookeries of St. Giles's aimed to rid the city of these slums, with their notorious, densely populated courts. The wide street replaced overcrowded hovels and made possible visual and moral surveillance. Not surprisingly, the poor resented such "improvements," for they erased the intricate sociability of the poor that was less readily policed. These urban renovations created much-needed thoroughfares but also implicit walls cordoning off the middle and upper classes from the poor.[50]

Balzac's fiction charts the transitional era of the Restoration and July Monarchy, in which the spatial organization of Paris profoundly altered. His boarding houses and apartment buildings, in their relegation of individuals to particular floors according to rank and ability to pay, retain a sense of social heterogeneity and mobility that by the second quarter of the century was being dismantled. Nowhere is this correspondence of income and physical location within an apartment building more explicitly depicted than in *Le Père Goriot*. As the retired merchant's financial situation declines, he moves from the best rooms in Mme Vauquer's establishment on the first floor to higher floors and to progressively smaller and less well-appointed rooms.

Although throughout the nineteenth century Paris became increasingly a city of large apartment buildings, the conception and typology of the buildings changed. In the second half of the century, new apartment buildings no longer provided lodgings for a diverse socio-economic clientele, but instead housed people of roughly the same social and economic rank; consequently, buildings began to be constructed with floors of equal size and height. In *La Cousine Bette*, Balzac describes how:

En bâtissant de belles et d'élégantes maisons à concierges, les bordant de trottoirs et y pratiquant des boutiques, la Spéculation écarte, par le prix du loyer, les gens sans aveu, les ménages sans mobilier et les mauvais locataires. Ainsi les quartiers se débarrassent de ces populations sinistres et de ces bouges où la police ne met le pied que quand la justice l'ordonne. (476)

By erecting substantial and handsome houses, with porters at the doors, by bordering the streets with footwalks and shops, speculation, while raising the rents, disperses the squalid class, families bereft of furniture, and lodgers that cannot pay. And so these districts are cleared of such objectionable residents, and the dens vanish into which the police never venture but under the sanction of the law.[51]

Apartment buildings and entire neighborhoods became segregated, with the upper and middle classes occupying more centrally located apartments and private homes, and the working classes pushed farther to the outskirts of Paris. As the city grew, the rich moved west, the poor toward the east.[52] Yet even within the bourgeois apartment building, subtle distinctions still marked the rooms of "monsieur du premier" just above the boutiques of the ground floor, from the renters on the fourth floor, whose more modest circumstances required suffering the inconvenience of several flights of stairs, and the "disagreeable" proximity to the servants' quarters.[53] The country of "liberté, égalité, fraternité" solved the problem created by the erasure of the ideological boundaries separating master from servant by relegating the servants to the top floor of the building, and thus imposed a physical barrier between bourgeois masters and their rarely devoted servants. Physical proximity did nothing to erode the great social distances that separated employer from employee. Balzac's fiction records the uneven "progress" of such changes. The narrator of *La Cousine Bette* describes how, in 1844, "l'aspect de la place de Laborde et de ses environs était encore peu rassurant . . . l'aristocratie [était] coudoyée là par une infime bohème" (476; "the purlieus of the Place de Laborde were still far from inviting . . . a [vile] bohemia dwelt cheek by jowl with the artistocracy," 467). Not until the second half of the century would the social segregation of Paris, begun during the Restoration, be realized.

Despite increasing attempts to segregate the family from the outside world, and thus keep its members and their secrets safe, the bourgeois family itself provided the means for both the creation of secrets and secret intrigues and their revelation to an outside world. Balzac's diptych *Les parents pauvres* (1846–47) indicates the degree to which, in July Monarchy France, family relations remained economic affairs in the middle and upper classes. Marriages were still alliances between families, not individuals. The arrangements joining two families involved the same kinds of bargaining and schemes that occurred in the world of business and finance; supposedly separate spheres were in fact quite intertwined. Balzac's Cousine Bette and Cousin Pons, the eponymous protagonists of his two novels about "poor relatives," offer contrasting examples of individuals on the margins of their families' emotional centers. Eavesdropping locates their liminal position in the family spatially, on the edge of its affective and financial center yet privy to family secrets. Although Dickens's fictional world repudiates arranged marriages in favor of those based upon mutual respect and affection, it reveals the extent to which private and public constantly overlap in other ways, despite attempts to keep them separate.[54] Morever, in both Balzac's and Dickens's novels, families stage scenes of intimacy and concord for other people; such displays of domestic felicity acknowledge the publicity of private life and its concerns.

At the same time, both novelists' representations of domestic spaces are suffused with a psychology of the private. Robin Evans notes how early modern literature and autobiography scant on their description of places, architecture, and furnishings. The space that people inhabit is mentioned in its barest essentials: only those elements that help provide a general sense of the setting or are integral to the plot.[55] In contrast, Balzac and Dickens's fictional dwellings are lavishly described and psychologically dynamic, revealing their inhabitants' anxieties and fantasies about physical and human environments. Such spaces disclose much about the people who occupy them: the image they wish to project, but just as often, the part of themselves they hope to hide.[56] In a milieu where one is judged by one's surroundings and possessions, the narrator of *Le Cousin Pons* declares with an air of hurt cynicism, "En médecine, le cabriolet est plus nécessaire que le savoir" ("for a doctor a cab is more necessary than a knowledge of medicine," 159).[57] In an era in which things and spaces foster the kind of life one wishes to have, architecture can be said to have "produced, permitted, and concretized not only a concept of history (be it collective or individual) but also, the staging of everyday life and of those rituals which expose social behavior." One does not merely possess; one "inhabits" a system of values.[58] Eavesdropping dramatizes this dwelling in ideology.

SECOND STORIES: BALZAC´S SCENES OF PRIVATE LIFE

In its examination of what constitutes a family and of what distinguishes the public from the private, Balzac's *Le Père Goriot* (1834–35) presents overtly the issues at stake in his more explicitly domestic dramas. In a novel about familial relations, Balzac represents the private lives and not-so-secret intrigues of individual lodgers in a *pension de famille* to trace the intricacies of what comprises a "family" and family feeling in Restoration France. Though seemingly about life in a semipublic place (the Maison Vauquer), *Le Père Goriot* falls under the larger rubric "Scènes de la vie privée" ("Scenes of Private Life") in *La comédie humaine*. It exploits the liminal status of the boarding house to investigate the boundaries to family life and its secrets. Not surprisingly, eavesdropping figures prominently in this border-space. Such a site offers shelter, yet in bringing together people unrelated by anything but the need for housing, it remains a semipublic site.

The eavesdropping and spying in the Maison Vauquer dramatize the tenuous quality of boarding-house privacy. As if to stress this fragile border between public and private, the novel's opening paragraph characterizes the story to be told as "dramatique," not in "le sens vrai du mot; mais, l'oeuvre accomplie, peut-être aura-t-on versé quelques larmes *intra muros* et *extra*" ("dramatic," not "in the real meaning of the term but, once the whole tale has been read, a few tears may well have dropped, perhaps privately, perhaps even in public").[59] Already, Balzac emphasizes the concept of boundaries – here between the fictional and real worlds – and the connections between the activities happening on both sides of such physical and psychological walls. Furthermore, in describing the subject of the novel as the "secrètes infortunes du père Goriot," secret misfortunes that "chacun peut en reconnaître les éléments chez soi, dans son coeur peut-être" (22; "you'll be able to recognize...in your own life, perhaps even in your own heart," 6), Balzac forces his reader to consider the private nature of the story about to unfold, containing events that could happen to the reader, "vous qui vous enfoncez dans un moelleux fauteuil" – ensconced in a comfortable armchair at home (22).

Balzac's text demonstrates early on the intimate relations between public and private spaces and stories. The high walls surrounding the garden of the Maison Vauquer and separating it from the street and the adjacent house (24), the bars on the ground-floor windows (25), its location in the "rues serrées" ("close-packed streets") of the particular neighborhood, "[le] plus inconnu" ("[least] known") of Paris (23; 5), cannot keep out inquisitive eyes and ears. At the same time as the narrator emphasizes the hidden or private nature of this world, he also exposes it to his readers' view. The narrative reveals how the proprietress, Mme Vauquer, would betray others to improve her lot, and characterizes her "pension bourgeois" as a place where privacy is continually threatened by idle curiosity, proximity of unrelated persons, and competing pecuniary interests.[60]

Despite the cynical view that the reader obtains of the *pension*, its inhabitants continually recast themselves as a family, albeit one eager to know the secrets of its members. This artificial family reveals the underlying currents of self-interest and conflicting desires pervading the idealized body it emulates: the bourgeois family. Those who take full room and board have breakfast together in a manner that has "l'aspect d'un repas de famille" because "chacun descendait en pantoufles, se permettait des observations confidentielles sur la mise ou sur l'air des externes, et sur les événements de la soirée précédente, en s'exprimant avec la confiance de l'intimité" (31; it "resemble[s] a family meal" because "they all came down in slippers, allowing themselves confidential remarks about what had been set out for them, or about the appearance of those who merely dined there, as well as on the events of the previous night, expressing themselves with the self-assurance of intimacy," 13). This "familial" atmosphere is marked by gossip. Those present chatter about those absent. Created by mere proximity, this community thrives on the speculations that transgress bounds of privacy. The affectionate sharing of news among family members is reduced here to intrusive curiosity. An assemblage of those rejected by or separated from their families, like Victorine "qui, tous les ans, se cognait contre la porte de la maison paternelle, inexorablement fermée" (36), and Mme Couture, whom she calls "Maman" (248),[61] or those who seem to possess none (Mlle Michonneau), the inmates of the boarding house affect traditional family roles by calling others and themselves "Papa" Vautrin and "Maman" Vauquer; the *pensionnaires* become her "enfants gâtés" ("spoiled children"; 154, 38, 239, 247, 31).

The familial position each occupies has a rough spatial correlative in the particular floor of the house on which each rents a room. Thus, Mme Vauquer has her apartment on the first floor of the building, while Vautrin inhabits the second, and Père Goriot and the student Rastignac each rent one of four rooms on the third floor, the story closest to the garret, where the cook and the man of all work sleep (30–31).[62] The self-named "Papa Vautrin" convincingly presents himself as a "bon bourgeois" and hence beyond suspicion.[63] Moreover, in this world of surveillance and speculation, only Vautrin keeps his secrets impenetrable, while learning everyone else's: "Il savait ou devinait les affaires de ceux qui l'entouraient, tandis que nul ne pouvait pénétrer ni ses pensées ni ses occupations" (38; "he knew or could guess at the private lives of those around him, though no one could figure out either what he was thinking or what he did," 19). Significantly, he has a gift for opening locks (37; 18). Few secrets or hidden caches are safe from him. "Papa Vautrin" and "Maman Vauquer" supervise the lodgers and manage their secrets.

This artificial family stands in direct contrast to the "real" family drama of the eponymous Père Goriot whose relationship with his daughters is suspected by the other boarders to be less than familial, and whose generous paternal spirit does not guarantee him the filial affection he craves. Although initially "Monsieur Goriot" rents a three-room apartment on the *piano nobile* of the house, as he gives more and more of his money to his rapacious daughters, his straightened finances compel him to move upstairs to smaller and smaller quarters. He ends up on the third floor in a tiny room; his ascension to progressively higher floors provides the inverse spatial correlative to his reduced status within the boarding house. The representative of familial affection and responsibility, "Père Goriot" deserves the accurate, if dismissive, nickname that Madame Vauquer gives him and that the other boarders adopt as his finances deteriorate ("Old Goriot," 49).

Because Goriot does not act like one of the "family" – because he isolates himself from the other boarders and does not gossip – they assume he has something to hide (50). For them, reserve implies a secret. His attempt to maintain a degree of privacy insures that people will be curious about his life; they act accordingly. Mme Vauquer and the cook Sylvie eavesdrop on his conversation with a woman whom Sylvie describes as "une fille trop jolie pour être honnête, *mise comme une divinité*" (Balzac's emphasis; "far too pretty to be a decent woman, *and dressed like an angel*"). "[S'étant] mi[ses] aux écoutes" ("set[ing] themselves to listen"), the spies "surpri[s]ent plusieurs mots tendrement prononcés pendant la visite" ("manag[e] to catch the old man and his visitor speaking a few tender words") and assume that he is keeping a mistress, despite his declaration that she is his daughter (51; 30).

The lodgers and their "Maman Vauquer" speculate about the mysterious, ill-defined relations between Goriot and the two beautiful women who visit him periodically. Putting this information together with his reticence about his personal life, they fabricate extravagant, criminal scenarios about him: he is a "fripon," "un vieux drôle," (a "rascal," "a queer old fish"); he has ruined himself on the stockmarket and gambled away whatever was left; he is a spy for the police; "on en faisait tout ce que le vice, la honte, l'impuissance engendrent de plus mystérieux. Seulement, quelque ignobles que fussent sa conduite ou ses vices, l'aversion qu'il inspirait n'allait pas jusqu'à le faire bannir: il payait sa pension" (49–50; "they turned him into whatever vice, shame, and helplessness could make the most mysterious. But however awful he or his horrible way of life might be, their dislike never reached the point of evicting him: he paid his rent," 22). Despite the criminal verdict that everyone pronounces on Goriot, they allow him to keep his place in the boarding house because his behavior does not affect their own privacy – indeed, suspicion of him deflects attention from them – and because he contributes regularly to the financial stability of the house: he pays his rent. But they continue to suspect, watch, and listen.

Even the naïve Eugène de Rastignac, returning home late at night, spies and eavesdrops on his nextdoor neighbor, rather than directing his attention to where the real shady dealings are being committed, in Vautrin's chamber on the floor below.[64] The narrative relates how:

un soupir...troubla le silence de la nuit...Il ouvrit doucement la porte, et quand il fut dans le corridor, il aperçut une ligne de lumière tracée au bas de la porte du père Goriot. Eugène craignit que son voisin ne se trouvât indisposé, il approcha son oeil de la serrure, regarda dans la chambre, et vit le vieillard occupé de travaux qui lui parurent trop criminels pour qu'il ne crût pas rendre service à la société en examinant bien ce que machinait nuitamment le soi-disant vermicellier...Mais serait-ce donc un voleur ou un receleur qui, pour se livrer plus sûrement à son commerce, affecterait la bêtise, l'impuissance, et vivrait en mendiant? se dit Eugène...Le père Goriot regarda tristement son ouvrage...il souffla le rat-de-cave...et Eugène l'entendit se coucher en poussant un soupir. – Il est fou, pensa l'étudiant.
– Pauvre enfant! dit à haute voix le père Goriot.
A cette parole, Rastignac jugea prudent de garder le silence sur cet événement, et de ne pas inconsidérément condamner son voisin. Il allait rentrer quand il distingua soudain un bruit assez difficile à exprimer...Eugène prêta l'oreille, et reconnut en effet le son alternatif de la respiration de deux hommes. Sans avoir entendu ni le cri de la porte ni les pas des hommes, il vit tout à coup une faible lueur au second étage, chez monsieur Vautrin.
– Voilà bien des mystères dans une pension bourgeoise! se dit-il. Il...se mit à écouter, et le son de l'or frappa son oreille. Bientôt la lumière fut éteinte, les respirations se firent entendre derechef sans que la porte eût crié. Puis, à mesure que les deux hommes descendirent, le bruit alla s'affaiblissant. (62–63)

[t]he deep silence [was] broken by a long, drawn-out sigh...Stepping carefully into the corridor Eugène saw a bar of light etched under Père Goriot's door. Worried that his neighbor might be sick, he peered through the keyhole and, looking around the room, saw the old man busy at so transparently a criminal activity that Eugène could not...but perform a service for society, were he to learn just what the so-called manufacturer of vermicelli was plotting, there in the dead of night...Could it be that Goriot was a thief, or a fence, pretending to be a helpless old clod and living like a beggar, the better to practice his

trade? ... Goriot stood looking sadly down at his night's work ... he blew out the wax candle ... then, sighing, he could be heard stretching himself out to sleep.

"He's insane," the student thought.

"You poor child!" Père Goriot suddenly declared.

Hearing this, Rastignac decided he'd better say nothing about the entire affair, nor ought he to thoughtlessly pass judgment on his neighbor. He was just going back into his room when he suddenly heard an odd noise ... Listening carefully, he could make out the sound of two men breathing. No one had knocked at the door, nor had he heard footsteps, but suddenly he spied a faint light down on the second storey, where Monsieur Vautrin lived.

"This is a strange business for a private boardinghouse!" he told himself. He ... stopped to listen, and heard the unmistakable clink of gold. Then the light went out, he could hear the two men breathing once again, but there was no sound of a door opening or closing. Slowly, as the two men went back down the stairs, the sound of breathing got weaker and weaker. (40–42)

In these back-to-back night-time investigations, Rastignac's suspicions of wrongdoing are aroused by aural cues, which he then verifies with visual and aural surveillance.[65] Proximity tempts him to listen in. Sound rather than sight first triggers curiosity, as thin partitions between apartments insure that one is more likely to overhear than see one's neighbors. The self-assumed moral rectitude of the inmates makes them take on the role of citizen-policeman, a vestige from revolutionary times when neighbors informed on each other and no one felt safe from the Terror. By the Restoration (*Le Père Goriot* is set in 1819), such urban paranoia changes focus; everyone judges his or her neighbors on their moral probity, rather than their revolutionary zeal. The infractions most imagined are those involving the two obsessions of the bourgeoisie: money and sex. No wonder then that Goriot, called "un vieux matoux" ("an old tomcat") by Mme Vauquer and his fellow-lodgers, is a prime suspect, unlike Vautrin, who presents himself as a businessman and who fraternizes with the other lodgers (52; 32). Because Goriot hides while Vautrin displays generosity and "family" feeling, suspicions fall on the wrong "father." After his prowling, Rastignac remains "distrait par les soupçons qui lui venaient sur le compte du père Goriot" (64; "distracted by Goriot's suspicious behavior," 42), not Vautrin's indistinct financial dealings. The narrative begins to reveal Vautrin's secrets through a conversation between the two servants, Sylvie and Christophe, that only the reader overhears. In other words, "Papa" Vautrin's authority can be contested only by institutional and narrative forces outside the "famille" Vauquer. We learn that both servants have been approached by a stranger asking questions about Vautrin, but that "Papa" has bought their silence (65–66). If, for the Maison Vauquer, actions speak louder than words, sometimes it pays to silence both. Money buys information or its witholding.

As Rastignac's listening suggests, although both visual and aural spying riddle this fictional world, eavesdropping provides most of the crucial information in *Le Père Goriot*: the snippets of information that pique one's curiosity, produce more clandestine looking and listening, and provoke all kinds of narrative and financial speculation. Thus when Rastignac overhears "à la fois la voix de madame de Restaud, celle du père Goriot, et le bruit d'un baiser," the incongrous relationship between a high-society woman and the "vieux vermicellier" seems mysterious and, therefore, all the more interesting (87; "simultaneously, Madame de Restaud's voice, and Père Goriot's voice, and the unmistakable sound of a kiss," 63). When Goriot leaves "par un escalier dérobé" (110; "by a back staircase," 85), the young student burns to find out "quelles étaient [les] relations [de Madame de Restaud] avec le père Goriot" ("what [Madame de Restaud's] relationship to Père Goriot was all about"), and in solving this mystery, hopes to "régner en souverain sur cette femme si éminemment Parisienne" (93; "rule this magnificently Parisian woman," 69). An understanding of the quasi-secret, intimate relationships between men and women determines one's success in the high-society world Rastignac wishes to enter.[66]

Hence, in this narrative world of petty bourgeoisie and aristocracy, although everyone would hate to be labeled a spy or a snitch, everyone watches and eavesdrops. Vautrin warns Rastignac, "Dites que je suis un infâme, un scélérat, un coquin, un bandit, mais ne m'appelez ni escroc, ni espion!" (159; "Tell me I'm a swine, a scoundrel, a dirty rascal, a gangster – just as long as you don't call me a swindler or a spy!," 130). Clearly, such unauthorized listening does not function as the moral litmus test that it does for Dickens, whose villains always eavesdrop by design, but whose virtuous characters "inadvertently" overhear. Even Mme de Beauséant, one of the noblest figures in the novel, deliberately overhears conversations and commands to servants when it is in her best interest (103). Vautrin positions himself in the salon after dinner so that he can secretly listen to and observe Rastignac with Victorine (210). The deliberate quality of his eavesdropping is more pronounced, more calculated, and often more successful than other characters. He is also able to keep his own clandestine dealings safe longer from inquisitive eyes and ears. In order to speak privately to Rastignac, he leads the young man into the garden, noting, "Là, personne ne nous entendra" (145; "[Here,] no one will hear us," 118).

If Vautrin's power can be measured by the degree to which he is able to keep his secrets safe, Goriot's inability to contain the flow of information about him or have others accept his own story registers his lack of social position and authority. Goriot's precautions not to be overheard almost always fail.[67] Eugène finds himself again inadvertently, then deliberately, listening to a conversation between Goriot and Delphine (295; 260). Justifying his eavesdropping first by asserting his privileges as Delphine's lover, Rastignac soon finds that the content of the conversation overcomes his scruples and excuses further listening. In *Le Père Goriot*, characters can always invent a justification for eavesdropping or spying. Rastignac learns the depths of Anastasie's economic and marital troubles and breaks into the conversation between Goriot and his two daughters to offer the money the elder sister desperately needs. Rather than thanking the young man for his financial proposal, Anastasie is horrified to discover that he knows her most intimate secrets (including the paternity of her children). But her financial distress impels her to accept Rastignac as one of the family; she calls him "frère," because implication in her romantic and economic secrets makes him part of the family as well. Confidences, common interest, or financial complicity bind people together more than genuine affection.

The degree to which the inmates of the Maison Vauquer abhor overt spying, even as they secretly practice it, becomes clear in the scene of Vautrin's dramatic capture. The tenuous bond holding this "famille Vauquer" together disintegrates the moment the police expose him as the archcriminal "Trompe-la-Mort" ("Cheat-Death"),[68] whose capacity for deception seems more than mortal. Yet the decisive event that prompts collective outrage and disbands the *pensionnaires* is not Vautrin's arrest but the discovery of a snitch, "un mouchard," among them. One would think the revelation of a dangerous criminal living in their midst and posing as an honest merchant would cause more of a stir than the discovery that Mlle Michonneau has turned informer for the police. But la Michonneau's status as a *traitor*, the one who tells "family" secrets, provokes her housemates' decree of expulsion. What else might she reveal to the police, if offered the right fee? Her transgression of the unwritten but sacred house rules – one can gossip within but not outside the walls of the "famille Vauquer" – is more egregious than Vautrin's evident criminality. While he is "merely" a notorious criminal, as an informer la Michonneau represents the threat of what living in such intimate proximity with strangers may produce: the danger of having one's secrets made public and handed over to the police. She must be expelled, so that the imaginary security of private space can be maintained.

Notably, the medical intern Bianchon, a recurring character in *La comédie humaine* and one of its few honestly successful figures, is the first to call for her eviction. He had suspected the older woman of questionable activities when he overheard her conversation with Poiret and "avec le monsieur qui paraissait à bon droit suspect" in the Jardin des Plantes (220; "with the man who had seemed suspicious, and rightly so," 189). Bianchon's distrust grows when he catches bits of a second conversation in which "[il a] l'oreille frappée du mot assez original de Trompe-le-Mort" (227–28; he "heard the strange name, 'Death-Dodger,' and was struck by it," 196). The police chief cannot infiltrate the *pension de famille* directly, but must convince its members to act on his behalf. His rendezvous with Poiret and la Michonneau take place in a public garden, where characters of all walks of life and their literal and metaphoric "paths" converge – where families and secrets are not at all safe.

Michelle Perrot explains that attitudes toward the police and the law changed between the eighteenth and nineteenth centuries in France. Whereas in the earlier century "the police had served as protectors and confidants, in the nineteenth century they gradually relinquished that role. No longer did victims turn to the police for help; the police increasingly intervened on their own. People turned instead to the courts, accentuating a tendency to substitute the force of law for private vengeance."[69] The *pensionnaires* in *Le Père Goriot* demonstrate this less welcoming attitude to the police; they pity Vautrin during his arrest. In contrast, they show no sympathy for la Michonneau and her partner Poiret, who epitomizes bourgeois mediocrity and blind obedience to authority, and who justifies his betrayal of a fellow-boarder by evoking the law (228).

Vautrin himself identifies the extent to which la Michonneau has transgressed the unwritten laws of both "respectable" and criminal societies. He declares, "C'est toi [qui m'a trahi] ... vieille cagnotte, tu m'as donné un faux coup de sang, curieuse! ... je n'ai jamais trahi personne! Tiens, cagnotte, vois-les ... Ils me regardent avec terreur, mais toi tu leur soulèves le coeur de dégoût" (266–67; "It was you [who betrayed me] ... you old slut, you set off that fake fit, you busybody! ... I've never betrayed anyone! Hey, you old bitch, look at all these people ... I scare them silly, but you, you make them feel like throwing up," 232). In this pronouncement, Vautrin defines the difference between them: although he may defy the laws of society, he has not been a traitor. Her transgression inspires not terror – which contains an element of respect – but disgust. Her "curiosity" exceeds acceptable bounds, for it allows information to circulate among a much larger public than the *pension*. Such an offence makes her forfeit her right to live among the other boarders; hence their cry "A la porte, la moucharde" – a cry that expresses graphically her new relation to the group: on the other side of a divide (271; "Out [the door], you stool pigeon!," 236).

One lodger presents Mme Vauquer with an ultimatum: either she tells Mlle Michonneau to leave, or the rest of the *pensionnaires* will publicize that, "il ne s'y trouve que des espions et des forçats" ("the only people who can stand it here are spies and convicts"). His threat to tell stories, like Bianchon's declaration to leave if la Michonneau does not (269), reveals the degree of obloquy with which they regard "la moucharde" in their midst. It also demonstrates the extent to which even the most honest of the *pensionnaires* recognizes the tenuous security of domestic secrets. His later pronouncement about the difficulty of distinguishing bourgeois from felon indicates a universal paranoia about the infiltration of "les meilleures sociétés" ("the best of circles") by those whom some would prefer to mark on their forehead rather than their shoulders with an obvious sign of their criminality (270; 235). But ultimately, the boarders' threats expose the extent to which all citizens – "bon bourgeois" and "galérien" alike – are complicitous in the dissemination of secret information, and how this information raises disturbing questions about privacy, identity, and morality. Little separates the criminal from the upright citizen, when it comes to curiosity. We all want to know; we all want to tell. Success resides in knowing when and how to listen, when to tell, when to threaten to tell; almost all secrets have value on the diverse markets of Restoration Paris.

Although Mme Vauquer accedes to the group mandate of expulsion, as her boarders dwindle, she seeks someone to blame for her precarious finances and turns upon the departed Michonneau. From being simply an informer, Mlle Michonneau becomes, for Mme Vauquer, "capable de tout, elle a dû faire des horreurs, elle a tué, volé dans son temps. Elle devait aller au bagne à la place de ce pauvre cher homme . . ." (286; "capable of anything, she's surely been guilty of ghastly things, in her time – murders, thievery. She ought to be the one to go to jail, instead of that poor man," 250). In a society where private interests take precedence over all else, for Mme Vauquer the greatest criminal is the one who deprives her of her income. From being a "curieuse" (266), it is merely a step to being "capable de tout," behavior that deserves incarceration.

Le *Père Goriot* may expose Vautrin as Trompe-la-Mort, but its more subtle revelation is the hypocritical stance that the bourgeois boarders – and readers – take regarding the publicity of the private. Some forms of curiosity are more sanctioned than others. Eavesdropping, a liminal and suspect activity, exposes how the borders – of public and private, of respectability and criminality – are malleable constructs. Although the Sûreté identifies Vautrin by the brand on his shoulder, when he reappears in *Splendeurs et misères des courtisanes* (1847), the telltale mark is missing, and with it, the police's certainty of linking Carlos Herrera with Vautrin (or Jacques Collin).[70] Balzac intimates early in his *Comédie* how quickly confused are many social categories: public and private, the criminal and the law-abiding, working class and bourgeois. A novel that begins with the minute identification of a mistress with her dwelling-place ends with the tacit admission that such social markers and social walls are quite fragile.

***

The diptych of novels that forms *Les parents pauvres* (1846–47) intensifies Balzac's examination of private spaces, families, and their infiltration by concentrating on marginalized family members and their relationships with nuclear families. Eavesdropping in *La Cousine Bette* and *Le Cousin Pons* manifests Balzac's fascination with the threshold, be it spatial, psychological, metaphoric, or sexual. In both novels, scenes of secret listening stage problems of knowledge and intimacy – the limits to each, the urge to exceed such limits, the ability or inability to do so, and the implications of such transgressions.[71] Balzac explores the manner in which these "poor relations," relegated to the borders of bourgeois domestic life, represent opposing figures of family neglect and offer very different responses to such marginalization. The contrast between the two characters obtains in their position either as an eavesdropper who gathers compromising information about her family to use it against her supposed loved ones (Bette), or as a kind-hearted, unwitting victim of other people's snooping, whose own affective and material treasures are stolen (Pons). The degree to which each is accepted into the family corresponds with how many family secrets each cousin is privy to. The female concierge, or *portière*, is the other figure playing a central role in the eavesdropping configurations of *Les parents pauvres*; her ability to infiltrate private spaces and learn virtually all family secrets aligns her uneasily with Balzac's omniscient narrator.[72]

The ambivalent attitude toward acquiring secret information presented in the confrontation with the *moucharde* (snitch) in *Le Père Goriot* manifests itself more explicitly in terms of gender in the double story of poor relations. In *Les parents pauvres*, Balzac displaces the reader's curiosity about private lives onto the old maid, middle-class prostitute, or working-class concierge. By associating transgressive activities such as eavesdropping with figures who are socially, morally, and economically marginalized, the narratives distance the bourgeois reader's own interest in the secrets of private life from the obviously suspect investigations of Lisbeth (Bette) Fischer, Valérie Marneffe, and Madame Cibot. In *La Cousine Bette*, the story of eavesdropping focuses primarily on the Hulot family and its internecine struggles for money, sex, and power; Bette represents the family outsider whose control of secret stories is almost equal to that of the omniscient narrator. The alignment of eavesdropping with narrative ominiscience and a subtle discomfort with such positioning assumes more overt form in *Le Cousin Pons*, where the concierge capitalizes on her position as official regulator of the threshold to infiltrate private spaces and learn family secrets. The endings to the two novels and the corresponding fates of female eavesdroppers distinguish between the narrative in which individuals turn strangers into kin and form alliances that break down families, and the story in which the analogous activities of the narrator and the avaricious *portière* form part of a larger narrative in which kin become strangers to justify exploiting their relations.[73] In *Bette* and *Pons*, the definitions of family and outsider, of private and public, are determined by aims of ambition, greed, revenge, or lust rather than by biological or affective connection. In the Paris of the 1830s and 1840s, building lots and family plots impinge upon each other; few spaces or narratives are safe from infiltration or appropriation.

Balzac composed the first account of these "poor relations," *La Cousine Bette*, in 1846, while lavishly furnishing his home for the long-awaited arrival of his lover of thirteen years, Eveline Hanska. Graham Robb suggests this is why the novel is "so much a novel of interiors."[74] Several rooms that Balzac describes are similar to the ones he himself was decorating at the time. *Le Cousin Pons*, written during the following year, reveals Balzac's related passion for collecting. Although Balzac elsewhere devotes large passages of exposition to more public buildings, in *La Cousine Bette* his descriptions are almost exclusively those of domestic spaces. The layout or contents of Victorin's law office, of Vautrin's quarters at the Sûreté, of the Prince de Wissembourg's rooms at the ministry, are never portrayed. Instead, this novel about family life describes in scrupulous detail the domestic interiors of this "drame domestique" (domestic drama) and its less than scrupulous characters (165). In *Bette*, characters are continually moving, changing homes, and in doing so, altering their relations with people. Lived space is social space; how and where one lives affects one's interactions with others. The novel's intimate spaces represent not sanctuaries from the world of business, but the sites where the commerce of secrets, loves, and bodies takes place. Eavesdropping registers the instability of families, their homes, and their secrets in Balzac's bourgeois-monarchy Paris. Just as people move from one apartment to another, so, too, do they maintain more than one dwelling at a time.[75] Such infidelity to space parallels the emotional and sexual infidelity of most of *Bette*'s characters.

This attention to interior space – the place of confidential conversation – and to the tenuousness of its existence, appears as early as the first scene of the novel. *La Cousine Bette* opens with the arrival of a carriage at the door of "une grande maison nouvellement bâtie sur une portion de la cour d'un vieil hôtel [particulier] à jardin. On avait respecté l'hôtel qui demeurait dans sa forme primitive au fond de la cour diminuée de moitié" (51–52; "a large, newly-built [*sic*] house, standing on part of the courtyard of an ancient mansion that had a garden. The old house remained in its original state, beyond the courtyard curtailed by half its extent," 4). Already this description suggests an encroachment upon private space and a subdivision of land hardly conducive to privacy. The lot that belonged exclusively to the older edifice has been taken over to provide housing for the baron Hulot and his family, whose apartment occupies the entire ground floor of the building. The erection of this newer apartment building has halved the area of the court that functions as an intermediate space between public and private realms. The buildings' proximity to each other makes it difficult to separate families, their activities, and their secrets. The setting of *Le Cousin Pons* presents a similarly encumbered privacy: Pons lives in an apartment that once formed part of a larger *hôtel particulier* that is now broken up into an assortment of variously sized and shaped individual dwellings. Both novels thus stress at the outset the artificiality and fragile privacy of the domestic spaces that each narrative will explore.

The beginning of *La Cousine Bette* further emphasizes a concern for privacy and confidentiality. Baroness Hulot (née Adeline Fischer) leads her visitor, M. Crevel, through the grand salon into a smaller room and carefully closes all doors and windows before she will speak to him. She shuts "la croisée et la porte du boudoir [qui n'est séparé du salon 'que par une légère cloison'], afin que personne ne pût y venir écouter. Elle eut même la précaution de fermer également la porte-fenêtre du grand salon, en souriant à sa fille et à sa cousine," whom she has asked to step into the garden (53–54; she shuts "the window and the door of the boudoir [which is separated from the drawing room 'only by a slight partition'], so that no one should get in and listen. She even took the precaution of shutting the glass door of the drawing-room, smiling on her daughter and her cousin," 6–7). However, she leaves the card-room door open:

afin d'entendre ouvrir celle du grand salon, si quelqu'un y entrait. En allant et venant ainsi, la baronne n'étant observée par personne, laissait dire à sa physionomie toute sa pensée; et qui l'aurait vue, eût été presque épouvanté de son agitation. Mais en revenant de la porte d'entrée du grand salon au salon de jeu, sa figure se voila sous cette réserve impénétrable que toutes les femmes même les plus franches, semblent avoir à commandement. (54)

to hear if any one should open that of the drawing-room to come in. As she came and went, the Baroness, seen by nobody, allowed her face to betray all her thoughts and any one who could have seen her would have been shocked to see her agitation. But when she finally came back from the glass door of the drawing-room, as she entered the card-room, her face was hidden behind the impenetrable reserve which every woman, even the most candid, seems to have at her command. (7)

The baroness's elaborate efforts to forestall intrusions and to ensure that her conversation with the retired merchant will not be heard hint at the compromising nature of information to be exchanged. Yet in its representation, we are given access to precisely that information kept from the public. The Balzacian novel is built upon this paradox. The baroness's extraordinary measures to keep her conversation with Crevel private provide one of the few effective private exchanges in a narrative that more often displays the unrelenting plot to reveal the Hulot family's disgraceful secrets by one of its "beloved" members. Although the novel exposes Bette's incremental usurpation of clandestine information, this initial gesture of shutting her and other potential eavesdroppers out is one of the few that succeeds; although Valérie Marneffe learns of Crevel's adulterous proposition to the baroness and her eventual renegotiation of the offer, Bette never does. The narrative's elaborate, self-conscious exposure to readers of this conversation and of the baroness's efforts to contain the skeletons in the Hulot closet emphasizes that it is almost the only secret that Bette does not discover. In revealing this secret to readers while keeping it from the most avid eavesdropper of the novel, the narrative distances our acquisition of private information from that of the scheming spinster and her allies. It also forms a pendant to the secret betrayal that Bette hides from her family to the very end. In a novel whose central story revolves around female competition and alliances, whose major plot and plotting spring from an old maid's desire for revenge against her successful, beautiful cousin, the crucial secrets that each keeps from the other frame the entire narrative. Such narrative framing reminds us of the sibling rivalry at the base of *La Cousine Bette* – a rivalry that is explicitly sexual, but that concerns the stability or destruction of more families and fortunes than those of the Fischer women.

The title of the first chapter, "Où la passion va-t-elle se nicher?" ("Where will passion nest?") raises the problem of finding a space that is cozy, intimate; it reminds us that space is psychologically charged. The word "nicher" also contains the sense of something hidden (a recess). Much of the novel focuses on this concern about "où... se nicher," about creating a private area impervious to discovery. The "petit paradis" that Crevel establishes for Valérie Marneffe represents the extreme example of this need to construct a *lieu sûr* where clandestine affairs can be conducted. This little house is "entièrement cachée à la vue par la loge et par l'encorbellement de l'escalier" ("entirely hidden by the lodge and the projecting mass of the staircase"). It is accessible through the adjoining furniture store, which Crevel rents out

> à bas prix et au mois, afin de pouvoir... punir [le marchand de meubles] en cas d'indiscrétion, puis par une porte cachée dans le mur du corridor assez habilement pour être presque invisible. Ce petit appartement... était donc à peu près introuvable. A l'exception du marchand de meubles d'occasion, les locataires ignoraient l'existence de ce petit paradis. La portière, payée pour être la complice de Crevel, était une excellente cuisinière. M. le maire pouvait donc entrer dans sa petite maison économique et en sortir à toute heure de la nuit, sans craindre aucun espionnage. (251)

> at a low price, and only from month to month, so as to be able to get rid of [the furniture-dealer] in case of his telling tales, and also through a door in the wall of the passage, so ingeniously hidden as to be almost invisible. The little apartment... was very difficult to find. With the exception of the second-hand furniture-dealer, the tenants knew nothing of the existence of this little paradise. The doorkeeper, paid to keep Crevel's secrets, was a capital cook. So Monseiur le Maire could go in and out of his inexpensive retreat at any hour of the night without any fear of being spied upon. (217)

The narrative itself is complicitous in maintaining the "invisibility" of this hidden paradise, protected from infiltration by the neighbors' ignorance of its existence. The readers, like Hulot, do not learn of it until several years into the affair and many pages into the novel. Hulot remains more uninformed than the readers, for he has no suspicions that Valérie – his mistress as well as Crevel's – is unfaithful to him. The narrator reveals this love-nest just before it changes from being the site of secret liaisons to that of public exposure. Instead of hiding Crevel's affairs, the house becomes a trap for Hulot; the cozy space becomes confining, as the sexual secrets it once guarded are instead displayed to the public and its institutions.[76] If the mayor can enter his little home without fear of "espionnage," others cannot. Once Marneffe and the police catch Hulot *in flagrante delicto* with Valérie, the affair, until then an open secret within the family, becomes officially a crime. Written down by the judge's secretary, the official report of the "secret" affair offers Valérie's husband the opportunity for blackmail. One man's crime against the family provides another man's questionable means to "support" his own family. Balzac's numerous references to eyes, glances, and whispers even at the moment of official censure stress the law's complicity in such plots that profit from clandestine spaces and activities (328, 329, 331).

Balzac creates an aural correlative of Crevel's "petit paradis" in his description of the little room in which Valérie later conducts her intimate affair with Wenceslas. The space corresponding to this relationship is smaller, consisting of a single room in a "maison, grosse de paradis et de mystères" (456; "house, full of paradises and mysteries," 446). Designed for secret meetings, the layout of each floor and room of this establishment is the same. The narrative describes how:

Chacune de ces pièces, flanquée de deux gros murs mitoyens, ... se trouvait totalement isolée, au moyen de portes battantes très épaisses qui faisaient une double fermeture sur le palier. On pouvait donc causer de secrets importants en dînant sans courir le risque d'être *entendu*. Pour plus de sûreté, les fenêtres étaient pourvues de persiennes au-dehors et de volets en dedans. (456, e.m.)

Each of these rooms, built between thick party-walls, ... was entirely shut in by very thick double doors on the landing. Thus the most important secrets could be discussed over a dinner, with no risk of being *overheard*. For greater security, the windows had shutters inside and out. (446, e.m.)

Supposedly impervious to eavesdropping, this protected chamber, with its double-doors and window coverings, nevertheless suffers a staged exposure like the one in Crevel's love-nest. In each betrayal, an extra key unlocks the space and reveals its secrets. Despite the obsessive shutting of doors and windows in *Bette*, no space, no secret is safe from discovery, for none remains the exclusive territory of a single person or couple. There is always someone else – a go-between, confidante, or accomplice – who can be corrupted. If individuals can be paid to be silent, like the *portière* for Crevel's love-nest, so, too, can they be bribed to reveal secrets. Each of these scenes of aural and visual spying represents a set-up, and one that reveals all too conclusively the monetary base of the relations between most individuals in Balzac's Paris.

The solid family dwellings with their multiple rooms and more numerous related occupants are no safer from detection and discovery than the two sites of forbidden pleasure. Every location is a potential stage for eavesdropping or spying.[77] In *Bette*, a "drame domestique," aural or visual spying occurs repeatedly; people act to convince others of their loyalty or their love, while secretly plotting to betray them. Individuals employ intermediaries to gain the secrets of a third party. After the revelation of everyone's secret motives and fears, the Hulot family assembles for dinner, and the narrator relates how, "Quiconque eût vu cet intérieur de famille, aurait eu de la peine à croire que le père était aux abois, la mère au désespoir, le fils au dernier degré de l'inquiétude sur l'avenir de son père, et la fille occupée à voler un amoureux à sa cousine" (101; "Any one seeing this domestic scene would have found it hard to believe that the father was at his wits' end, the mother in despair, the son anxious beyond words as to his father's future fate, and the daughter on the point of robbing her cousin of her lover," 57). Such "scenes" are precisely that: staged spectacles of intimacy. Even the marriage of Crevel's daughter Célestine with the Hulots' son, Victorin – the single stable conjugal relationship in the novel – has been arranged through fathers who met at their mistresses' homes. The most publicly sanctioned union thus has at its base private, illicit relationships that threaten the institution of marriage.

In a narrative of relatives and secret relations, everyone is engaged in numerous clandestine confidences and double-dealings; everyone eavesdrops on friends, lovers, and family members in an attempt to understand and profit from the secret exchanges of money, information, and resources. Whispers, side glances, tiptoes, cocked ears abound.[78] Bette confides her secret love to Hortense, who proceeds to "steal" her lover from her (140); Wenceslas confesses the couple's financial predicament to Bette, who uses the information to deliver Wenceslas to Valérie (272); everyone hides troubles from Marshal Hulot, who is deaf, and therefore cannot covertly acquire the information necessary to help Adeline or her family (76). Conversely, everyone hears the *maréchal*'s voice or footsteps before he enters a room, so that they are able to screen crises from him (316). Baron Hulot is simultaneously the individual from whom secrets are often hidden, and who always has something to hide. Almost everyone conceals something from those they love or hate, and almost everyone does not keep the confidences they swear to maintain. Secret stories create secret desires (and vice versa), desires that implicate everyone in the novel.

Valérie and Bette's collusion is the most complicated relation in a narrative of confidences and betrayals. Initially the baron encourages Bette's acquaintance with Valérie "pour avoir un oeil dans [l]e ménage [des Marneffe]" ("that she might keep an eye on the couple"), while for her part, Valérie, "voulant avoir une oreille dans la famille Hulot, caressait beaucoup la vieille fille" (150; "anxious to have an ear in the Hulot house, made much of the old maid," 108). Instead of guarding herself from Bette, Valérie wisely makes "un complice de l'espion" (161; "an ally of the spy," 120); she agrees to help the Alsatian cousin ruin her family while furthering her own ambitions. In their secret pact Valérie proposes, "Voulez-vous que nous soyons comme deux soeurs? Voulez-vous me jurer de n'avoir pas plus de secrets pour moi que je n'en aurai pour vous, d'être mon espion comme je serai le vôtre? . . . Voulez-vous surtout me jurer que vous ne me vendrez jamais, ni à mon mari, ni à M. Hulot, et que vous n'avouerez jamais que c'est moi qui vous ai dit. . ." (153, Balzac's ellipses; "Shall we henceforth be sisters? Will you swear to me never to have any secret from me any more than I from you – to act as my spy, as I will be yours? – Above all, will you pledge yourself never to betray me either to my husband or to Monsieur Hulot, and never reveal that it was I who told you –," 113).

Their agreement completed, the two "sisters" manage the flow of information and thus manipulate the individuals entangled in their plots. Through Bette, Valérie always knows how the Hulots react to her latest conquests or demands; Bette presents her role in Valérie's actions as that of the "unwilling" witness who limits the extent of the courtesan's expenditures and influence. Of all the schemers in the novel, these two women possess the most complete information, so that their machinations are largely successful. Such plots turn strangers into kin, yet such kinship is based upon complementary financial interests rather than mutual affection. This relation remains the novel's strongest, casts suspicion on the "natural" affective bonds of domestic ideology, and augurs ill for the bourgeois family's desire to erect a domestic fortress safe from infiltration. The physical proximity of the women's private spaces gives material form to the overlapping plots they construct to foster their mutual interests.

Bette's position as go-between and confidante serves both women's plans admirably. Bette "se surnomm[e] elle-même le confessionnal de la famille" (85; "call[s] herself the Family Confessional," 39). Except for the wary baroness, the family members, using Bette as a safe repository for secrets, unknowingly deliver themselves up to her intrigues. Bette also assures Crevel that she is a safe confidante, one who "hears all" but "knows" and "repeats" "nothing" (172; 132). A double agent, Bette abuses everyone's trust in order to bring the Hulot family to financial ruin and dishonor. She divulges just enough of people's secrets to their enemies to maintain her role as confidante while convincing both parties that she listens in their own interest. Information not readily "confessed" to her she gleans through watching and eavesdropping. This female Hermes, the "god of the third ear,"[79] works to be everywhere and privy to everything at once. The consummate infiltrator of clandestine spaces and information, she understands the importance of privacy. While conspiring with Valérie, Bette is careful not to speak until "après avoir mis le verrou à la porte du cabinet" (162; "[after having] bolted the door of the room," 122).

All characters in the novel display this justified fear of betrayal and attempt to keep private information secure. Accordingly, the phrase "parler" or "dire" "à l'oreille" ("to whisper") occurs with increasing frequency as the plotting and intriguing become more intricate, and as everyone shares information with accomplices, often in the presence of those they wish to dupe.[80] Bette figures most prominently in these semiprivate exchanges, not only as whisperer and ready listener, but as the individual who observes and overhears as much as possible.

No scene stages the publicity of secret dealings more brilliantly than the one in which Valérie manages all four of her lovers at once by placing them in different corners of her apartment building. In a comedy of illicit manners, Valérie first asks Montès to speak more softly, because her other lovers are beginning to suspect he is not her "cousin" (230–31); that failing, she takes him into the bedroom, at which point, "Hulot ... alla sur la pointe du pied écouter à la porte de la chambre, et il fit un bond prodigieux en arrière, car M. Marneffe ouvrit la porte" (233; "Hulot ... went on tiptoe to listen at the bedroom door; but he bounded back with a prodigious jump, for Marneffe opened the door," 197). When this attempt at private conversation miscarries, Valérie hides Montès in Bette's apartment. But Hulot, suspicious, follows his lover there; in reassuring him of her devotion, she makes Montès jealous, because he "avait évidemment tout entendu" ("had heard everything") while hidden in Bette's *cabinet de toilette* (236; 201). As her explanations become more complicated, her domestic space becomes increasingly congested, and her amorous intrigues more precarious (243; 210). Yet despite the threat of overheard conversations and avowals, this female Machiavelli succeeds in placating, cajoling, and finally convincing each lover that he is her true beloved. Like her apartment itself, which "respirait l'honnêteté" in the public rooms but reveals its luxurious sensuality in the bedroom decor, Valérie possesses "tous les dehors de l'honnêteté" (203, 159) ("appears the very model of respectability").

Indeed, Valérie would have prevailed over the united Hulot efforts to frustrate her ambition, but for the family's recourse to an extrafamilial authority. Victorin turns first to the police for help. But Vautrin, now the head of the Sûreté, cannot intervene in domestic matters. He admits, "On nous a défendu, monsieur, de nous occuper de vous, mais Mme de Saint-Estève est marchande, elle est à vos ordres" (436; "We are forbidden, Monsieur, to meddle in your affairs; but Madame de Saint-Estève is in business, and will attend to your orders," 425). Vautrin makes clear how, officially, the nineteenth-century family and its concerns have become "sacred," off-limits for any state interference or surveillance (423). The press, the institution that publishes intrigues of all kinds, manages "la police correctionnelle de l'opinion," and guarantees the effectiveness of this interdiction.[81] The narrative confirms the power of the press to disseminate information, to shape public opinion, and to manufacture the "truth."[82] In this novel of the bourgeois monarchy, family secrets are treated as delicately as state secrets; if the official police cannot directly concern themselves with family matters, they turn, as Victorin does, to private investigators.

Unlike Rastignac in *Le Père Goriot*, who refuses Vautrin's problematic offer of a wealthy wife, Victorin reluctantly strikes a bargain with Mme de Saint-Estève, Vautrin's aunt. This woman, who knows the secrets of high-society families but refuses to divulge them (420–21), represents the link between the police and Sûreté and the clandestine institutions that regulate society. Mme de Saint-Estève's familial relations with the official forces of the law suggest the less than separate relationship between these two kinds of discipline. She is, in effect, a disinterested Bette, a professional eavesdropper who acknowledges her position on the threshold of private life and the profits she gleans from this listening post. Both secret investigators are never suspected, much less caught. Mme de Saint-Estève uses Valérie's own romantic plots against her. She provides the jealous Montès with the irrefutable proof of Valérie's infidelity, inciting him to poison his unfaithful lover (457). And although Bette dies, "elle garda le secret de sa haine... Elle eut d'ailleurs la satisfaction suprême de voir [toute la famille] en larmes autour de son lit, et la regrettant comme l'ange de la famille" (488; "she kept the secret of her hatred... And, indeed she had the supreme satisfaction of seeing [the entire family] standing in tears round her bed and grieving for her as the angel of the family," 480). Her alliance with Valérie undisclosed, the Hulots mourn the death of their domestic guardian "angel."

The departure of this angel leaves the Hulot family emotionally and physically reunited. Célestine and Victorin, Hortense and Wenceslas, Adeline and a "contrite" Hector all live on different floors in the house that Victorin had the foresight to buy years earlier. The narrative relates how "Chacun de ces ménages jouissait donc d'une fortune particulière, quoique vivant en famille... Ce père prodigue reconquis donnait la plus grande satisfaction à sa famille" (489; "Each household, though living as one family, had its own fortune... This reclaimed prodigal [father] was the joy of his family," 481). Despite its trials, the family appears consolidated and strong. The separation of family fortunes seems to ensure domestic harmony, since would-be snoops have no incentive of material gain; proximity yet compartmentalization of family members seems to literalize and regulate the emotional intimacy presumed of the building's inhabitants.

Yet physical closeness of individual, sexual bodies rather than family branches once more threatens domestic happiness based on spatial propinquity and financial segregation. Eavesdropping again dramatizes the confluence of spaces and bodies, rather than their careful regulation. The baroness, who earlier in the novel "se bouchait les oreilles" ("stopped her ears") so as not to hear of "la conduite de son mari audehors" (75; "her husband's proceedings outside his home," 30), suffers a fatal attack after overhearing her husband in his latest infidelity, which occurs literally under the roof of this domestic bastion:

Adeline, réveillée par un bruit étrange, ne trouva plus Hector dans le lit qu'il occupait auprès du sien... elle monta d'abord à l'étage supérieur occupé par les mansardes où couchaient les domestiques, et fut attirée vers la chambre d'Agathe, autant par la vive lumière qui sortait par la porte, entrebâillée, que par le murmure de deux voix. Elle s'arrêta tout épouvantée en reconnaissant la voix du baron, qui, séduit par les charmes d'Agathe, en était arrivé... à lui dire ces odieuses paroles: "Ma femme n'a pas longtemps à vivre, et si tu veux tu pourras être baronne." Adeline jeta un cri, laissa tomber son bougeoir et s'enfuit. (490)

Adeline, roused by some unusual noise, did not see Hector in the bed he occupied near hers... She went upstairs to the floor occupied by the servants, and there was attracted to the room where Agathe [the maid] slept, partly by seeing a light below the door, and partly by the murmur of [two] voices. She stood still in dismay on recognising the voice of her husband, who, [seduced by] Agathe's charms,... went to the length of saying – "My wife has not long to live, and if you like you may be a Baroness." Adeline gave a cry, dropped her candlestick, and fled. (483)

Adeline's eavesdropping provides incontrovertible evidence that her errant husband will never change and provokes her death three days later. Making the family impregnable against temptations or infiltration is not physically or psychologically possible; there will always be someone willing to assist the bourgeois family in its own destruction. But the fictional representation of such dysfunctional families and the revelation of their secrets – the spectacle of intimacy gone astray – confirms the relative security of the reader's domestic bliss. Hulot's monstrous sexual energies serve as a *monstrum*, or warning, of what can happen when sexuality is not properly regulated. In Balzac's Restoration and July Monarchy Paris, transgressive energies – sexual or epistemological – are nearly impossible to contain. In Balzac's fiction, only those who are willing to manipulate stolen information can achieve any measure of success. Recognition of the futility of trying to keep public and private spaces and stories separate ends only noble lives, not seductive plots.[83]

* * *

In *Le Cousin Pons*, the *portière* Madame Cibot epitomizes another form of domestic spy: the servant or paid employee. The narrator of *La Cousine Bette* declares:

Dans tous les ménages, la plaie des domestiques est aujourd'hui la plus vive de toutes les plaies financières. A de très rares exceptions près... un cuisinier et une cuisinière sont des voleurs domestiques, des voleurs gagés, effrontés, de qui le gouvernement s'est complaisamment fait le recéleur, en développant ainsi la pente au vol... A qui tente de les surveiller, les domestiques répondent par des insolences, ou par les bêtises coûteuses d'une feinte maladresse; ils prennent aujourd'hui des renseignements sur les maîtres, comme autrefois les maîtres en prenaient sur eux. (213)

In every household the plague of servants is nowadays the worst of financial afflictions. With very few exceptions,... the cook, male or female, is a domestic robber, a thief taking wages, and perfectly barefaced, with the Government for a fence, developing the tendency to dishonesty... If any attempt is made to interfere with them, the servants reply with impudent retorts, or revenge themselves by the costly blunders of assumed clumsiness; and in these days they enquire into their master's character as, formerly, the master enquired into theirs. (175–76)

Les parents pauvres confirms this pronounced fear of theft by those whose labor produces the well-ordered bourgeois household. The domestic betrayals in *Bette* are rivaled if not surpassed by the unrelenting, underhand dealings of Mme Cibot, so notorious that she is referred to as "*la* Cibot." She is the consummate concierge, that emblematic French Cerberus who guards the entrances to all dwellings in the city, and who, even as she protects inhabitants from unwelcome intrusions, is suspected of being a police informant.[84] Mme Cibot's regulation of what and who constitute the categories of public and private – visitors, information, secrets – determines the outcome of the novel and the varying success of its characters. Although she readily admits Rémonencq into the two musicians' apartment in their absence because "il vivait en bonne intelligence avec les Cibot" (131; "he lived on good terms [was in cahoots] with the Cibots," 103), she refuses repeatedly to let the honest Topinard visit the dying Pons (328).[85]

La Cibot's hypocrisy knows no bounds. Although continually repeating to Pons and Schmucke how "désintéressée" (disinterested) she is (143; 170), Mme Cibot's decisions about whom to admit foster her own interests, not her lodgers'. She constantly warns the two gullible musicians to be wary of nurses and other servants ("c'est tout voleuses... Vous allez voir comme elles sont intrigantes"), while engaging in the very activities she cautions them about (169; "nurses are thieves... I could tell you something about their scheming ways," 138). The narrative of *Pons* repeatedly links interest in other people's affairs – curiosity – with interest in their *financial* affairs. In this milieu, eavesdropping reveals not just family secrets, but financially rewarding information. Even more than *Le Père Goriot*, *Le Cousin Pons* demonstrates the utter fiction of the separation of public from private secrets and lives. And covert listening spatially maps the impossibility of this division.

Mme Cibot's domination over Pons and Schmucke is all the more complete because of their estrangement from or lack of family. As Pons's relations begin to close their doors to him, he relies increasingly on the *portière* even for food, thereby giving her greater access to his apartment and the collection of precious objects it houses. *Pons* reveals the danger of trusting those hired to provide what one's family cannot or refuses to offer. Figures of nurturance are the individuals most likely to betray. A self-styled "rivale de la Maternité" (197; "Maternity's rival"),[86] la Cibot spreads malicious reports about Pons's relatives, the Camusots and Popinots, attempting thereby to usurp their place in Pons's heart, and thus in his will (177). Similarly, when Pons dies, the lawyer Fraisier places his "nourrice" (nurse) in the chamber of the dead man to help take care of the body and to help Schmucke, but really to place in the apartment "un espion et un gendarme" over his own accomplices (310; "a spy, a police-officer,"267). Serving as Pons's and Schmucke's factotum, la Cibot enjoys an access to their most intimate spaces and an ability to control entry to them that are virtually unlimited. Consequently, her domestic thefts are not limited to the money that a cook can skim off the food budget (as the quotation from *Bette* suggests), but consist of information and material objects, both equally invaluable.

As in *Le Père Goriot* and *La Cousine Bette*, everyone suspiciously watches and listens to everyone else within earshot. When Hélène Brisetout visits Pons, "toutes les portes étaient entre-baillées" (288; "every door in the house was ajar," 248). Anyone with anything to hide takes the precaution of locking his or her door or of retiring to a more private location: when the concierge comes to consult him, Fraisier "met le verrou pour que sa ménagère ne vînt interrompre les confidences de la Cibot" (208; "bolt[s] the door to make sure that his housekeeper [cannot] come in and interrupt [la] Cibot's confidential utterances," 173); Poulain asks her to walk into the salon, so that the servant will not hear their conversation (197). One chapter title puns on this vain desire for secrecy: "Pour ouvrir une succession on ferme toutes les portes" (333).[87] Yet these precautions are ineffective when crafty types like la Cibot and Fraisier are concerned; they control private space and its secrets so masterfully that, at one point, their conversation escapes even the omniscient narrator's purview (265).

Mme Cibot regulates not just the exits and entrances to her own apartment building; through a dubious professional courtesy, other concierges give her access to places otherwise closed to her (224–25). In a novel where locking doors provides the only defense against an ever-intrusive, inquisitive world, la Cibot possesses an almost foolproof "open sesame." No private space or conversation is safe from her pryings. Even when the two musicians, suspecting her treachery, lock her out so that they can confer undisturbed (286), the narrative stresses the aural cue this action provides: "la Cibot en entendant ce bruit significatif... [cria] 'vous me paierez cela, mes petits amis'" (286–87; "[la Cibot] heard the significant click of the bolts" and cried "I'll pay you out for it, my fine friends," 246). She may not hear the conversation, but she realizes that the suspicions of the two lodgers require a change in her tactics.

More than visual spying, eavesdropping in *Le Cousin Pons* signals not just who is secretly listening to whom, but who capitalizes effectively on illicit information. The innocent Pons's accidental overhearings reveal to him only how much his family and their dependants despise him (51, 65). Similar to Bette in his humble position as an "égout aux confidences domestiques" (a "drain down which domestic confidences were poured"), the bachelor finds himself more bound to discretion than his female counterpart, for "un seul mot hasardé lui aurait fait fermer la porte de dix maisons" (62; "one rash word would have barred him from ten households," 38). Rather than giving him power over his relatives, listening threatens to exclude him from their homes.

In contrast, Mme Cibot – whose schemes make her more akin to Bette than her male counterpart – represents the most successful eavesdropper in the novel. She overhears the conversations both of her gullible victims and of her collaborators, Fraisier and the collector Magus (265). Her covert listening acquires greater subtlety as the novel progresses. At first, the concierge merely hides out of sight in Pons's bedroom, so that when he complains to Schmucke about her treatment of him, she can twist whatever Pons says to her own advantage (255). Later, when she wishes to know the content of Pons's will, she pretends to exit his room. Then, arming herself with a hand-mirror and positioning herself behind the door (which she keeps ajar), she can observe and hear all that transpires (283). When Pons catches a glance of her in the bedroom mirror, however, he has the notary lower his voice so that she cannot hear the terms of the will (284). Undaunted, the inquisitive *portière* returns at night with Fraisier to sneak a look at the sealed document; caught in the act by the musicians, she pleads, "C'est pure curiosité!...c'est le défaut des femmes, vous savez!" (298; "It was only curiosity!...It's a woman's failing, you know!," 257). Seeing that this explanation fails to satisfy her lodgers, la Cibot leaves, still playing the innocent, but not before hiding under her dress a painting to sell to Magus (299). Although Fraisier suspects that she has duped him, he never learns exactly how (338). At the end of the novel, she has escaped at least two deadly punishments: the fortune-teller's dire prophecy of assassination (154), and the poison that her second husband prepares for her but drinks by mistake (367). The doorkeeper to private rooms and information, la Cibot embodies an emphatic denial of the platitude "crime does not pay." Her eavesdropping, unlike that of the *honnêtes gens* of the narrative, pays all too well.

Sharon Marcus notes how *Le Cousin Pons* links the omniscient narrator, who has access to virtually every space and conversation, and the *portière*. Both possess "limitless mobility and vision;" both "enter private space without knocking, precisely because it is private." For Mme Cibot, private space holds objects worth stealing and circulating on the open market; for the narrator, privacy "signifies a story worth recounting because it is not already in the public domain." From this affiliation Marcus concludes that the narrative "exonerates" la Cibot for her crimes.[88]

Yet the omniscient narrative voice of *Les parents pauvres* distances itself from the female eavesdropper – whether the *portière* in *Pons* or the spinster cousin and her "sister" in *Bette* – and her illicit activities in subtle ways. In the earlier novel, although Bette dies with her secret intact, her attempt to revenge herself on her cousin's family brings about the death of the man she wished to marry, Marshal Hulot. Her plot to destroy the family is "all too successful" ("avait trop réussi," 383). Both Bette – the spinster who loves a younger man and avenges herself on her female cousins for depriving her of this beloved – and Valérie Marneffe – the middle-class prostitute who uses her façade of respectablity to ply her trade – directly threaten the bourgeois family. Their infractions of social codes are of an explicitly sexual nature, and they are punished accordingly: Valérie's passionate Brazilian lover infects her with a deadly poison that disfigures and kills her; Bette dies from the frustration of seeing all her schemes (to destroy the Hulots, to marry the maréchal) fail.[89] Mme Cibot's punishment is more discreet, since her transgressions are so close to the narrator's and the bourgeois family's. Her machinations to acquire Pons's collection represent a more debased form of his own relatives' scheme. Mme Cibot does not die in the country as a fortune-teller predicted because she does not allow herself to leave Paris. Her liberation – from the bonds of matrimony and from the fortune-teller's prophecy – comes at a cost. Although the *portière* may roam the metropolis freely, gathering its secrets and secret possessions and selling them to the highest bidder, the city constitutes a virtual prison, a space open to her but at the same time confining her. And whereas the omniscient narrator and the Camusots-Popinots get off scot-free,[90] their fictional, female, working-class counterpart does not; she has learned her place.

In contrast to such wily manipulators of secrets, the poor stagehand Topinard, the only person besides Schmucke who cares for Pons, can do nothing with the information he has overheard to protect the gullible German from the intrigues of Pons's greedy relatives. Although he overhears the plot to deprive Schmucke of his legacy from Pons, Topinard cannot gain entrance to the room where the unsuspecting musician is signing away his inheritance until it is too late (333). Significantly, Schmucke's response, when informed of the deception against him, is silence: "Il mourut en dix jours sans se plaindre, car il ne parla plus" (364; "He died in ten days without uttering a single complaint, because he had lost the power of speech," 317). What more is there to say, what indeed *can* one say, when one's words and secrets will always be used against oneself? Balzac's pessimism about the possibilities for domestic bliss in a city filled with eavesdroppers could not be clearer.

Topinard appears to be the only figure in *Pons* who lives in happy domesticity, free from the anxieties of domestic infiltration. Balzac describes his tiny sixth-floor apartment in detail. It consists of a kitchen and two bedrooms: "Dans la première de ces deux chambres se tenaient les enfants... La seconde était la chambre des époux Topinard" (350; "The children slept in the first of these... and the Topinards had the second as their marital chamber," 303). Despite its limited space, this home provides separate quarters for parents and children and offers a degree of privacy for the couple whose bedroom is a "lieu réservé," off-limits for the children (353). In this meager lodging, Schmucke finds hospitality after his eviction from the apartment he shared with Pons (345). The fragility of this one space that is truly a home, its scanty proportions and furnishings, stand in marked contrast to the opulent Camusot home that opens the novel and that is the site of repeated eavesdropping throughout the first half of the narrative. The only space free from infiltration is a home so poor that its domestic secrets have no value on the open market. Potential snoops would gain nothing in penetrating its interior – a significant attribute in a novel where most of the characters are bought ("acquis," 361) as easily as the paintings and other objects that the collectors connive to obtain.

However, the narrative does not grant even Topinard – one of the few uncorrupted creatures in this plot of theft, bribery, and avarice – full protection from narrative "speculation." Although his home may be safe from intrigue, his story is not. A man whom such plots have turned taciturn and misanthropic, Topinard "passe pour avoir commis un crime, et les mauvais plaisants du théâtre prétendent que son chagrin vient d'avoir épousé Lolotte" (367; "Rumour has it that he committed some crime; malicious wits at the theatre claim that his moroseness is due to his having married Lolotte," 319). In a culture perversely attached to the publicity of the private, the public will manufacture skeletons in a family's closet if they do not already exist, for broadcasting other people's scandals confirms, through contrast, the illusions of one's own privacy and domestic bliss.[91] Be it ever so humble, there's no place like home. But even a humble home is subject to gossip and some form of speculation. If an individual cannot afford the attentions of the *portière*, the public will find a way to fabricate and spread a story about him to protect its own secrets.

OF HOUSE AND HOME: *DOMBEY AND SON*

At the same time that Balzac was producing *Les parents pauvres*, Dickens began writing *Dombey and Son* (1846–48) while vacationing on the Continent. More than the French novels, it represents the urgent desire to establish a home that is impervious to the intrusions of the marketplace.[92] A novel about the longing for a domestic haven, begun when its author was away from his own in London, *Dombey and Son* demonstrates a distinctly nineteenth-century sense of the word "home." Unlike an earlier conception of the house, in which domestic dwelling was often combined with or located next to business enterprise (as the term "cottage industry" suggests), the nineteenth-century image of "home" as a reified, nucleic space evokes a zone defined precisely in its separation from the space of work and business.[93] *Dombey and Son* exposes the misfortunes of a man who focuses on the prosperity of his financial house at the expense of his domestic and emotional home. The novel examines the confluence, in the word "house," of concepts of domestic dwelling, family genealogy, and family business.[94] This multiple use of the term denies the separation that the ideology of separate spheres would imply. An intrusion into the world of domesticity generates an incursion into the commercial world, and vice versa. Mr. Carker, Dombey's business manager, commits or directs the most insidious eavesdropping that occurs in the novel. The fact that he represents the "sordid" business world from which the "pure" domestic realm is to be protected intensifies the import of his infiltrations into domestic space and makes them transgressions that jeopardize all the "houses" of Dombey.

In staging the demise and resurrection of the "House of Dombey" through eavesdropping, Dickens reaffirms the ideology of separate spheres even as he uses the publicity of the private to educate his readers about the virtues of domestic life and the threats to it. In contrast to the "contracted sympathies" of Dombey and Carker, who conflate public and private spheres and hire others to be their "confidential agent[s]," Dickens opposes sympathetic listeners, those within the narrative – characters and the omniscient narrator – as well as his own readers.[95]

His narrator assumes the role of a "good spirit" who takes "the house-tops off" "with a potent and benignant hand" to expose social ills and stir citizens "to make the world a better place" (738, 739).[96] Dickens formulates a complex relation between public and private spheres and secrets – one that extolls the virtues of domestic ideology yet grants license to the novelist or other moral managers to intrude on private life and its spaces in the interests of social and moral improvement. All eavesdroppers are not created equal. The conclusion of the novel establishes the safety of the Dombey household and family narrative, even as it suggests that true privacy is dependent on narrative reticence as much as on the willful construction of public and private spheres, spaces, and subjects. Eavesdropping in *Dombey and Son* suggests that the ideology of separate spheres is as much a construct as the fictions that celebrate it.

The continual repetition of the word "house" in a novel replete with eavesdropping also reminds us of the distinct manner in which the English language articulates this act of surreptitious listening. In English "to eavesdrop" originally meant to position oneself underneath the eaves of a house in order to listen secretly to private conversations. The expression contains a concrete reference to domestic architecture and a positioning of the subject within a specific architectural space. In contrast, French does not have a single word for the activity of eavesdropping, but instead offers expressions such as "être aux écoutes" or "surprendre une conversation," neither of which contains an allusion to architecture or a distinct place. Although French also cautions that "les murs ont des oreilles" and "il ne faut pas écouter aux portes," these locutions lack the precise location of an individual actively listening that eavesdropping conveys. Not surprisingly, eavesdropping figures prominently in *Dombey and Son*, a novel preoccupied by domestic spaces and the kinds of psychological and ideological implications they carry.

In his biography of Dickens, Peter Ackroyd asserts that "the London of his novels always remains the London of his youth, a city with its heart still in the eighteenth century."[97] By and large, this statement can be applied to the architecture and layout of the great houses that Dickens describes in his novels. In *Dombey and Son*, the businessman's apartments on the first floor of his house consist of a sitting room, a library *cum* dressing room, and a conservatory *cum* breakfast room (75). As this catalog suggests, the identification of specific spaces with particular activities is still in flux; Dombey's private apartments are located on a floor that later in the century functioned primarily as public space. Thus, Paul's postbaptismal dinner is served in the library (115). However, the psychological resonances with which the novelist imbues these domestic spaces reflect a transition toward a Victorian sensibility and ideology.

In fact, many of the more modest dwellings that appear in Dickens's fiction already associate domestic comfort and harmony with privacy. The snug cottages offering refuge to Little Nell and Oliver Twist, the cozy if humble accommodations of the Toodle home in *Dombey and Son*, provide a degree of psychological security and familial affection that greatly exceeds their physical proportions. They stand in marked contrast to intimidating, stately homes like *Bleak House*'s Chesney Wold or Dombey's dreary mansion.[98] In *Great Expectations*, Wemmick's castle, equipped with moat and drawbridge, not only literalizes the sanctity of the domicile ("a man's home is his castle"), but associates this private space with a private persona and the telling of secrets. Division of self accompanies compartmentalization of information. When Pip asks Wemmick, in his home, to relate the secret story of Jaggers's housekeeper, the clerk replies, after hesitating, and only after assurances of confidentiality, "what I do know, I'll tell you. We are in our private and personal capacities, of course."[99]

Dombey and Son's obsession with the multiple meanings of the word "house" suggests a distinction between it and the domestic ideal of "home" that is established by the end of the novel and that resurrects the financial as well as familial "House." Witold Rybczynski explains how the word "'[h]ome' brought together the meanings of house and of household, of dwelling and of refuge, of ownership and of affection. 'Home' meant the house, but also everything that was in it and around it, as well as the people, and the sense of satisfaction and contentment that all these conveyed."[100] Significantly, Carker's house is filled with beautiful objects but is bereft of familial presence or warmth. If his carpets are "soft and noiseless," they suggest not comfort and domestic tranquility but rather the possibility of keeping his activities inaudible (554).[101] Dickens contrasts this house with a true home: the modest cottage that Carker's estranged, impoverished brother and sister inhabit on the outskirts of London.

Dombey and Son demonstrates the dangers of not distinguishing between house and home, of confusing or conflating the public and the private, and in so doing allowing the public world access to secret information, thus endangering an individual's position in both worlds. In a novel primarily about Dombey's family life, its lengthy full title – "Dealings with the firm of Dombey and Son, Wholesale, Retail and for Exportation" – foregrounds the firm's financial matters, and suggests the problematic priorities of the business's "Head" even before the story gets underway.

It begins with the birth of Paul Dombey, Junior, an event that his father perceives in terms of its effect on his firm, rather than on his dying wife. The opening of the narrative wryly reflects Dombey's consideration of family event as business venture:

> Dombey sat in the corner of the darkened room in the great armchair by the bedside, and Son lay tucked up warm in a little basket bedstead, carefully disposed on a low settee immediately in front of the fire and close to it... "The House will once again, Mrs. Dombey," said Mr. Dombey, "be not only in name but in fact Dombey and Son... There is some inconvenience in the necessity of writing Junior," said Mr. Dombey, making a fictitious autograph on his knee; "but it is merely of a private and personal complexion. It doesn't enter into the correspondence of the House. *Its* signature remains the same." (49–50)

Dombey fails to value the "private and personal." Instead, he privileges the counting house over the domestic house and denies any difference between public and private behavior. He considers his son merely as an extension of the firm. Through the course of the narrative, Dombey and the reader are taught to value the separation of public and private spaces, activities, and stories. At the same time, this education depends upon the exposure of Dombey's private story to the vast reading public avidly consuming Dickens's fiction.

The narrative playfully imitates Dombey's dangerous conflation of public and private in its third chapter title, "In which Mr. Dombey, as a Man and a Father, is seen at the Head of the Home-Department" (74). Dombey's proud adherence to the outward display of success and his reversed priorities of producing a family that will sustain the business House of Dombey and Son lead him to neglect his daughter Florence, whom he considers "[i]n the capital of the House's name and dignity... merely a piece of base coin that couldn't be invested – a bad Boy – nothing more" (51). Using a metaphor of spatial exclusion, Dickens contrasts Dombey's estrangement from his daughter with other fathers' love of their children. Unlike Florence, children blessed by paternal affection "had won their household places long ago, and did not stand without, as she did, with a bar across the door" (424). The trope presents the house as the space of familial tenderness. Being barred from the literal space indicates exclusion from the figurative one. Florence's nightly visits to her father's closed door provide the ritualized enactment of this emotional separation (396). Just as his rooms suggest a lack of defined private space, Dombey demonstrates a disregard for the private interactions that should take place in such areas. Like its "Head," the firm disregards the usual familial relations and sets up "unnatural" ones, so that the Carker brothers' positions are reversed: the "Senior in years" is the "Junior in the House" (245).

Privileging public appearance over intimacy, Dombey does not recognize private interaction as the foundation for public success. Although he jealously guards Paul from other people's love, Dombey fails to understand how he must protect and manage familial affection. Refusing to nurture private feeling and the spaces conducive to it, he also prohibits any expression or display of intimacy between his second wife and his daughter primarily because "it is likely to be noticed" and, by contrast, cast his own interactions with them in an unfavorable light (686).

This affective failure takes spatial form. Dombey's domestic house provides merely the semblance of a respectable Victorian home, with none of the familial warmth or ease that constitute the idea of home. Despite lavish redecoration, the magnificent house is "no home . . . for any one" (592). The narrative ironically relates how, "If none of the new family were particularly at home in private, it was resolved that Mrs. Dombey at least should be at home in public, without delay" (593). In the impersonal language of the board meeting ("it was resolved"), the text indicates that for Dombey, the private is merely a show put on for the benefit of the public and for the ostentatious display of the "Firm's" respectable foundation. Dombey manages properly neither counting house nor domestic home, but instead hires Carker to be the "confidential agent" of his joint domestic and financial affairs. In giving Carker free admission to both houses, in allowing him access to spaces and secrets normally reserved for the family, the businessman enables his treacherous manager to plot the fall of both Dombey "Houses" (653, 683).[102]

In marked contrast to Dombey, other characters understand the need to protect personal space, private information, and intimate interactions. They also recognize the profit or knowledge that the infiltration of others' private spaces can provide. As in Balzac's novels, everyone in *Dombey and Son* is continually poking his or her nose into other people's business: prying, snooping, watching, listening. Major Bagstock observes Miss Tox's apartment across the court "with a double-barrelled operaglass" (147) and commands his servant to keep "in constant communication with Miss Tox's maid" in order to be informed of her association with the Dombey family (186). He describes himself as having "lived in the world with his eyes open . . . and his ears cocked" (349). The walls of Mrs Pipchin's establishment are "brittle and thin" (160); she devotes "much of her time to concealing herself behind doors, and springing out on [her maidservant] whenever she [makes] an approach towards

Mrs. Wickam's apartment" (167). Mrs. Skewton and Carker listen so intently to the conversation between Edith and Dombey that their own exchange is distracted and random (465–66).[103] Conversely, Susan Nipper distinguishes herself as a trustworthy servant and loyal friend by indicating that she does *not* eavesdrop, calling herself the little "Pitcher as I might have been" (476).

Even the saintly Florence inadvertently overhears a private conversation, although the information she gleans merely confirms that her father's lack of affection for her is public knowledge. In a prolonged exchange between a little orphan and her guardian aunt, the narrative forces Florence and the reader to recognize the extent to which her position is worse than that of the conventional Victorian object of pity: unlike the orphan, who cannot hope for a parent's love, Florence has a father who deems her unworthy of affection. The aunt concludes, "your misfortune is a lighter one than Florence's; for not an orphan in the wide world can be so deserted as the child who is an outcast from a living parent's love" (423). Overhearing the truth she would deny, Florence collapses, although moments later she resolves to act so as to refute the opinion "in one mind certainly: perhaps in more – the belief that [Dombey is] cruel and unnatural" (423). The narrative's vagueness about which "mind" holds this belief suggests that Florence herself knows the extent to which her father is "cruel and unnatural." Her banishment from the parental hearth and the public circulation of her story will come back to haunt Dombey. For if the home and House of Dombey are inseparable, so, too, are their narratives; the disgrace of the one affects the other. If Florence's exile is cause for pity, other scandals will do greater harm to family and firm.

Just as everyone ferrets out secrets, everyone worries about other characters' intrusiveness. Captain Cuttle lives in such fear of the prying Mrs. MacStinger that when he moves to Sol Gills's shop he "curtain[s] the glass door of communication between the shop and parlour, on the inside; fit[s] a key to it from the bunch that had been sent to him; and cut[s] a small hole of espial in the wall" (438). Edith fears that Carker may have heard her conversation with the gypsy woman. Each is suspicious of what the other knows or suspects: he saw that "she saw in *his* eye that her distrust was not without foundation" (461). Most of the figures, like Edith, try not to speak before "looking round to see that they [are] quite alone" (503), or like Mr. Toots, speak "in a suppressed voice, to prevent its reaching...jealous ears" (547). When Florence arrives at Sol Gills's shop after having fled her father's house, she begs Captain Cuttle to hide her, worrying that someone might be "listening and watching" (763). Yet such attempts to protect private spaces and stories always fail. There is always someone – even if only the omniscient narrator and his readers – who is privy to the delights and horrors of intimate life. Characters or the narrator publicize domestic bliss only by exposing that sphere thought impervious to infiltration.

In a novel obsessed with protecting private space and its secrets from exposure, the fact that its archcriminal Carker explicitly enlarges the definition of eavesdropping to encompass both watching and listening cannot be overestimated. At a key moment, Carker confers with his minion, Rob Toodles, the wayward son of the family representing working-class domestic harmony and affection:

> "Halloa!" he cried, calling him roughly back. "You have been – shut that door."
> Rob obeyed as if his life had depended on his alacrity.
> "You have been used to eaves-dropping. Do you know what that means?"
> "Listening, Sir?" Rob hazarded, after some embarrassed reflection.
> His patron nodded. "And watching, and so forth." (678)

Carker expands the scope of eavesdropping to include any spying that encroaches upon a domestic space. He thus returns the word to its etymological sense of being positioned under the eaves of a house and gives concrete, social form to transgressions of intimate space and its secrets. Hence Carker's caution to "shut that door." The scene also reminds the reader that, in hiring someone to eavesdrop for him, Carker links those spheres that Victorian ideology wished to segregate: the public world of business and the private world of the home. Despite the fact that his discussion with Rob takes place in his own secure home, he fears being unable to keep the conversation private, for his own activities deny the assurance of privacy that the ideology of separate spheres would maintain. Emphasizing Carker's double manipulation of private space and information, the narrator relates how, although continually listening to and observing others, Carker himself is "always closely buttoned up and tightly dressed" (239). A would-be covert information monopolist, Carker ferrets out other people's secrets, but holds the sole right to transmit them to a larger public. He repeatedly threatens Rob not to reveal his own affairs, yet engages the boy to eavesdrop on other people's; he also listens to his spy's private conversations (385).[104] Carker's house is filled with carpets and cushions that "are too soft and noiseless, so that those who move or repose among them seem to act by stealth" (554). His private environment reveals the hidden nature of its master. Rather than a space of intimacy, comfort, and ease, his house represents an extension of his plotting to a more private space.[105]

Carker's fears of having his secrets disclosed are justified, for Dombey discovers his treachery through covert listening. In fact, two of Hablot Browne's illustrations for the novel emphasize the significance of this expanded sense of eavesdropping and explicitly juxtapose Carker's vicarious eavesdropping with the retaliatory, clandestine listening of his employer. The pictures present first Rob and later Dombey secretly spying on other characters in modest homes (Solomon Gills's shop and parlor, and Mrs. Brown's urban hovel), where the division of space and opportunities for privacy are limited (413, 823). Be it ever so humble, no house is safe from inquisitive eyes and ears. After allowing Carker to manage his understanding of people and information, Dombey finally acts as his own agent. Mrs. Brown invites him to "stand behind the door, and judge [Rob's story] for [him]self" (821). Rob's coaxed confession gives Dombey the location of Carker and Edith's rendezvous in France.

Using Carker's own tricks and servant against him, Dombey ascertains the runaways' whereabouts, and follows them. Edith escapes because, in the Dijon hotel suite with multiple doors, she discovers a hidden doorway leading to a secret passage. The "betrayer" now "betrayed," Carker also flees via this secret path (860, 862). The narrative represents aurally his radically altered fortunes. The most successful eavesdropper earlier, Carker now fears every noise, every knocking, every bell, every voice, real or imagined (861, 862, 866, 868). His story concludes in a series of ominous aural cues and apocalyptic visions, culminating in Dombey's belated shout of warning, the rumble of an approaching train, and Carker's shriek just before it crushes him (875).

Yet Carker's death cannot halt the destruction of the Dombey houses that he has instigated. The violations to the domestic house jeopardize the secrets of the business house as well. The secrets of both kinds of house become common knowledge, the subject of gossip. Tellingly, the firm's messenger, Mr. Perch, provides the easy passage of private information into public knowledge. As his name implies, Perch occupies a strategic position in the outermost office, the go-between of counting house and enterprise. Accepting the newspapermen's offers of drinks at the "public house" in return for providing insider information, Perch leaks private intelligence of the Dombey firm's financial woes into the vast public domain of other businesses and the press (836). Private House secrets become public-house gossip. Perch also confirms the firm's failure to Dombey's domestic servants. The narrative positions him as a voice with an authority equal to that of the *Gazette*, the paper that published bankruptcy listings, and reinforces his associations with the publicity of the private (924). From counting house to public-house, from public-house to private house, Perch represents the intermediary who offers secret information to two public bodies: the large, anonymous public who reads the papers, and the smaller, if equally damaging one of the household servants. As in *Le Père Goriot*, such communities thrive on secret-sharing.[106] In *Dombey and Son*, these public and semipublic groups are constituted from the invasion of private bodies and bodies of knowledge:

The council in the Servants' Hall whispered so among themselves, and shook their heads... This observant body had plenty to say of Mr. and Mrs. Dombey, and of Mr. Carker, who appeared to be a mediator between them... They all deplored the uncomfortable state of affairs... but upon the whole, it was agreeable to have so good a subject for a rallying point, and they made a great deal of it, and enjoyed themselves very much. (743)

Although the servants "deplore" the misfortunes of the Dombey household, the news fosters their own concord and pleasure. In a similar manner, when the clerks learn of the firm's financial woes, they stop working and pass the time speculating about the bankruptcy, its origins, and its implications (814–15). In their festivities, both servants and clerks become "quite dissipated, and unfit for other service" (816). Such riotous behavior anticipates the imminent break-up of both Dombey House and home. At the same time, the disarray in the Dombey House occasions "reconciliation" and celebration among other "observant" bodies (815). It suggests in an exaggerated register the unity in the households assembled to read Dickens's novels. Contemplating another family's tribulations makes one's own home seem comparatively prosperous and safe – or encourages individuals to ensure that theirs are.

From whispered exchange to overheard conversation, from "doubtful rumours" to published fact, the bankruptcy of Dombey and Son becomes public knowledge, its "great mysteries, the Books" opened and pored over by outside accountants, its undeniable truth verified by the newpapers (910, 924). The description of Perch whispering stories to "gaping listeners, in a low voice, as if the corpse of the deceased House were lying unburied in the next room" figures the bankrupt firm as a cadaver, the one Carker had earlier meticulously "dissected" to discover its secrets (909, 722). Dickens extends this metaphor to its domestic counterpart. The Dombey home is subjected to the same invasive probings, with "herds of shabby vampires...opening and shutting all the drawers...There is not a secret place in the whole house" (928). Every secret spot is opened up, subjected to inspection, and marked for resale. The creditors suck every drop of blood from the dying corporate and domestic bodies.[107]

Dickens stresses the psychological violation that occurs when the public and its organs have access to domestic space by describing the physical disarray of the Dombey household. Literal and affective space are one; everything is out of place: "[m]attresses and bedding appear in the dining-room; the glass and china get into the conservatory;" food is brought in from the "public-house" and consumed on "pieces of furniture never made to be eaten on" (928). The material bedlam literalizes the emotional and financial "ruin" of the House of Dombey (923). The orderly, respectable household, which compartmentalized things and individuals and hid Dombey's emotional bankruptcy, disintegrates with his financial failure. Domestic and financial house founder because neither can count on the emotional security of a true home. Business house and private home collapse into each other, as domestic space becomes the site of and object for sale (929). The invasion of all spaces and things normally kept private – drawers, bedrooms, bodies – is the more pronounced because the physical house containing them remains impervious to decay: "It is a great house still" (928, 923). Since Dombey's house has been the semblance of a home, its ruin leaves only the material shell intact; the physical edifice now embodies the emotional vacuum it previously housed.[108]

The novel's prolonged dénouement stresses issues of aurality, secrecy, the generation of stories, and stories of regeneration. Sounds proliferate: ringing signals danger, like the bell at the gate through which Carker escapes (862); conspicuous silence or a tolling bell denotes death (933–34, 887); wedding bells and the chinking of glasses convey joy (806, 888, 970). The last two hundred pages are also marked by a series of effective or frustrated eavesdropping scenes. These moments of overhearing accentuate aurality's central role in relaying information and stories.

The self-effacing Mr. Morfin offers the most significant example of how benevolent as well as evil characters can marshal the flow of information through eavesdropping. Despite his attempts to muffle the sounds of conversation emanating from Carker's office, Morfin overhears the manager's treacherous plot (841). His knowledge produces not ambitious schemes or gossip but sympathy for the subjects of these conversations, Carker's maligned elder brother John and his sister Harriet. Although he cannot avert the financial disaster of Dombey and Son, Morfin satisfies most of Dombey's creditors. Using confidential information to help and not to harm, Morfin is also blessed with an exceptional aural inviolability. The narrator mentions twice that his landlady is deaf, and therefore cannot eavesdrop upon him (912, 917). Until he shares the firm's secrets with Harriet and John, Morfin confides only in his violoncello (913). Indeed, the narrative invests both his person and his personal space with a singular aural integrity. When Walter Gay and John Carker need a secure, private space to confer in, they withdraw to Morfin's office (249). Dickens never describes Morfin's home in Islington, and sets only one conversation in it, a conversation that arranges a restitution of funds to Dombey. Harriet and John's charity remains hidden, known only to them and their truly "confidential agent" Morfin. Harriet cautions that they must keep the knowledge of the gift so secret that "it may seldom be whispered, even between" themselves (915). She recognizes the vulnerability of even the most carefully guarded secrets: if whispered, they may fall on the wrong ears. Their gift is one of the few stories that the public in the novel never discovers, even if the omniscient, eavesdropping narrator reveals it to his readers (912–17). Not coincidentally, the two reminders of the landlady's deafness bookend this episode, creating a wall of privacy that characters within the narrative cannot penetrate. The only good landlady or concierge is a deaf one. Dickens thus underscores the fact that – within the text – this magnanimous act will not become public knowledge.

The final secret, also revealed by the narrator only to the novel's readers, concerns the house of Dombey. By the end of the novel, Florence and her husband have created a home of their own, a refuge for Dombey from the inquisitive "world" that constantly seeks to expose his secrets. Toots's declaration that "there is a foundation going on, upon which a – an Edifice... is gradually rising... [f]rom his daughter, after all, another Dombey and Son will ascend... triumphant" recalls the convergence of family line, domestic structure, and family business in the "House" of Dombey (974). Florence, the spurned daughter, not only builds a sanctuary for her family, but, with her husband, restores to her father all he had lost. The narrative confirms Miss Tox's early pronouncement, "to think... that Dombey and Son should be a Daughter after all!" (298). The house of Dombey-Gay depends upon its *domestic* managers for its emotional wellbeing. Within this haven, Dombey learns to treasure his child and grandchildren for their own sake, not as indices of his firm's vitality. The narrative relates how the story of the bond between Dombey and his grandson "goes about and follows them... But no one, except Florence, knows the measure of the white-haired gentleman's affection for the girl. That story never goes about. The child herself almost wonders at a certain secrecy he keeps in it. He hoards her in his heart" (975). *Dombey and Son* ends by alluding to a tale of love so private that it cannot be told. Dombey has learned the virtues of domestic ideology. He considers his love for his granddaughter too precious, too intimate to be mentioned. Like a miser, he will not present it to a public that may not treasure it properly. He has become a true Victorian.

Yet despite casting this story as utterly private, its narration belies the secrecy to which it refers, places the love before a larger reading public, and offers it up as a subject for conjecture and gossip. Narrative reticence about this most private tale is half-hearted at best. It emphasizes that the novel itself assumes a transgression of privacy to exist and to appeal to its readership. The Victorian novel's financial success was premised on the exposure of fictional domestic secrets to a larger public, the public that eagerly awaited each installment of the serialized text. More generally, the ideology of separate spheres depended upon the publicizing of the myth of secure boundaries between public and private, a fiction that the extensive eavesdropping in *Dombey and Son* and most mid-nineteenth-century novels undermine even as they proclaim its authority.

The nineteenth-century novel reiterates the longing for safe spaces, places where family secrets can be kept, yet tacitly acknowledges that private space is only tentatively secure. Even the most "homely" house, in both senses of the word, is constantly subject to surveillance and infiltration. No matter how many walls a family erects to shelter its intimate life, it will always be vulnerable to eavesdropping. In a culture perversely attached to publicizing the ideal of privacy (and with the technological means to do so), intimate secrets almost inevitably seep out. The yearning for home carries with it a secret acknowledgment of its precarious existence. Its constant recreation in nineteenth-century fiction bespeaks a willful determination to construct these spaces even as they are continually transgressed, and even as the narratives about them deny the privacy that they represent. The last sentences of *Dombey and Son* imply the secret that Victorian domestic would repress: the only truly safe haven lies in "an invisible country far away," about which the sea's voices can only "whispe[r]... in our childish ears" (976).

If Dickens's novel whispers its doubts about keeping the home and its secrets safe, Wilkie Collins's *The Woman in White* (1860) sensationally stages the perils and pleasures of transgressions of domestic space and ideology. It intensifies the discussion of eavesdropping and its relation to private spaces and identities in earlier nineteenth-century texts by concentrating them in the English country house – the exemplary private space – and in the female narrator. Like Balzac's novels, *The Woman in White* foregrounds a female character who eavesdrops and thus defies spatial, social, and ideological boundaries – a character uneasily aligned with an implied male author or narrator. However, in presenting Marian Halcombe as a prime *narrator* in a story that sets itself up to rival the authority of the law, Collins's novel links concerns about privacy and private activities with more pronounced anxieties about the relation between gender and narrative and social agency. In the central episode of covert listening, Marian eavesdrops upon two men in the library and then records their secret plot in her diary. *The Woman in White* explores the role that writing plays in establishing public and private identities; it dramatizes the dangers and delights of secret listening and reading that produce acts of telling and writing. If its narrative dwells longer on the pleasures of transgression and on the correspondence between sexual and textual bodies than earlier nineteenth-century texts, it also increases the punishment of all who would defy the constructions of domestic ideology and its spaces.

CHAPTER 4

The madwoman outside the attic: Eavesdropping and narrative agency in The Woman in White

> The hiding of a crime, or the detection of a crime, what is it? A trial of skill between the police on one side, and the individual on the other. When the criminal is a brutal, ignorant fool, the police in nine cases out of ten win. When the criminal is a resolute, educated, highly-intelligent man, the police in nine cases out of ten lose. If the police win, you generally hear all about it. If the police lose, you generally hear nothing. And on this tottering foundation you build up your comfortable moral maxim that Crime causes its own detection! Yes – all the crime *you* know of. And what of the rest?
>
> *The Woman in White*

Frederick Walker's poster for the Olympic Theatre's 1871 dramatic adaptation of *The Woman in White* portrays a woman clothed in white passing through a doorway or large, shuttered window (Figure 1).[1] The background's dark, starlit sky and the woman's frightened glance evoke a nighttime setting of mystery and suspense. The woodcut could represent any of several women in Collins's 1860 novel *The Woman in White*: the first woman in white whom Walter Hartright encounters, later identified as Anne Catherick; Laura Fairlie, who, dressed in white on the first evening of Walter's stay at Limmeridge House, possesses an uncanny resemblance to Anne; or, as the black-and-white print suggests, a reversed image of Marian Halcombe as she embarks on her aural surveillance mission in the middle of the narrative. That the evocative woman of the title can refer to many of the text's female characters indicates the tenuousness of women's identities in the narrative. The ambiguity of the woman depicted and the fear she exhibits as she leaves a protected space reflect the novel's preoccupation with individual identity and with the danger that women incur in leaving the spaces and activities deemed proper to them.[2] Eavesdropping – an improper activity on the border between inside and outside, private and public – figures transgression in the novel. An eavesdropper steals the secrets of private life and controls their

Figure 1. Frederick Walker, RA, *The Woman in White*, 1871 (Tate Gallery, London/Art Resource, New York)

dissemination in the public realm; by withholding or disclosing people's secrets, the eavesdropper determines their social identity. In *The Woman in White*, illicit overhearing stages anxieties about and pleasure in the complex relations between gender, identity, and narrative and social agency. Eavesdropping in the novel also hints at Collins's own ambivalent attitude toward conventional gender roles and transgressions of them.

Although numerous critics have examined issues of gender, identity, and agency in Collins's novel, none has considered specifically how eavesdropping represents the intersection of such concerns and the transgression of conventional attitudes toward them in the novel – that is to say, how this narrative device helps tell the story and comments on the tale being told and its ideological implications.[3] Peter Thoms is one of the few critics to look in detail at Collins's "use of structure for thematic purposes."[4] However, in reading the characters' development as a "movement from a false story or a 'plot' to the possession of a true story," he considers all three protagonists' stories (Walter's, Marian's, and Laura's) as forming a single, collective tale standing in opposition to the conspirators' intrigue (55). Consequently, Thoms does not consider how the repeated emphasis of composite construction calls attention to the problematic relations in the novel between narrative agency, identity, and *gender*. Women have very different narrative opportunities than do men in the novel. Although Marian and Walter appear to contribute equally to solving the mystery, Walter ultimately controls what is told to whom. Tamar Heller argues convincingly that Walter, representing the "professional man who, by the novel's end, reasserts the division between male professionalism and domesticity," acts out Collins's need to distinguish himself from the realm of domesticity and women in order to establish himself as a professional male writer.[5] This intratextual competition between male and female writers for authorial control parallels Collins's anxious rivalry with female authors such as Charlotte Brontë, creator of the original "madwoman in the attic," as well as George Eliot, the "masculine" and socially unconventional woman writer whose recent *Adam Bede* (1859) had established her as a major English novelist.

In the complicated narrative and social environment of *The Woman in White*, eavesdropping represents spatially the interaction of social, institutional, and narrative forces operating in the novel.[6] Eavesdropping, the usurpation of other people's private information, suggests the unsanctioned transfer and use of narrative information from speaking subject to listener, and from writer to reader within a text. Ideologically, given its liminal position in the space between the private conversation and the realm of public knowledge, eavesdropping dramatizes the struggle for the control and dissemination of a story. The recurrent acts of illicit overhearing in Collins's text suggest that this particular novel, and perhaps novels in general, are composed of deviant activities and attempts to suppress them. The novel itself represents a space of female narrative activity and mobility that is eventually contained and enclosed within reassuring, conventional, patriarchal structures.[7] Moreover, because the distinction between private and public spheres is bound up with middle-class Victorian assumptions about gender, eavesdropping in *The Woman in White* foregrounds the relationship between narrative agency and the determination of sexual and social identity.

The foremost transgression in *The Woman in White* is, in fact, against conventions of gender: specifically, Victorian assumptions about women's passivity and men's activity.[8] Declaring that "This is the story of what a Woman's patience can endure, and what a Man's resolution can achieve,"[9] the authoritative narrator of the preamble asserts that gender roles are fixed and absolute. Initially unidentified, this narrator delegates to Walter Hartright the power to "be heard first" and establishes him as the prime organizer of the narrative (33).[10] Thus the pen begins firmly in the male hand, and the power to write or tell represents the ability to act or do. The opposition of woman's passive endurance and man's active will, however, quickly breaks down. Although the conclusion confirms and legitimates the fixed gender categories of the beginning, the narrative itself revels in, thrives on, indeed owes its existence to, transgressions of all kinds of social and narrative codes: gender, law, privacy. In such an environment, eavesdropping serves as both narrative strategy and metaphoric representation of this subversive activity.

The narrative space of *The Woman in White* presents a struggle for authority that ultimately reaffirms the social and institutional status quo. Those individuals who threaten and transgress conventional boundaries of law, narrative, and gender are punished.[11] Sir Percival's and Count Fosco's attempt to rewrite Laura's identity and hence usurp her fortune ostensibly stands as the central crime in *The Woman in White*. Yet in this story of complicated plots and plotting, eavesdropping reveals not just the collusion between men to steal a particular woman's social identity and the wealth that accompanies it, but, more radically, a collaboration between narrative representation and female confinement. Far from demonstrating that good characters, whether male or female, triumph over evil ones, *The Woman in White* exposes a collusion of male narrative forces to limit female narrators and characters. Multiple patriarchal figures competing among themselves for control of stories and identities further complicate the narrative. The final confrontation between the male antagonists Walter and Fosco can occur precisely because Marian, like Anne Catherick, "a dangerous woman to be at large" (177), has been enclosed within the "asylum" that Walter provides for her; her narrative voice has been silenced.[12]

Indeed, Collins's novel portrays women's institutional fate in the male-dominated socio-economic, medical, and legal establishment. As Count Fosco tells Marian, "English Society, Miss Halcombe, is as often the accomplice as it is the enemy of crime" (258). *The Woman in White* relates the story of this secret crime. Sir Percival appears to be the villain of the piece, and only later do characters and the reader realize that Fosco is the more deadly criminal. A third, even more insidious enemy of female narrative agency lurks within the pages of the novel: Walter Hartright, the principal narrator and apparent ally of female characters. His crime goes undetected by the novel's characters and its more conventional readers.[13]

The opening of *The Woman in White* suggests why this central crime and hidden danger pass unremarked, proposing as it does an absolute division between public and private spheres, sanctioned and unsanctioned eavesdropping, authorized and unauthorized narratives. This section is entitled the "preamble," a term usually referring to the preliminary statement of a formal, legal document. As such, the beginning asserts that the narrative itself imitates the proceedings of a court of law and mimics the presentation of a legal case, with each individual narrative representing the account of a different "witness" (33).[14] The narrative makes explicit that both readers and characters become invested with the powers of judgment and must be convinced of an individual's social and moral legitimacy; social institutions determine personal identity.[15] The court represents a public, sanctioned overhearing that is always accompanied by a written account of the proceedings. This oral and written act purports to "set the record straight" by establishing the "truth" and writing it down, thus lending the act legitimacy and permanency. Such writing is always in the public domain. In turn, the judgment or verdict forms part of a larger legal narrative of case history and precedent, so that a ruling in one case establishes the authority of an argument in succeeding ones.

In contrast, both private conversations and diaries operate under the assumption of confidentiality. However, in *The Woman in White*, all writing falls in the public domain; private notes, letters, and diaries are subject to interception and circulation among a larger audience than the one for which they were intended. The lawyer Mr. Gilmore notes the danger of being "obliged to commit to writing questions which ought always to be discussed on both sides by word of mouth" (163). Yet even such discreet conversations, in this novel, may be overheard; private and secure conversations or writing seem impossible. Eavesdropping and unsanctioned reading of private documents stand as the criminal correlatives of the public, sanctioned overhearing with which the court of law regulates all forms of transgression.

By invoking "the Law" as the ultimate authority, and by investing the reader with the same powers of judgment as legal justice ("As the Judge might once have heard it, so the Reader shall hear it now"), the preamble establishes the novel as a substitute tribunal where transgressions of social order are punished, since "the machinery of the Law [cannot] be depended upon to fathom every case of suspicion, and to conduct every process of inquiry" (33).[16] In a novel where written narrative stands in for oral testimony, the acquisition of oral information and its transcription into written document must be guarded and controlled, for such acts confer legitimacy upon both the story and its teller.[17] The struggle for narrative authority thus involves both the power to control an individual's identity and the public account of it.

In *The Woman in White*, crime often centers on acts of eavesdropping or forgery: aural or written trespassing, intruding on or appropriating the property of other individuals. The information an individual gathers aurally (or through secret reading of private writing) provides the material to write another person's story, to usurp that individual's identity, and the titles to rank and property that accompany it. In addition to the attempted theft of Laura's identity and fortune, the crimes that Sir Percival and Count Fosco have perpetrated are, respectively, forgery (creating a false legitimacy and title by adding a line to a marriage register) and counter-revolutionary spying (illicitly acquiring information about others to prevent them from challenging the political establishment). In such a narrative milieu, eavesdropping spatially situates and figures acts of narrative, whether they aim to uphold or subvert the narrative or social order.

Yet just as individual characters eavesdrop on each other and decide which pieces of information are relevant to them, here the reader is specifically enjoined by the preamble to overhear other people's stories and make judgments about them. Does this imply that the reader, as a metanarrative eavesdropper, is to be punished for his or her listening in on stories about others? Hardly. Because readers' listening is, as the preamble indicates, a sanctioned overhearing, one that the narrative itself sets up, it affords us the seductive position of committing a seemingly illicit activity, yet without fear of punishment. Our eavesdropping provokes judgment in us, the judgment that the narrative requires in order to accomplish its stated purpose of proving the guilt of certain characters, reestablishing the identity of Laura Fairlie Hartright, and in doing so, asserting the right of other characters to positions of rank, title, and authority. But the "truth" that the novel presumes to tell "always in its most direct and most intelligible aspect" is actually a narrative of devious strategies that performs its own textual usurpations and incarcerations (33).

Collins described the "central idea" of his work as "a conspiracy in private life, in which circumstances are so handled as to rob a woman of her identity ... The destruction of her identity represents a first division of the story; the recovery of her identity marks a second division."[18] He alludes to the novel's heroine, Laura Fairlie, whose husband Sir Percival Glyde conspires with his friend Count Fosco to replace her with the mentally and physically frail Anne Catherick and imprison Laura in Anne's place. Once the false Lady Glyde had died, Laura's fortune would pass to her husband and his partner in crime. Part of the "conspiracy in private life" is the fact that this novel is not "private," but consists of a plot against privacy and private information. Laura recovers her identity through the dissemination of private information to a larger public audience, and through public recognition of her by the male villagers and laborers on her estate, who collectively vote her into existence at the end of the novel. Like the reader, they are told only part of the story upon which they render a verdict. However, *The Woman in White* relates the usurpation of not just Laura's identity, but also that of the other female protagonist in the novel, and one of its central eavesdroppers and narrators: Marian Halcombe. Besides the overt subjects of crime and punishment, *The Woman in White* presents Marian's transgression of the unwritten laws of proper female behavior, and the ensuing discipline and incarceration to which she is subjected. The three other women in the novel – Madame Fosco, Anne Catherick, and her mother, Mrs. Catherick – offer similar examples of transgressive female energies and the retributive, male efforts to curtail their activity.

In an age where "'moral insanity' redefined madness not as a loss of reason, but as deviance from socially accepted behavior," any woman could be called "insane" who exhibited behavior considered "abnormal or disruptive by community standards."[19] Anne Catherick represents mental disorder; *The Woman in White* critiques the Victorian system of benevolent, paternal "moral management" to care for her mental and physical illness. The novel more subtly enacts the same kind of "management of women's minds" on other female characters who stand as figures of deviance and transgression. In doing so, it offers to Collins's more conventional readers a reassuring reestablishment of the social order and woman's place within it.[20] In a text that foregrounds the importance of writing and narrative control in determining social power, this institutionalization of "mad" women and other deviants takes place on a narrative level: they are written into limited roles or written out of the story altogether.

The first number of *The Woman in White*, published in *All the Year Round* (1859), concludes with the following exchange, overheard by Walter Hartright, between a policeman and two men in a carriage:

> "Policeman!" cried the first speaker. "Have you seen a woman pass this way?"
> "What sort of woman, sir?"
> "A woman in a lavender-coloured gown –"
> "No, no," interposed the second man. "The clothes we gave her were found on her bed. She must have gone away in the clothes she wore when she came to us. In white, policeman. A woman in white."
> "I haven't seen her, sir."
> "If you or any of your men meet with the woman, stop her, and send her in careful keeping to that address. I'll pay all expenses, and a fair reward into the bargain."
> The policeman looked at the card that was handed down to him.
> "Why are we to stop her, sir? What has she done?"
> "Done! She has escaped from my Asylum ... " (55)

Overhearing that the woman whom he has just spoken with and helped had escaped from an insane asylum causes Walter to reexamine his actions. He wonders whether his promise "to leave her free to act as she pleased" was "ill-considered," despite the fact that in their encounter, "the idea of absolute insanity which we all associate with the very name of an Asylum, had ... never occurred to me, in connection with her;" "nothing, in her language or her actions," appeared "to justify" her incarceration (55). Indeed, when asked by the policeman what this person has "done," the only crime of which she can be accused is having fled the place where she was held against her will. Yet Walter ponders whether he has "[a]ssisted the victim of the most horrible of all false imprisonments to escape; or cast loose on the wide world of London an unfortunate creature, whose actions it was [his] duty, and every man's duty, mercifully to control" (55). Walter's reevaluation not only expresses a desire to evaluate, categorize, and sentence women; it also recalls the novel's initial self-presentation as a space of judgment. Significantly, the preamble confers upon Walter a privileged status: it gives him the right to "be heard first" and establishes him as the narrative's prime organizer, who determines what (or who) fits where (33). Just as effete Mr. Fairlie hires him to "arrang[e] and moun[t]" his masterpieces, the unidentified narrator engages Walter to arrange all the pieces of this master's story (*Riverside*, 9). Walter's need to decide whether this unidentified woman should be permitted to remain at liberty parallels the larger narrative's demand to determine where women in general belong, when they should be allowed freedom, and when it is "every man's duty, mercifully to control" them.

Hidden until the lawyer Mr. Gilmore begins his section of the narration is the fact that Walter himself devised the plan of "presenting the story to others, in the most truthful and most vivid manner" by having it told "at each successive stage in the march of events, by the persons who were directly concerned in those events at the time of their occurrence" (150). Walter introduces himself as merely a witness and veils his role as the preamble's author. By associating the preamble with the authority of the law – a distanced, anonymous, impartial institution – Walter hides the fact that such institutions, like the preamble, are manmade, and that they, too, often assert the rights, privileges, and authority of some individuals (and their stories) over others.[21]

The end of the first installment raises the question of the need to contain a potentially dangerous woman, the mysterious "woman in white" whom Hartright met on a deserted road in the middle of the night. Just as Walter considers whether or not he behaved properly in permitting her to remain free to act, the narrative itself oscillates between freedom and containment of female power. D. A. Miller has registered the confusion of distinct, rigid gender categories in this novel. In his argument about readerly feeling in Collins's sensation novel, Miller stresses homosocial relations and the repression of homosexuality in the construction of gender.[22] He inverts the traditional formulation of male homosexuality as a woman's spirit imprisoned in a male body and suggests that Marian Halcombe, the most compelling female narrator in the novel, represents "*anima virilis in corpore muliebri inclusa*": a man's spirit imprisoned in a female body.[23] Yet *The Woman in White* is not primarily the story of, "on the one side, a passive, paranoid homosexual feminization; on the other, an active, corroborative, heterosexual masculine protest."

Miller assumes that the reader is male,[24] whereas Collins presumes an audience of men and women in the preface to the second edition of the novel, and fluctuates in addressing a male or a female reader (or both) in the body of the novel (32, 76, 79, 88). Subsuming "the sequestration of the woman" into an argument about how normative heterosexuality represses homosexuality, Miller does not explore the implications of Marian as a woman writer, nor, by extension, the relation between women's narrative agency and social power.[25] By focusing on only one aspect of her character, his reading replicates the novel's incarceration of the female narrative subject; he puts Marian's story to his own (gay) male ends.[26] Moreover, Miller's argument relies on a vocabulary of visual surveillance rather than eavesdropping, which specifically involves the control of language, and thus offers greater resonances for a discussion of narration and narrating subjects.

The narrative space of *The Woman in White* represents a region less of either/or, than of liminality. It manifests a resistance to dichotomies of black or white, masculine or feminine.[27] The narratable defies such ordering activities; not surprisingly, narrative closure involves the reestablishment of fixed social positions and absolute gendered identities. Mr. Fairlie, whose "effeminately small" feet are shod in "little womanish bronze leather slippers" and who has "a frail, languidly-fretful, over-refined look," offers an appearance that is "unpleasantly delicate in its association with a man, and, *at the same time*, something which could by no possibility have looked natural and appropriate if it had been transferred to the personal appearance of a woman" (66, e.m.). But Mr. Fairlie's pale delicacy appears to be a *Fairlie* trait, a characteristic passed down on the *father's* side that both Laura and her half-sister Anne inherit, but that Marian, daughter of Mr. Halcombe, does not.[28] In this way, Collins renders suspect the contemporary belief that women were primarily responsible for the hereditary transmission of madness, as characterized by weakness, nervousness, and languor.[29] The contradictory doublings among characters indicate how Collins complicates the dichotomies established in the novel.[30] The effeminate Fosco offers a very different image of the criminal from brutal, macho Sir Percival, just as his massive presence makes a striking foil to his compatriot, the diminutive Pesca. However, "unfeminine" Marian is Fosco's closest narrative double, and his equal in intelligence and plotting; their similarities and attraction to each other provide a distinct counterexample to the traditional couple represented by Laura and Walter.[31] For this reason, eavesdropping, an act that takes place on the boundary between inside and outside, private conversation and public knowledge, and that foregrounds its liminal, transgressive status, serves as a particularly resonant trope for the narrators themselves and the narrative activities occurring within this novel.

The first eavesdropping scene distinctly contradicts the first sentence's announcement of fixed gender roles and opens up a narrative space in which the primary narrators present exceptions to orthodox generic characteristics rather than the rule. Instead of exhibiting manly "resolution," Walter is characterized by indecision. Possessing few of the characteristically "masculine" attributes associated with decisive activity, he has so bungled his control over his own finances that he must return to a female space, his mother's cottage. His self-portrait acknowledges his position of economic dependence, limited mobility, and marginal status, a situation very similar to that of a Victorian woman (34). In order to be hired by Mr. Fairlie, Walter must "produce testimonials – letters that speak to his character," letters that speak for him and confirm his identity (41). As drawing master at Limmeridge, Walter holds the position of a privileged servant analogous to the Victorian governess. Dependent on a capricious employer for his livelihood, he has no sexual identity: "I had trained myself to leave all the sympathies natural to my age in my employer's outer hall, as coolly as I left my umbrella there before I went upstairs...I was admitted among beautiful and captivating women much as a harmless domestic animal is admitted among them" (89).[32] Miller emphasizes Walter's lack of "manliness" in the novel's first half, but he mistakenly locates the origin of Walter's "feminization" in Anne's touch. In fact, Walter's "immatur[ity]" obtains even before his encounter with Anne, as his economic and social dependency suggests.[33] Walter must embark on an imperial adventure to Central America to return a virile, "changed man," determined to wrest back not only Laura's identity and inheritance from Fosco and Sir Percival but also control of the narrative from his presumed ally, Marian Halcombe (427).

In contrast, Marian violates established Victorian assumptions about gender even as she continually utters them. For instance, she declares, "I am as inaccurate as women usually are" (60). Rather than supporting such behavioral norms, this incongruity suggests their invalidity.[34] In his first encounter with her, Walter describes Marian first in terms of her figure, which is "comely and well-developed, yet not fat; her head set on her shoulders with an easy, pliant firmness; her waist, perfection in the eyes of a man, for it occupied its natural place, it filled out its natural circle, it was visibly and delightfully undeformed by stays" (58).

In this catalog of attributes, traditional notions of feminine beauty combine with hints of the woman yet to be encountered. She is shapely, yet that shape is visible because, unlike other women, she does not restrict her body with the accoutrements of fashion: the stays that confine a woman's body. Even her body resists enclosure.[35] Her head rests with "pliant firmness" upon her shoulders, yet combines compliancy with will, a characteristic attributed to men in the Victorian gender dichotomy.

This combination of "masculine" and "feminine" traits is succeeded by the realization that Marian is not a passive object to be evaluated by "the eyes of men." Instead, approaching her, Walter gasps to discover the strong, unconventional, and thereby "ugly" features of his new pupil. He describes how:

> The lady's complexion was almost swarthy, and the dark down on her upper lip was almost a moustache. She had a large, firm, masculine mouth and jaw; prominent, piercing, *resolute* brown eyes... Her expression – bright, frank, and intelligent – appeared... to be altogether wanting in those feminine attractions of gentleness and pliability, without which the beauty of the handsomest woman alive is beauty incomplete. To see such a face as this set on shoulders that a sculptor would have longed to model – to be charmed by the modest graces of action through which the symmetrical limbs betrayed their beauty when they moved, and then to be almost repelled by the masculine form and masculine look of the features in which the perfectly shaped figure ended – was to feel a sensation oddly akin to the helpless discomfort familiar to us all in sleep, when we recognise yet cannot reconcile the anomalies and contradictions of a dream. (58–59, e.m.)

Walter reveals the discomfort that a "resolute" woman provokes in him, an uneasiness particularly acute since he has demonstrated a tendency to be less than resolute in his own actions and thoughts. In general, Walter's first narrative emphasizes Marian's "resolution" and "will," which bolster his own lack of "manhood" (96, 63).[36] In response to her "fearless sympathy which [meets him] on such mercifully equal terms," Walter evinces a "loss of self-control" and "weakness" (95, 97). He holds the position of emotionally overwhelmed, speechless, and submissive femininity; she that of "fearless," self-possessed, determined masculinity. When he leaves Limmeridge, she presses his hands "with the strong, steady grasp of a man" while, he admits, his "voice faltered," his "eyes moistened in spite of [himself]" (148).

In a novel asserting it will tell the story of what "Man's resolution can achieve" and "Woman's patience can endure," such characterization initially seems incongruous. Marian hardly seems the epitome of ladylike submission, but instead embodies a mixture of traits usually considered masculine or feminine, as does Walter, although he seems less conscious of this fact. Marian appears more aware of such gender oppositions yet more dubious of their validity. In describing herself and Laura, Marian declares, "She is an angel; and I am – Try some of that marmalade, Mr. Hartright, and finish the sentence, in the name of female propriety, for yourself" (61). Refusing to identify herself as a devil, Marian resists classification in binary terms, even though she uses the excuse of "female propriety" to escape such taxonomy. Her ability to manipulate oral and written language appears early on. Aware of her situation as a middle-class Victorian woman, she puts ironic self-consciousness into words. Nina Auerbach points out how an old maid's "overt supremacy... must cover itself with self-effacing rhetoric."[37] For Marian, irony becomes the rhetorical signature of doubleness.

Like her male counterpart Count Fosco, she combines masculine and feminine attributes in a manner that complicates Victorian assumptions about gender. Marian's description of the Count as "strikingly original and perplexingly contradictory" could be equally applied to herself (242). Just as Anne Catherick does not fit into easy categorization according to class (she has "not exactly the manner of a lady, and, at the same time, not the manner of a woman in the humblest rank of life," 48), Marian refuses classification as essentially "feminine." To Walter her lack of "gentleness and pliability" and all too "masculine form and masculine look" make him "almost repelled," and feel "helpless discomfort" (59), because such attributes remove from him the assurance of control. In her passion and her resolution, Marian exemplifies the "strong-minded" Victorian woman writers and heroines castigated for being "denatured" or "unwomanly" because they thought and acted in a manner that contradicted normative feminine behavior.[38] Neither completely feminine nor masculine, Marian's indeterminate status places her in an intermediary position between the men and women in the novel, communicating first with Laura, then with Walter, with Madame Fosco as with Fosco himself.[39]

This defiance of gender stereotypes makes Marian attractive not only to Count Fosco but to readers as well.[40] Marian embodies what Barthes calls an erotic space of "intermittence" or betweenness, the space of textual pleasure, for she represents liminality.[41] She constantly refigures conceptions of masculine/feminine, public/private, outside/inside as character-narrator in the novel. Her boundary-crossing takes literal form and becomes narrative and narratable event when she eavesdrops on Fosco and Percival's conversation in the library. Her eavesdropping provides a doubly layered, spatial representation of such liminality, since the act of deliberately overhearing is itself a transgression of boundaries. Because of its illicit nature and the threat of discovery, eavesdropping involves this Barthesian fascination for the reader (the metanarrative eavesdropper), the continual possibility that the flow of information will be cut off and the eavesdropper caught and punished. Moreover, in preparing to listen to the conspirators' conversation, Marian supplies further narrative titillation, for she divests herself of her "white and cumbersome" undergarments, those clothes that hinder her unrestricted movement on the ledge of the roof. Marian consciously notes how, in her "present dress... no man could have passed through the narrowest spaces more easily than I" (342). Just as she spies on the two men, gathering information about and from them, the reader can observe her as she performs her utterly clandestine activity in a semiclad state. We are privileged with doubly private information, for we acquire information about her and about the secret conversation between Fosco and Percival.[42]

To eavesdrop on the conspirators, Marian assumes a position similar to the figurative place of the reader or an omniscient narrator surveying events from on high: she installs herself on top of the veranda roof, above the two men in the library. In this post, she believes herself to be more protected than she would have been downstairs, "within reach of Sir Percival and the Count" (342). In listening to and then writing down Fosco's private conversation with Sir Percival, Marian transforms private knowledge into a form that can be easily circulated, reproduced, and transmitted to others to frustrate the criminals' plots. By transcribing the secret conversation she overhears into her diary, Marian establishes her possession of the information necessary to forestall their devious plans – or so she thinks.

Marian's two previous significant actions have been scriptural as well, in the form of letters. Her first letter to Laura's lawyer telling him of Percival and Fosco's activities temporarily obstructs their plans to force Laura to sign a document that would give Glyde access to her money and diminish her children's inheritance. When Marian writes a second letter informing the lawyer of Percival's physical abuse of and threats to his wife, she considers her writing as a surrogate male weapon. Echoing yet refuting the novel's opening sentence, she declares, "our *endurance* must end, and our resistance must begin" (321, e.m.). Marian refuses the role of feminine passivity in favor of linguistic, legal, and later, physical action. Nevertheless, she emphasizes how she "[writes] with Laura's authority" but entreats the lawyer "to *act* in her name" (329, e.m.). Marian's writing enlists the larger institutional power of the law to frustrate Percival and Fosco's plan, and turns the bruise or "mark" on Laura's arm into a "weapon to strike [Percival] with" (321). The mark on the body is translated into a mark on the page, as the battlefield becomes explicitly textual. Hence Marian determines to record the information she obtains in the central eavesdropping scene, for "the words those two men [would say] to each other would furnish us, not only with our justification for leaving the house, but with our weapons of defence against them as well" (357). Later, Walter hopes to rely on writing (the duplicate marriage register) to expose Percival's original crime.[43] In both instances, control of someone's private story – the threat or the act of putting it into circulation, and its inscription and dissemination in the public sphere – represents the greatest power over him, for it establishes him as virtuous citizen or monstrous criminal.

In her rooftop eavesdropping on the conversation in the library (the room embodying narrative power and the written evidence of its authority) and in the transcript of her listening, Marian more fully arrogates the male privileges of mobility, writing, and agency. Unlike the reader's or an omniscient narrator's sheltered listening, Marian's aural transgression involves no small risk. Her emphasis on the aural aspect of her spying ("Laura's life itself... might depend on my quick ears and my faithful memory," 340) acknowledges the particular danger in this kind of transgressive behavior: the reciprocal threat of being caught, through being overheard in turn. Michel Foucault notes that Bentham had initially envisioned "acoustic surveillance" in his *Panopticon*, but that he abandoned the idea "perhaps because he could not introduce into it the principle of dissymmetry and prevent the prisoners from hearing the inspector as well as the inspector hearing them."[44] Eavesdropping rarely involves a unidirectional flow of information, as Marian learns all too well. An unsanctioned listener, she is punished by the person whose space she has trespassed upon: Fosco retaliates with an extreme violation of her private textual space.

Collins's 1860 and 1861 revisions of the text for book publication accentuate the correspondence between textual and physical bodies in *The Woman in White*. One of the most significant changes occurs as Marian eavesdrops on the Count and Percival. She learns that Madame Fosco has stolen the two letters that she gave to Laura's maid Fanny to mail. In the serialized text, Marian states, "The letters had never left my own possession, till I placed them in Fanny's hands at the inn" (*Riverside* 251).

The revised account has Marian wonder "how could [the Count] have examined the letters when they had gone straight from my hand to the *bosom* of the girl's dress?" (*WW* 346, e.m.). This second version emphasizes that the abuse of a servant's private, sexualized body by Madame Fosco, her husband's "instrument" (329), precedes the violation of Marian's private text by Fosco himself. With the help of his wife, the Count substitutes a blank sheet of paper for the letter Marian was sending. Here, Fosco erases her writing, whereas later he writes in her diary; the second intrusion is greater, as he alters her most private textual space.

Marian hears of this violation as she herself commits an act of aural trespass. In an escalation of crime and punishment, Marian's eavesdropping provokes the violation of her physical and textual bodies. The language of "exposure" suffuses this part of the narrative and reinforces the bidirectional danger of Marian's illicit listening. Just as she hopes to "expose" Percival and Fosco's plot (323), by removing her womanly garments and leaving the domestic space – by transgressing the boundaries of "appropriate" behavior – she exposes herself to the elements and to the men's retributive actions. Consequently, she catches a fever from having crouched outside in the rain; Count Fosco not only reads her private journal in which she has transcribed the conspirators' conversation (thereby revealing her private thoughts to his gaze), he then writes comments in it. Fosco later relates how "Miss Halcombe unhappily exposed herself to be wetted through by a heavy rain" (373). His language is eroticized, invasive, and indicative of the textual violation that follows her physical exposure.

By reading Marian's diary, Fosco reappropriates the narrative agency – the ability to direct and shape the course of events – she had stolen from him. Writing in her journal and inscribing his name after his entry, Fosco reclaims his own plot from her and claims her most private narrative space. Doubly violated, her textual body becomes his;[45] he possesses her narrative and controls its ending. Critics have considered this act a textual "rape," but in doing so, they regard Marian as the object of male narrative and desire, without considering what happens to her as writing *subject*.[46] Fosco's appropriation of her intimate narrative space – his writing in and on her textual body – redefines its shape, giving it narrative stays limiting its expansion and power. His literary eavesdropping and punishment of her narrative theft ensure that Marian becomes a docile tool in Hartright's hands, just as Madame Fosco, the woman who once read Mary Wollstonecraft, has been "tamed" to become her husband's "willing instrument" (329). If, according to Victorian gender norms, Marian had exemplified an "unwomanly woman," Fosco's narrative usurpation removes from her the position of desiring, writing subject and redefines her as feminine, narratable object. Like Madame Fosco, her identifiable sound becomes not the "scraping of [her] pen" but the "rustling of her dress" (330). Fosco's writing on her textual body reestablishes the gender binary that her writing and eavesdropping would defy.

Fosco speaks of his reading her journal in terms of narrative and sexual satisfaction: "I can lay my hand on my heart, and declare that every page has charmed, refreshed, delighted me" (358). In his self-designated "paternal lines" (359), Fosco admires Marian's "tact," "discretion," "easy grace of style," and "charming outbursts of womanly feeling." Although he commends her "accurate observation of character," Fosco's critique echoes Victorian literary reviewers who, though complimentary, established patronizing and constraining standards for woman writers (358).[47] Instead of confirming her narrative authority, his admiration further diminishes it. Rather than a loss of maidenhead, the textual violation of Marian's diary deprives her of her "head" and leaves her a mere "maiden," albeit one who has forfeited consideration in the novel's sexual economy.

Fosco's unauthorized reading of Marian's diary serves another function in the narrative. His readerly eavesdropping represents a satisfaction of narrative desire, for he possesses the textual body of the woman who fascinates him. By presenting Fosco's inscription in her diary without previously signaling the reader that such transgressive activity has occurred, Collins does more than surprise the reader and heighten the suspense of his larger narrative. He also suggests the parallel between Fosco's illicit activity and our own. By surprising us with the information that we are not the only readers of this private document, Collins draws a further analogy between Fosco's intrusive behavior and our sanctioned eavesdropping on Marian's private words and thoughts; he makes us recognize the potentially transgressive nature of all reading.[48] We are in the same position as Fosco, yet because our reading is acknowledged, even solicited, by Walter with Marian's approval, we are absolved of Fosco's crime, even as we experience his titillation. As readers, we hold a privileged position of legitimate eavesdroppers, safe from punishment. Fosco, however, has read Marian's complete diary; we have read only those portions that she reads to Walter, who then determines what he should transcribe (456–57). Fosco's narrative trespass is thus more complete and invasive than ours, but his, like Marian's, will not go unpunished.

Marian's reinsertion into a traditional gender role occurs spatially as well. The eavesdropping madwoman who ventured outside the attic and defied male narratives is domesticated, enclosed within the house. Instead of describing Blackwater Park as "suffocated," "stifled," Marian herself is "shut in," restrained within the mansion whose power to confine rather than shelter she had noted earlier (220, 227). Marian's claustration contains those threatening, monstrous energies that challenge male hegemony. Fosco's inscription excises her role of active narrator, so that she becomes "nothing but a woman, condemned to patience, propriety, and petticoats for life" (221). She is given a life sentence, "condemned" to wear the narrative petticoats that she had removed to eavesdrop. Like Bertha Mason, imprisoned in the attic of Thornfield, Marian is confined in an abandoned wing of the mansion. There, sick, drugged, and powerless, she poses no threat to Fosco and Percival's plot.[49]

When she eventually recovers from her illness and flees, Marian in turn helps her sister escape. But the two women's attempt to prove Laura's identity fails when confronted with narratives attesting to the death of Lady Glyde and the incarceration of Anne Catherick: the doctor's death certificate (425–26), the "Narrative of the Tombstone" (426), the asylum director's testimony, even the labels on the linen Laura wears that identify her "in good marking ink" as "Anne Catherick, as plain as print!" (448). In a letter asserting narrative domination and female incarceration, Fosco warns Marian to stay inside and not meddle (468–69). Marian can no longer contest such male narratives herself; her hands, once "as awkward as a man's" and used to wielding the pen, now perform only housework, the task that she herself defines as "what a woman's hands *are* fit for" (253, 453). Fosco's writing insures that she will not foil his scheme to usurp Laura's identity (and with it, her property and wealth), and that his primary narrative opponent becomes Walter Hartright. The story becomes one of male pens competing to write women's stories, as well as their own.

The second half of the novel stresses Marian's diminished position in the narrative as passive character rather than narrating subject – as the male hero's confidante, rather than as his advisor or the chief plotter. Accordingly, Marian's eyes, once so "resolute," continually fill with tears, not "like men's tears, with sobs that . . . frighten every one around [her]," as they once did (187); rather, her tears "fall slowly over her cheeks" (453). In his first encounter with her after returning from America, Walter describes her "eyes large and wild, and looking at me with a strange terror in them . . . Pain and fear and grief written on her as with a brand"

(430–31). This impression could be equally applied to Laura, for both women have experienced a great trauma. Both have been incarcerated in different madhouses and stamped with the sign of "sorrow and suffering" (120), the mark that was once missing from the blank page of Laura Fairlie. Fosco's "large, bold, and firmly regular" handwriting in Marian's diary parallels the "hard, clear, cruel black letters" on Laura's tombstone. Both women have been "branded" deviant; both written out of the narrative in different ways and denied their respective identities as living, sane Lady Glyde, and as active, resolute narrator. One of these acts of stolen identity appears as a most serious crime; the other passes almost undetected.

Walter abets the male criminals' narrative and physical incarceration of Marian. Once in control of the story, he refuses to allow her to act outside the house, holding her back when she wants to help him confront Fosco (603). He treats Marian as the criminals treated Laura and Anne Catherick, keeping her indoors, ostensibly to offer her "care and protection" but effectively to curtail her physical activity and silence her story (211). In Walter's second narrative, Marian appears completely femininized. Her first words to Walter simultaneously invoke patriarchy and designate him as prime actor: "Father! strengthen him. Father! help him in his hour of need" (431). Instead of telling him what to do, Marian continually seeks and follows his advice. Walter's control of the narrative downplays Marian's successful rescue of Laura and foregrounds his own exploits (569, 570). Fosco rightly refers to the home that Marian, Laura, and Walter establish together in London as a "new asylum" (468), for in it woman's opinion and narrative are locked up.[50] Nevertheless, Marian's deferential attitude appears forced and suggests that Walter's narrative here overcompensates for her earlier dominance. Particularly since Fosco, not Walter, removed Marian from the position of narrative agency, Walter's appropriation of Fosco's achievement reminds us that, in the battle over control of stories and identities, one person's victory may abet an enemy's plot.

The ending of *The Woman in White* reiterates Marian's status as reformed "good angel" of the house, an angel given leave to speak by the new patriarch Walter, who, by the conclusion of the novel, has written himself and his wife into legitimacy, and produced male issue (646). Although at the end of the novel Marian presents Walter's son to him, we cannot conclude that she represents a form of narrative and sexual potency. Instead, Walter grants her this position, suggesting "let Marian end our Story." Moreover, the final lines of the novel are his; the narrator-scribe writes down for us her last words and encloses them in his own, a narrative gesture that repeats earlier incarcerations. Just as Fosco calls his wife "my angel" (328), Walter's dubbing Marian "the good angel of our lives" underscores the curtailment of her agency.[51] Holding "the Heir of Limmeridge" may imply Marian's ability to direct his education and acculturation, but her authority is indirect, oblique; she represents the conventional feminine power behind the throne.

Consequently, the second half of the novel foregrounds *Walter*'s narrative activity, for storytelling constitutes his primary means to regain Laura's identity and patrimony. After stating his "position" and his "motives," he declares that "the story of Marian and the story of Laura must come next" (435). Walter asserts:

I shall relate both narratives, not in the words (often interrupted, often inevitably confused) of the speakers themselves, but in the words of the brief, plain, studiously simple abstract which I committed to writing for my own guidance, and for the guidance of my legal adviser. So the tangled web will be most speedily and most intelligibly unrolled. (435)

He boldly claims the right and the power to tell other people's stories better than they can. He even presumes to "guid[e]" his own "adviser." He admits that "Laura Fairlie" is a "feigned" name for the woman whose identity the narrative has set out to establish; he has, in fact, changed all the characters' names (563). In substituting a fictitious name for the real one of the woman whose identity has been stolen, Walter reenacts her dispossession, ostensibly to protect her. Arrogating to himself the Adamic act of naming, he takes from her the identity that the narrative supposedly returns to her. He reestablishes the male control of a female textual space, a space to be written on and taken over.

Having revealed this secret, the narrative turns to silence the remaining deviant still at large: Count Fosco. Through his own rash acts, Percival has been punished in the very place where he forged the history of his legitimacy. Because his confession dies with Percival, Walter does not have the story in writing, the "proof" the lawyer considers necessary for the assertion of "Laura's" identity (463). Hence Walter vows "to wrest from Fosco the confession [he] failed to obtain from his accomplice" (579). By possessing the narrative Walter will have control over the person.

Walter accomplishes this feat through a series of sanctioned and illicit transmissions of information, notably involving eavesdropping and the transcription of the spoken word on to the page. When he points out the Count to his friend Pesca in the hope that the Italian can identify his compatriot, a man with a scar overhears their conversation. Although Pesca cannot identify Fosco, the Count recognizes him and flees, followed by the man with the scar. We learn through Pesca's voluntary confession that he is the secretary of a "Brotherhood," the name of which he whispers to Walter, and thus places his life in Walter's hands. Pesca authorizes him to tell his secret story; he shows him the "secret mark" "identified with the Brotherhood," an indelible emblem that all members bear (596). Walter becomes the depository of all secrets, the man who has the power of life and death in his speech and written stories. As secretary, the record-keeper of the group, Pesca has a similar power over other members. We learn of Fosco's "false" name (599), and of the fact that he has repudiated the Brotherhood whose objective is "the assertion of the rights of the people" (595). Seeming to represent lawlessness and transgression, Fosco is actually a counter-revolutionary wishing to maintain "the rights of the aristocracy and the sacred principles of Order" (644).

The final battle between Fosco and Walter is one of narrative authority, a contest to see who has the greatest "faculty of arranging his ideas" and controlling their dissemination (613). Walter has sworn he will extract a confession from Fosco; he does this through a blackmail of letters – threatening public exposure – for his note to Pesca brands Fosco as a traitor to the Brotherhood. To avoid being so identified, Fosco writes the confession of how he "took [Laura's] identity instead" of her life (632). In return for his freedom, Fosco gives Walter the narrative enabling him to reassert "Laura's" identity. Essentially, the two men transfer ownership of a woman's story and with it, narrative control. Now Walter possesses the right to tell; he has heard the story prepared for his own "private ear," and can do with it what he pleases (614). Later, his careful editing of the "narrative of the conspiracy" for the Limmeridge tenants is a testament to his complete control over the story (638). Walter ensures that Fosco will have only "the *fact*" of Walter's communication with Pesca, not the letter itself, the "written evidence" that would give Fosco leverage (612).

Yet even when compelled to write a statement of guilt, Fosco signs it, like his letter to Marian, with a "flourish" (469, 614). Although a confession, whether forced or voluntary, offers an acknowledgment of crime, Fosco turns a statement of presumed contrition into one of criminal prowess. If the flourish ending his "confession" suggests an ostentatious display, the confession itself exhibits more *braggadocio* than repentance. Moreover, in the Count's two other languages, Italian and French, the word for "flourish" suggests other meanings pertinent here. The French word *paraphe* (or *parafe*) and the Italian *paraffo* have an equivalent in the English *paraph*, a word meaning "a flourish made after a signature, originally as a kind of precaution against forgery."[52] A paraph makes forgery difficult, so that the Count's final narrative gesture offers a mark of authenticity. Fosco's "flourish" represents both the brandishing of his weapon in front of Walter – a gesture of defiance – and a guarantee of the authenticity of his writing and his identity. However, Fosco's identity is as questionable as his activities. Just as his narrative displays his skill at counterfeiting other people's identities, the story of his own proves difficult to decipher. If, as we have learned, the Count's name and face are as self-authored as his narrative about Laura, how genuine can this mark of authenticity be? What is the value of a genuine mark of a false name? Even Fosco's confession, where mysteries are supposedly solved, hints at further secrets and concealment. At the end of his verbal sparring with Walter, it seems as though Fosco has had the last word.

But although Walter has agreed not to implicate the Count, he does not control the man who eavesdropped upon his conversation with Pesca and who discovered Fosco to be a lapsed member of the fraternity. This spy's pursuit ends when he cuts on Fosco's physical body the kind of decisive inscription that Fosco put on Marian's textual one: the killer carves a "T" (for *Traditore*) over the mark of the Brotherhood on the Count's arm. This action identifies him as both a former member and a traitor to the cause. Fosco loses control of his life and his life-story. His physical body – bared and barred from the embellishments he used to create its contours – is exposed, just as his textual imposture is revealed in the narrative (643).[53] The Count's transgression of social laws outweighs Marian's and incurs a graver punishment. His body is fatally violated; his secret story is made more public than hers, "exposed to the flippant curiosity of a French mob" (643). The public that views his private body is more universal and impersonal than that which views Marian's. In Victorian England, the only way to silence a man is to kill him; women can simply be shut up.

Although Fosco's body is displayed and "identified" (644), supposedly "the hand that struck him [is] never traced" (643). However, Walter deduces that the man with the visible scar killed Fosco. He discovers this crime by overhearing two conversations: one between Pesca and the assassin, in which the secretary says he will forward a report (641), and the other among people who have just visited the Morgue and seen Fosco's corpse (642). Walter becomes the true "master" storyteller (599), the one who can identify all individuals and place his mark upon them. Establishing a new patriarchal law and order – of bourgeois, not aristocratic origins – Walter's narrative reassures the more conventional readers of

Collins's fiction. However, the narrative overkill required to produce the restoration of order subtly contests its permanence. Walter's own radical transformation appears suspect and reminds readers of the consummate puppetmaster behind the marionettes: Collins himself. Although Walter may know Fosco's plot about Laura Fairlie, he never learns the full story of the Brotherhood or "the secret history of [Fosco's] life" (644). Having established his own professional and social legitimacy and having fended off competitors, he lets other conspiracies proceed unchecked. Walter refrains from narrative or legal interventions that might impede the machinations of the Brotherhood; his concerns, like Collins's, center on establishing his narrative legitimacy and creating a professional identity clearly separate from the world of domesticity and women.

The recurrence of *The Woman in White*'s narrative incarcerations suggests an excessiveness that has significant implications about Collins's ambivalent, sympathetic yet defensive attitude toward women's narrative and social agency. His fiction, like his life, demonstrates an anxiety about offering women social and economic parity. Although Collins portrays numerous intelligent, resourceful women, his novels usually retreat toward a more conventional stance regarding women's narrative and social agency in their conclusions. Such narrative conservatism reflects both his need to satisfy a wide array of readers – from those who accept normative assumptions about gender to those who, like Collins himself, displayed a marked degree of unconventionality in their private social relations – and his rivalry with successful women authors.

The endings to most of his novels intimate that Collins's rebellion against conventional social mores was accompanied by a discomfort with granting women complete social and economic equality. In the major novels with an active, transgressive female character, narrative resolution requires her to be chastened before she can be accepted into the community. In some cases, such as that of *Armadale*'s Lydia Gwilt (1866), only death can expiate her crimes against society. Others, like *No Name*'s Magdalen Vanstone (1862), must be punished and suitably contrite before they are allowed to marry and reenter the fold of respectability, as Magdalen does when she weds the aptly named Captain Kirk. In *The Law and the Lady* (1875), Valeria Macallan goes further in establishing the legitimacy of women who actively investigate and solve crimes; she proves that her husband did not murder his first wife. But when forced to choose between publicly declaring his innocence or becoming his ministering angel and the mother of his child, she elects the conventional alternative, and allows her male cohorts to piece together the narrative that explains the mysterious death of the first Mrs. Macallan. Here, however, although the two men have the last word in solving the puzzle, Valeria is the novel's primary narrator. Like Walter Hartright, who permits Marian to conclude the narrative, Valeria grants the men the semblance of control, while she finishes the novel and continues to protect her morally and physically enfeebled husband. Although Valeria wields narrative power, by allowing male figures to appear in control and by presenting conjugal devotion as a justification for her actions, Collins was able to create subversive figures to critique normative gender ideology while, at the same time, courting the conventional readership he needed for popular success.

Collins's life reflects a similar tension between identification with transgressive characters that challenge social conventions and uneasiness about the full economic and legal empowerment of attractive, resolute women. His unconventional lifestyle was an unabashed rejection of normative social relations. He lived with one mistress, Caroline Graves, and her daughter from a previous marriage. At the same time, he established another woman, Martha Rudd, in a separate household; Martha bore him three children whom he acknowledged in his will. Yet Collins maintained a relatively traditional stance regarding women's economic equality. Whereas he acknowledged his illegitimate children by Martha Rudd in his will, he distinguished between male and female heirs. Although he granted life interests to Caroline and her daughter, and to Martha and his two daughters by her, only his son, Charles William Collins Dawson, received his share as a capital sum.[54] In addition, despite his defiance of conventional attitudes toward marriage, Collins constructed one "William Dawson," solicitor, as a cover for his visits to Martha Rudd Dawson. By posing as her husband, Collins provided the semblance of propriety for their relations and protected his children from public stigma. Although *The Woman in White* was written several years before his relationship with Martha began, its ending with two domesticated angels anticipates Collins's disinclination to unite himself with a single woman and reflects his contradictory attitudes toward traditional gender roles within the institutions of marriage and family.

Collins entered the literary marketplace at a time when his most obvious rivals in sensation and realist fiction were women. Tamar Heller's persuasive analysis of Collins's relation to the female Gothic and its nineteenth-century heirs explains how such plots are simultaneously "the source of inspiration and ambivalence."[55] Mrs. Henry Wood's and Mary Elizabeth Braddon's sensation fiction vied directly with Collins's own. At the same time, the professionalization of literature that was taking place in mid-century emphasized a division between male labor and female domesticity.[56] Collins's handling of a "resolute" female narrator thus has implications for his own situation in the literary marketplace, within both sensation fiction and the larger category of the novel. The acclaimed writer George Eliot can be seen as the original Mary Ann who, highly intelligent and not conventionally attractive, inspired his Marian Halcombe; the character's domestication and silencing by would-be male authorities and authors within the text suggests Collins's desire imaginatively to control and contain powerful female competitors.[57] In her representation of imprisoned madwomen, Charlotte Brontë offered Collins a compelling precursor; Emily Brontë's *Wuthering Heights*, with its series of framed narratives and multiple narrators, presented an impressive model for Collins's complicated narrative structure in *The Woman in White*. Elizabeth Gaskell, a regular contributor to Dickens's *Household Words* and *All the Year Round*, presented another powerful rival. In fact, Dickens solicited serial novels from Eliot and Gaskell to follow *The Woman in White* immediately in *All the Year Round*. Although both women declined, Gaskell produced "The Grey Woman," a Gothic tale that ran in three parts in the magazine in January 1861.[58] She also wrote "A Dark Night's Work," a novella that directly followed Collins's *No Name* as the front-page serial in *All the Year Round* in 1863. Although Collins's novels depict powerful, subversive women, their endings suggest a critical but not radical attitude toward gender ideology. More specifically, they intimate Collins's anxieties about asserting and maintaining his position in the competitive market of mid-century Victorian novelists, particularly female rivals.

The Woman in White reveals Collins's ambivalent and sometimes contradictory attitude toward the complex relations among gender, identity, and narrative agency. It suggests his sympathy for seductive, socially transgressive figures. But the novel also displays his need to court more conventional readers for financial and critical success. It presents Collins's attraction to resolute, marginalized women, yet his hesitation about granting such women complete economic and social equality. Finally, it traces his identification and nervous competition with successful contemporary women writers. The result is a novel that, in its repeated and increasingly violent suppressions of subversive energies, paradoxically suggests the inability of such measures to contain subversive agents, identities, and narratives. For although Walter may control our access to the narrative, it is the earlier, defiant Marian and Fosco who linger in our minds, long after we close the book. Like the secret Brotherhood that survives in the margins of Walter's narrative,

The Woman in White's subversive narrators, the illicit means by which they acquire information, and their transgressive stories continue to seduce and to produce readerly pleasure even as they are relegated to the attic – or the eaves – of the house of Victorian fiction.

If *The Woman in White*'s conclusion would restore the distance between transgressive characters and their readers, between two communities of secret listening and reading, Marcel Proust's *A la recherche du temps perdu* constantly diminishes that distance, setting up even closer parallels between our activities and those of his central character and narrator. "The last of the great French Realists," Proust provides a fitting end to a study of eavesdropping in the nineteenth-century novel.[59] His novel explicitly extends the prior century's preoccupation with public and private spaces and identities into the realm of sexual identity and sexual desire. Representations of covert listening remind us that we are situated knowledge-seekers; Proust's narrative dwells on and in this precarious position between desire and fear, safety and danger. More overtly than Collins's novel, *A la recherche* aligns erotic and epistemological drives. In doing so, it establishes a theory of narrative desire that encompasses the reader in the painful and pleasurable process of coming to knowledge. Eavesdropping here represents separation from an object of desire yet tantalizing proximity to it. *A la recherche* explores the transformative energy of transgressive curiosity. In Proust's novel, the vicarious act of eavesdropping holds a privileged place in the understanding and forging of selves and others.

CHAPTER 5

La double entente: *eavesdropping and identity in* A la recherche du temps perdu

> *Hearing* is a physiological phenomenon; *listening* is a psychological act.
>
> Barthes, *The Responsibility of Forms*

> Notre sagesse commence où celle de l'auteur finit, et nous voudrions qu'il nous donnât des réponses, quand tout ce qu'il peut faire est de nous donner des désirs.[1]
>
> Proust, *Contre Sainte-Beuve*

It is a critical commonplace to speak of Marcel Proust's visual sensibility. Numerous studies have focused on John Ruskin's influence on Proust, on the predominance of visual imagery, description, and perception in his novel, and on his theories about visual art in *A la recherche du temps perdu*.[2] In a well-known and often-quoted phrase, Proust declared his art to be one of the telescope, not the microscope.[3] Indeed, he compares well with the unnamed "romancier mondain" ("society novelist") at la marquise de Saint-Euverte's soirée who answers the question "Qu'est-ce que vous pouvez bien faire ici?" ("What on earth are you doing here?") by placing "au coin de son oeil un monocle, son seul organe d'investigation psychologique et d'impitoyable analyse" and responding, "d'un air important et mystérieux, en roulant l'*r*: – J'observe" ("into the angle of eyebrow and cheek a monocle that was his sole instrument of psychological investigation and remorseless analysis," and responding, "with an air of mystery and self-importance, rolling the *r*, 'I am observing!'").[4]

Less noticed, but equally important, is Proust's reliance on aural stimuli, perceptions, and sensations to evoke particular moments, scenes, or *ressentiments* that resound from "le violon intérieur" ("the violin within," III: 18).[5] Proust's fascination with aural mechanisms of perception and his aural sensitivity were pronounced,[6] and they manifest themselves in the significant role that sounds, voices, the telephone, listening, and music play in his work.[7] Declaring, "tout peut se transposer... un univers seulement audible pourrait être aussi varié que l'autre" ("everything is capable of transposition... a universe that was exclusively audible might be as full of variety as the other"), Proust describes other senses by means of sound, so that the intermittent scent of the hawthorns becomes "le murmure de leur vie intense" ("the murmuring of an intense organic life") and the street sounds that Marcel hears from his bedroom register the weather outside (*La prisonnière*, 75; III: 78; *Swann*, 112; I: 123; *La prisonnière*, 3; III:1). Surprisingly for an author whose sensitivity to sound is legendary, the attention paid to the role that this sense plays in *A la recherche* remains minimal, except for that of music in his oeuvre. Even then, scholars focus on music in Proust as a formal structuring element, rather than as an experience unto itself, with its own psychological weight and sensory affectivity.[8] The critical discussion of Proust's work seems to commit an "oculocentrism" pervasive in the Western literary tradition to which I would offer an aural corrective.[9]

Although not denying the centrality of vision in *A la recherche*, I would argue that hearing, and more specifically eavesdropping, plays a critical role in Proust's oeuvre, particularly in scenes usually considered voyeuristic. These episodes register an anxiety about private spaces – both literal and psychological – and yet suggest the near impossibility of keeping them protected from inquisitive ears and eyes. In *Le temps retrouvé*, the narrator describes how his composition must use "par opposition à la psychologie plane dont on use d'ordinaire, d'une sorte de psychologie dans l'espace" ("not the two-dimensional psychology which we normally use but a quite different sort of three-dimensional psychology," III: 1087).[10] *A la recherche* explores the psychological and epistemological weight attached to certain spaces and categories, such as the opposition of public and private, masculine and feminine, gay and straight.[11] Eavesdropping, a border activity, helps Proust figure and figure out such considerations. Both within the narrative itself, and on an extradiegetic level, the work offers strategies to frustrate incursions into secret or private realms, responses that help construct alternative spaces and selves, and in doing so, incorporate eavesdropping into their very operation.

Moments of illicit listening in *A la recherche* deal explicitly with the subject matter that nineteenth-century narratives often represent obliquely: sexual identity and desire. Such scenes represent instances of "epistemophilia": a primal impulse to know.[12] They dramatize Proust's intimate association of sexual knowledge with this larger epistemological urge and suggest a theory of narrative desire that extends to the reader of *A la recherche*. If "desire, in human sexuality, is always transgression...

something that is never completely fulfilled," moments of eavesdropping represent both the transgressive aspect of desire – the illicit acquisition of information – and its inability to be fully satisfied.[13] No matter how much we know, we almost always want to know more. Eavesdropping usually provides us with partial information and whets our appetite to possess the complete story. It not only dramatizes the exchange of information that forms the crux of storytelling, but in its incomplete acquisition of information, encourages us to create additional stories to account for what we may have heard. By the conclusion of Proust's novel, not only the characters and the narrator but the reader as well are implicated in this epistemophilic, narrative drive.

In particular, three eavesdropping scenes present an escalation of the kind of secret, sexual knowledge being obtained, and the supposedly "perverse" nature of this information. From the episode in the Combray section of *Du côté de chez Swann*, in which young Marcel inadvertently overhears Mlle Vinteuil's performance with her lover, to Charlus and Jupien's first encounter in *Sodome et Gomorrhe* at the center of the work, and finally to the scene at Jupien's sadomasochistic hotel in *Le temps retrouvé*, Proust links the aural acquisition of knowledge with issues of identity, sexuality, and desire. Although the novel is filled with moments of chance overhearing and deliberate eavesdropping, instances that provoke jealousy, misperceptions, and narrative delay, it is on the sustained, paradigmatic eavesdropping scenes that I wish to concentrate, where the actual epistemophilic mechanism is dramatized and offered as the subject of narrative itself. Like the Japanese paper forms in the teacup evoked in the Combray section that expand to create entire miniature narrative worlds, these episodes of clandestine listening in *A la recherche* open up narrative situations of exquisite complexity, depth, and resonance.

The first major scene occurs when the young Marcel, asleep in the bushes outside the Vinteuil home at Montjouvain, awakes to find Mlle Vinteuil and her lover inside the drawing room, "dont elle avait fait son petit salon à elle," a private space of her own (*Swann*, 157). At this point in the narrative, Marcel has already inadvertently overheard several conversations that indicate the gap between public and private personae: how one can construct a public persona by telling other people information about oneself or others that may be completely false.[14] Here, however, eavesdropping concerns precisely the personal information that one usually does not wish to disclose: that about sexual intimacy. The scene at Montjouvain immediately follows the narrative of Marcel's first exploration of solitary sexual pleasure, which occurred several years earlier; pleasure links the two episodes in his memory. In addition, both scenes contain a "fenêtre entrouverte" ("half-opened window") that connects, or affords communication between, two differently charged spaces (*Swann*, 156, 157; I: 172, 174).[15] In the initial onanistic scene, Marcel looks through the half-opened window to gaze upon the phallic tower of the castle-keep at Roussainville:

> Pendant qu'avec les hésitations héroïques du voyageur qui entreprend une exploration ou du désespéré qui se suicide, défaillant, je me frayais en moi-même une route inconnue et que je croyais mortelle, jusqu'au moment où une trace naturelle comme celle d'un colimaçon s'ajoutait aux feuilles du cassis sauvage qui se penchaient jusqu'à moi. En vain je . . . suppliais [le donjon] maintenant. En vain, tenant l'étendue dans le champ de ma vision, je la drainais de mes regards qui eussent voulu en ramener une femme. (156)

> With the heroic misgivings of a traveller setting out on a voyage of exploration or of a desperate wretch hesitating on the verge of self-destruction, faint with emotion, I explored, across the bounds of my own experience, an untrodden path which for all I knew was deadly – until the moment when a natural trail like that left by a snail smeared the leaves of the flowering currant that drooped around me. In vain did I call upon it now. In vain did I compress the whole landscape into my field of vision, draining it with an exhaustive gaze which sought to extract from it a female creature. (I: 172–73)

The narrator compares an episode of physical pleasure to a dangerous, heroic journey on an unfamiliar internal path, where the object of desire is distant and unattainable, abstract and imprecise, the "paysanne" of his wanderings. However ill-defined the object of desire, the indulgence in physical pleasure remains something forbidden, transgressive, and secret, occurring in the privacy of one's own room.

In the scene that follows in the reassembled chronology of memory (linking the onanistic moment with one several years later), Marcel observes a specific moment of interaction between Mlle Vinteuil and her lover. He is aware of the impropriety of remaining where he is, so close to the house, but he fears that the sounds he would need to make to leave would reveal his presence to her and make her believe that "[il] étai[t] caché là pour l'épier" (157; he "had been hiding there in order to spy upon her," I: 174). His scruples, however, are inconsequential, for Mlle Vinteuil deliberately sets up the scene with her lover as a performance for someone else. First, she stretches out along the sofa, leaving room for her friend, but then she reconsiders and, deciding that this position is "indiscrète," she takes up all the space; finally, she yawns, "pour indiquer que l'envie de dormir était la seule raison pour laquelle elle s'était ainsi étendue" (158; "as if to suggest that drowsiness was the sole reason for her recumbent position," I: 175). Soon "elle se leva, feignit de vouloir fermer les volets et de n'y pas réussir" (159; "she rose and came to the window, where she pretended to be trying to close the shutters and not succeeding," I: 175).

Her gestures and actions are enacted not only for her friend but also for some unnamed, unseen, and unheard third person. When her friend asks her to leave the windows open, Mlle Vinteuil protests, "Mais c'est assommant, on nous verra," and provokes the words "qu'elle avait en effet le désir d'entendre, mais que par discrétion elle voulait lui laisser l'initiative de prononcer," words that her lover "recites," namely, "quand même on nous verrait ce n'en est que meilleur" (159; "But it's too tiresome! People will see us;" the words "which she did indeed wish to hear but, from discretion, would have preferred her friend to be the first to speak"; "all the better that they should see us," I: 176). She also pretends that anyone watching would only see them reading together,[16] and declares, "c'est assommant, quelque chose insignifiante qu'on fasse, de penser que des yeux vous voient" (159; "It's so tiresome to think that whatever trivial little thing you do someone may be overlooking you," I: 176).

Significantly, Marcel both sees and *hears* the scene enacted before him, so that he receives the cues indicating the theatricality of the lovers' interaction, its staged quality, that would not be obvious if he could only see, as in a dumb show, their gestures from afar. The artificiality of the encounter leads the older, remembering narrator to describe how Mlle Vinteuil "cherchait le plus loin qu'elle pouvait de sa vraie nature morale, à trouver le langage propre à la fille vicieuse qu'elle désirait être, mais les mots qu'elle pensait que celle-ci eût prononcés sincèrement lui paraissaient faux dans sa bouche" (159; "reached out as far as she could across the limitations of her true nature to find the language appropriate to the vicious young woman she longed to be thought, but the words which she imagined such a young woman might have uttered with sincerity sounded false on her own lips," I: 176). The falseness of the role Mlle Vinteuil wishes to play (that of "la fille vicieuse"), the performative nature of her language, equal that of her lover, who whispers a final outrage contemplated toward her father, as if afraid yet secretly hoping that someone might hear this last "profanation rituelle" (160): to spit on his portrait, which his daughter had strategically positioned on the table near the sofa. Marcel initially cannot hear what the lover suggests, and learns of it only because Mlle Vinteuil responds with feigned incredulity, so that her lover repeats her intent "avec une brutalité *voulue*" (161, e.m.; "with a studied brutality," I: 178). At this point Mlle Vinteuil, "d'un air las, gauche, affairé, honnête et triste vint fermer les volets et la fenêtre" ("with an air that was at once languid, awkward, bustling, sincere and rather sad, came to close the window and drew the shutters close") so that the young Marcel "n'en entendi[t] pas davantage" (161; "heard no more," I: 178). Although she closes both the window and the shutters, so he can neither hear nor see, Marcel remarks only on the fact that he can *hear* nothing more. Listening has become more important than seeing, for it is more in overhearing the lovers' interaction than in seeing it that the young boy senses, even if he does not fully comprehend, the staged, ritualistic quality of the sexual encounter that then takes place behind closed doors. Like Vinteuil's "petite phrase" of music, the episode sends echoes of the compulsiveness and ritualization of desire throughout the rest of the narrative.

Marcel's complete awakening to a complicated sense of sexuality and self-fashioning takes place only later. The older Marcel emphasizes the theatricality of the scene he witnessed years earlier:

C'est à la lumière de la rampe des théâtres du boulevard plutôt que sous la lampe d'une maison de campagne véritable qu'on peut voir une fille faire cracher une amie sur le portrait d'un père qui n'a vécu que pour elle; et il n'y a guère que le sadisme qui donne un fondement dans la vie à l'esthétique du mélodrame. (161)

It is behind the footlights of a Paris theatre and not under the homely lamp of an actual country house that one expects to see a girl encouraging a friend to spit on the portrait of a father who has lived and died for her alone; and when we find in real life a desire for melodramatic effect, it is generally sadism that is responsible for it. (I: 178–79)[17]

In this melodramatic moment, Vinteuil's daughter wishes to create an "evil" self in order to experience "le plaisir sensuel," since she conceives such forbidden sensual pleasure as being the privilege "des méchants" (162).[18] Marcel does not actually witness much that is sexually explicit except for the kiss the lover plants in the bodice of Mlle Vinteuil's dress (160). Instead, he overhears and sees the enactment of a drama that creates the persona capable of experiencing sexual desire, a self-fashioning that erases the dutiful daughter and establishes the transgressive lesbian. Mlle Vinteuil's shutting the window signals Marcel's exclusion from the closed world of Gomorrah,[19] the world with which Albertine will be associated. This scene significantly concludes the depiction of "le côté de Méséglise."

The rest of the Combray section deals briefly with "le côté de Guermantes" as a means of introducing la duchesse de Guermantes – who will represent a figure of a different desire for Marcel, desire evoked and mediated through stories about the ancient family of the Guermantes and elite society – and as a prelude to recounting "Un Amour de Swann." Although the young Marcel believes in the utter separation of these two "ways," as the similar subject matter (love and desire) indicates, they are not as disconnected from each other as he believes them to be.[20]

The story of Swann's love for Odette continues the discussion of role-playing and theater in a different register than that of the Verdurins and their social masks (258). It stages an eavesdropping scene with Swann as a jealous lover who tries to listen to an unseen conversation, only to discover that he has mistaken the apartment of two gentlemen for Odette's. Swann imagines hearing "ce murmure qui révélait la présence de celui qu'était venu après son départ, la fausseté d'Odette" ("that murmur which revealed the presence of the man who had crept in after his own departure, the perfidy of Odette"), a murmur enabling him to experience "un plaisir de l'intelligence" (*Swann*, 269; I: 298). For Proust, this "pleasure of knowing" is the supreme, if most elusive, pleasure. However, the origin of the voices and the episode itself reveal more about Swann than about Odette; it registers the extent to which his love for Odette has changed Swann's behavior and character.

In more general terms, the scene suggests a concept that becomes more elaborated in the course of our reading *A la recherche*: the impossibility of knowing someone else completely or of reaching stable and universal truths, yet, despite this recognition, the continual attempt at this project.[21] "Le secret de la vérité" that young Marcel initially searches for between the pages of a book is ever elusive (83).[22] Even though

> on est comme emporté avec [l'âme] dans un perpétuel élan pour ... dépasser [cette prison spirituelle], pour atteindre à l'extérieur, avec une sorte de découragement, en entendant toujours autour de soi cette sonorité identique qui n'est pas écho du dehors mais retentissement d'une vibration interne. On cherche à retrouver dans les choses, devenues par là précieuses, le reflet que notre âme a projeté sur elles, on est déçu en constatant qu'elles semblent dépourvues dans la nature du charme qu'elles devaient, dans notre pensée, au voisinage de certaines idées. (*Swann*, 85–86)

we have the sensation of being always enveloped in, surrounded by our own soul, still it does not seem a fixed and immovable prison; rather do we seem to be borne away with it, and perpetually struggling to transcend it, to break out into the world, with a perpetual discouragement as we hear endlessly all around us that unvarying sound which is not an echo from without, but the resonance of a vibration from within. We try to discover in things, which become precious to us on that account, the reflection of what our soul has projected on to them;

we are disillusioned when we find that they are in reality devoid of the charm which they owed, in our minds, to the association of certain ideas. (I: 93)

Using metaphors of aurality (the echo, resonance) as well as vision (the reflection), Proust explains how our attempts to know the secret story behind the other, just like our love for him, are efforts to understand the other whom we project upon him, an other complicated by the layers of personae that we and he construct to obfuscate a changing, evolving self. Eavesdropping on this private self may expose less about the mysterious, often deceitful other, and more about one's own shifting identity and character. Instead of revealing Odette's secret life, the scene discloses the extent to which Swann's love has become obsessive, so that, like a fatal disease, "son amour n'était plus opérable" (*Swann*, 303; "his love was no longer operable," I: 336). Although eventually the narrative does validate Swann's jealous suspicions, his efforts here at uncovering the truth reveal primarily the essence of this "vibration interne."

The two histories of homo- and heterosexual desire come together in *Sodome et Gomorrhe*, when the narrator connects the activities such as "contempler un spectacle curieux et divertissant" ("look[ing] on at a curious and entertaining spectacle"), like the scene at Montjouvain, and "écout[er] le récit des amours de Swann" ("listen[ing] to the account of Swann's love affairs"). Seeing and hearing love stories unfold are preliminary steps in the internal "voie funeste et destinée à être douloureuse du Savoir" (*Sodome*, 500; the "fatal and inevitably painful road of Knowledge," II: 1152). The via dolorosa for Proust is an interior one of knowledge and desire, of which the most personal section becomes Marcel's love affair with Albertine. The narrator anticipates this recognition in the final pages of *Swann*, where Marcel overhears two of Odette's former lovers speaking of her past life (*Swann*, 412–14).[23] Marcel's awakening into a realm of transgressive sexuality and of secret self-creation at Montjouvain, a realm only fleetingly and incompletely revealed to him, signals a preoccupation with sexuality and identity that later eavesdropping scenes develop and complicate.

By opening *Sodome et Gomorrhe* – the volume of *A la recherche* literally and ideologically at the center of his text – with a second eavesdropping scene, Proust dramatically emphasizes its importance. At the beginning of this first encounter between Charlus and Jupien, Marcel has posted himself as a spy, watching for the return of the Duke and the Duchess in order to ask them about his invitation to a soirée. But instead of learning the truth of one communication (whether or not he has been invited), he makes "pendant la durée de mon guet, une découverte, concernant particulièrement M. de Charlus, mais si importante en elle-même que j'ai jusqu'ici, jusqu'au moment de pouvoir lui donner la place et l'étendue voulues, différé de la rapporter" (*Sodome*, 3; "in the course of my [watch I] had made a discovery which concerned M. de Charlus in particular but [which] was in itself so important that I have until now, until the moment when I could give it the prominence and treat it with the fullness that it demanded, postponed giving an account of it," II: 623). By the vocabulary of military intelligence ("j'avais épié leur retour," "mon guet"), the narrator signals the importance of the inadvertent "discovery" about Charlus. The French verb *rapporter* means "to report," "to mention," or "to bring back" but also "to snitch on" someone else.[24] All of these denotations come into play in this scene, although for the moment the narrator defers revealing the secret of his discovery and gives instead a discourse on insect pollination. The deferral reflects the narrative strategy of the novel as a whole: to present a scene, but to reveal its import only pages or volumes later. Thus the narrative replicates in the reader the same deferred understanding that its protagonist experiences.

Marcel relates that, although he had been "si confortablement aménagé au haut de la maison" ("so snugly contrived at the top of the house," II: 623), he left this cozy vantage point in order not to miss the Guermantes' return, and instead has "posted" himself on the staircase. Finally, "la curiosité m'enhardissant peu à peu, je descendis jusqu'à la fenêtre du rez-de-chaussée, ouverte elle aussi et dont les volets n'étaient qu'à moitié clos" (*Sodome*, 4; "my curiosity emboldening me by degrees, I went down to the ground-floor window, which also stood open with its shutters ajar," II: 623). The stealth with which this observation is conducted seems excessive for the reasons provided (the Guermantes' return or botanical enthusiasm), but is wholly in keeping with the scene that follows. Marcel first hears, then sees, Jupien "qui ne pouvait me découvrir derrière mon store où je restai immobile jusqu'au moment où je me rejetai brusquement de côté par peur d'être vu de M. de Charlus, lequel allant chez Mme de Villeparisis, traversait lentement la cour" (4; "who could not detect me behind my blind, where I stood perfectly still until the moment when I drew quickly aside in order not to be seen by M. de Charlus, who, on his way to call upon Mme de Villeparisis, was slowly crossing the courtyard," II: 624). Already the two states of curiosity and fear of discovery are intermingled as Marcel is himself engaged in "discovering" the secrets of other creatures, whether they be the professed exchange between insect and flower, or the verbal and physical one between the former tailor and the Baron that the botanical passage anticipates.

On this reconnaissance mission, the narrator notes how Charlus, believing himself not to be seen, "[a] relaché dans son visage cette tension, amorti cette vitalité factice, qu'entretenaient chez lui l'animation de la causerie et la force de la volonté" (5; has "relaxed that artificial tension, softened that artificial vigour in his face which were ordinarily sustained by the animation of his talk and the force of his will," II: 625). He has taken off the public mask of virile masculinity and reveals beneath it "quelque chose de si affectueux, de si *désarmé* . . . ce à quoi il me faisait penser . . . c'était à une femme!" (6, e.m.; "something so affectionate, so defenceless . . . what he suddenly suggested to me . . . was a woman," II: 626). Jupien, in turn, assumes a corresponding attitude so easily that Marcel marvels "qu'il fût capable de tenir à l'improviste sa partie dans cette sorte de scène des deux muets, qui . . . semblait avoir été longuement répétée . . . le truchement étant identique, et sans qu'on se soit pourtant jamais vu" (6–7; "that he was capable of improvising his part in this sort of dumb show which . . . seemed to have been long and carefully rehearsed . . . the means of communication being the same and, even though one has never seen [the] other before, the scene already set," II: 627). This description emphasizes the silent communication between the two men, in a scene that recalls Montjouvain in its quality of repetition and familiar "rituels" (*Sodome*, 8), although in the later episode the men do not know each other.

In an earlier (1909) version of this encounter, Proust ends the description of the meeting at this point, and the narrator concludes:

M. de Guercy [Charlus] s'avançait dans la cour mais il s'arrêta encore un instant pour demander à Borniche [Jupien] un renseignement que je ne distinguai <pas>. J'entendis seulement le commencement de la phrase: "Vous qui devez bien connaître le quartier vous pourriez peut-être me dire" puis il baissa la voix et j'entendis seulment les mots pharmacien et marchand de marron. Borniche que je voyais de face debout au milieu de la petite baie dorée, eut un air froissé, jaloux et digne. Il se redressa avec le dépit d'une grande coquette et d'un ton glacial, douloureux et maniéré il dit: "Je vois que vous avez un coeur d'artichaut." . . . Mais bientôt l'ivresse du commérage <noya la déception de son coeur>. Depuis ce jour M. de Guercy changea l'heure de sa visite à Mme de Villeparisis, et il ne s'en allait jamais sans acheter une rose à Borniche.

M. de Guercy [Charlus] moved forward into the court, but he stopped for a moment to ask Borniche [Jupien] a question that I could <not> hear. I only caught the beginning of the sentence, "You who know the neighborhood so well, could you tell me"; then he lowered his voice and I heard only the words "pharmacist" and "chestnut-seller." Borniche, whom I saw face-on, standing in the middle of the little golden opening, presented a hurt, jealous, and dignified demeanor. He held his head up high, with the pique of a great flirt, and in an icy, sorrowful, and affected tone said, "I see that you fall in love with everyone you meet."... But soon the intoxication of gossiping <overcame his heart's disappointment>. Since then, M. de Guercy changed the time of his visits to Mme de Villeparisis, and he never would go away without buying a rose from Borniche.[25]

In this earlier draft, Borniche-Jupien, recovering from his disappointment over his failure to attract Guercy-Charlus, becomes merely an "entremetteur" (a go-between, procurer) or "truchement" (intermediary) for Charlus. In the final, published text, a complicated and prolonged version of this scenario dwells on the aural cues that Marcel receives about the nature of this interaction. Rather than remain a "dumb show," the revised scene greatly augments Marcel's vicarious initiation into the world of Sodom through his extended eavesdropping.

When Jupien invites Charlus inside his shop, telling him "on vous donnera tout ce que vous voudrez" (8; "you shall have everything you wish," II: 629), the narrator relates how "la porte de la boutique se referma sur eux et je ne pus plus rien entendre" (9; "the door of the shop closed behind them and I could hear no more," II: 629). The narrative emphasizes Marcel's incomprehension of the scene before him. Rather than accept this dénouement, the curious Marcel, "fort ennuyé de ne plus entendre la conversation de l'ancien giletier et du baron" ("greatly annoyed at not being able to hear any more of the conversation between the ex-tailor and the Baron"), realizes that by moving to the adjoining, vacant shop, he can continue his surveillance. Choosing between a "prudent," subterranean route that "se ferait à couvert" ("would be made under cover") and from which "[il] ne serai[t] vu de personne" ("[he] should not be seen by anyone") or one by which "longeant les murs, [il] contourn[erait] à l'air libre la cour en tâchant de ne pas être vu" ("keeping close to the walls, [he would edge his] way round the courtyard in the open, trying not to let [him]self be seen"), Marcel opts for the latter path, exposing himself to possible counterespionage. As he reflects on the reasons for his choice, the narrator evokes the scene at Montjouvain and links both moments. He concludes that the revelation of secret knowledge requires a similar risk of detection. Finally, he relates this quest for knowledge to the heroic military exploits he has been reading about recently, and goads himself not to be "pusillanime, quand le théâtre d'opérations est simplement notre propre cours, et quand... le seul fer que j'aie à redouter est celui du regard des voisins qui ont autre chose à faire qu'à regarder dans la cour" (10; "show less courage when... the only steel that I... have to fear is that of the eyes of the neighbours who have other things to do besides looking into the courtyard," II: 631). The narrator thus divulges the reason for the continued vocabulary of heroism, and evokes the onanistic incident as well as his childhood reading of adventure stories.[26] In *Swann*, Marcel had referred to his search for truth through the pairing of reading and direct experience as a "*conquête* de la vérité" (*Swann*, 85, e.m.; a "*conquest* of truth," I: 93). In the current episode, the epistemophilic quest becomes analogous to a heroic search for truth, the "dangerous" interior path of the scene of onanism converges with reading's vicarious road to knowledge, and the comparison between the bookish narrator's activities and those of the reader becomes more apparent.

Very early in *A la recherche*, Proust associates reading with desire. Specifically, by replacing the mother's postponed goodnight kiss with her late-night reading of *François le Champi* to her son, the narrative implicates the mother's storytelling in an economy of desire. Although she leaves out the love scenes, the choice of Sand's novel for this unexpected maternal reading is telling. In *François le Champi*, a foundling eventually marries the woman who raised him; filial affection evolves into connubial love – a truly Oedipal fantasy. Psychoanalytic critics have stressed the orality of this episode and the manner in which the scene becomes fundamental to the representation of a forbidden love. They interpret reading aloud as the orality of eating, a fantasy of physically assimilating the beloved object.[27] I would emphasize instead the *aurality* of the mother's reading, an aurality that lays the groundwork for the importance of eavesdropping in Proust's novel. This early episode in the novel intertwines sublimated desire with aural experiences. If, for Proust's narrator, reading continually harkens back to this formative moment, then reading and reading in *A la recherche* offer opportunities to satisfy a particular form of desire, the desire to know. And if aurality is often associated with satisfying sexual desire, it follows that eavesdropping scenes in *A la recherche* link illicit listening with the acquisition of sexual information, although physical desire is often "exploited" to pose questions about the nature of identity and truth that are not exclusively sexual.[28] Indeed, vicarious experience holds a privileged place in understanding not just others but oneself. The narrator explains that "Nous ne connaissons jamais que les passions des autres, et... ce que nous arrivons à savoir des nôtres, ce n'est que d'eux que nous avons pu l'apprendre"

(*Swann*, 127; "It is only with the passions of others that we are ever really familiar, and what we come to discover about our own can only be learned from them," I: 140). For Proust, reading and eavesdropping – indirect experiences of someone else's life-story – provide significant ways of learning about the self, its complexities and contradictions.

Through its eavesdropping scenes, the narrative complicates the theory of scopophilia that Freud was developing at the same time that Proust was writing *A la recherche*.[29] In his analysis of infantile sexuality, Freud discusses an "instinct for knowledge or research" that cannot

> be classed as exclusively belonging to sexuality. Its activity corresponds on the one hand to a sublimated manner of obtaining mastery, while on the other hand it makes use of the energy of scopophilia. Its relations to sexual life, however, are of particular importance, since we have learnt from psycho-analysis that the instinct for knowledge in children is attracted unexpectedly early and intensively to sexual problems and is in fact possibly first aroused by them. (194)

Although later research has shown that Freud was mistaken in believing this "instinct to know" manifests itself initially between the ages of two and five years,[30] his association of sexual curiosity with a more general "epistemophilic impulse" articulates the correlation between investigations into two kinds of knowledge in *A la recherche*.[31] To a greater extent than the lesbian love scene, this second overheard sexual moment dramatizes the quest for knowledge associated with the discovery of adult sexual relations, when the child first mistakes pleasure for sadistic torture. The narrator describes how the sounds "étaient si violents que, s'ils n'avaient pas été toujours repris un octave plus haut par une plainte parallèle, j'aurais pu croire qu'une personne en égorgeait une autre à côté de moi et qu'ensuite le meurtrier et sa victime ressuscitée prenaient un bain pour effacer les traces du crime. J'en conclus plus tard qu'il y a une chose aussi bruyante que la souffrance, c'est le plaisir" (11; "were so violent that, if they had not always been taken up an octave higher by a parallel plaint, I might have thought that one person was slitting another's throat within a few feet of me, and that subsequently the murderer and his resuscitated victim were taking a bath to wash away the traces of the crime. I concluded from this later on that there is another thing as vociferous as pain, namely pleasure," II: 631).

In his exploration of possible non-heterosexual primal scenes and sexual desires, Proust extends and deepens Freud's study of desire. Proust's text recuperates the aural component of the epistemophilic urge that psychoanalytic theory, favoring the visual, gives scant attention to.[32]

This epistemological quest, the true *"reconnaissance* mission" in the Proustian world, entails recognizing something new in the already known, discovering an unsuspected aspect of someone or something. The psychoanalyst perceives how "the concept of instinct is... one of those lying on the frontier between the mental and the physical."[33] It comprises liminality. Eavesdropping – a word whose very etymology indicates a boundary and its trespass – spatially represents being neither in one category nor another completely. It situates a transgressive activity that evokes anxiety and fear of punishment; it thus provides a more evocative means of figuring an exploration of this liminal psychological territory than voyeurism. Through sounds, more than through sight, Proust makes Marcel aware of the close proximity between extreme pain and exquisite pleasure, between suffering and ecstasy in Jupien and Charlus's encounter.[34]

In contrast to the scene at Montjouvain, which terminates before the moment of consummation, Proust here presents a fully realized sexual act; yet despite its details, the narrative exposes less a sensual moment than one of epistemophilic insight, a sublimation of carnal pleasure into an instance of psychological understanding. The sexual scene is indeed a scene of desire, but its representation stresses metaphysical desire more than physical passion. Scenes of sexual encounter in *A la recherche* spur Marcel, and by extension the reader, to an understanding about human relations and sexual identities, their intricacies, their bewildering variety, their mixture of pleasure and pain. In listening to an "acte de possession physique" in which "l'on ne possède rien" (*Swann*, 230; "the act of physical possession" in which "the possessor possesses nothing," I: 255), Marcel learns not only about Charlus's sexual orientation and homosexual love, but also about the deceptive nature of appearances and the nearness of apparently opposed states or emotions. Just as the "deux côtés" of Méséglise and Guermantes are not so separate as the young Marcel believes them to be, the emotional and physical states of pleasure and suffering border each other as well. This recognition, far from being limited to the overtly homosexual relations in the book, becomes even more pronounced in Proust's lengthy discussion of supposedly heterosexual love in Marcel's relationship with Albertine, where the two cities of the plain, initially distinct from each other, approach each other and mingle with the world of heterosexuality. The boundaries between them disappear; they prove as illusory as many of Marcel's initial assumptions about the people whose sexual and amorous relations such categories chart. Eavesdropping, an activity that erases boundaries between public and private knowledge, reveals the tenuous boundaries between straight and gay identities.

A final eavesdropping scene in *Le temps retrouvé* further complicates the ideas explored in other moments of clandestine listening. Marcel, searching for a place to buy a drink, discovers what he initially believes to be a meeting place of spies (*TR*, 117). Despite his misgivings about the establishment, he decides to enter the building to quench his thirst and, at the same time, "tâcher d'assouvir, malgré l'inquiétude qui s'y mêlait, ma curiosité" (118; "attempt, although I felt nervous at the prospect, to assuage my curiosity," III: 839). Proust thus associates the satisfaction of physical need and psychological desire with the entrance into a particular place. Standing in the vestibule, he overhears a group of men whose conversation confirms his suspicion of shady dealings, though differently from what he had assumed. At first, the "banalité" of their talk stifles any desire to listen further. Only when, in allusions to chains and beating, it reveals something illicit, unexpected, and possibly criminal does he tremble and wish to know more (119). Proust again signals the proximity of seemingly opposed states, fear and desire.[35] Marcel concludes:

> ce n'était donc pas qu'un nid d'espions que cet hôtel. Un crime atroce allait y être consommé si on n'arrivait pas à temps pour le découvrir et faire arrêter les coupables. Tout cela pourtant, dans cette nuit paisible et menacée, gardait une apparence de rêve, de conte, et c'est à la fois avec une fierté de justicier et une volupté de poète que j'entrai délibérément dans l'hôtel. (119)

> it was not... a nest of spies. An appalling crime was about to be committed, unless someone arrived in time to discover it and have the criminals arrested. And yet the whole scene, in the midst of this peaceful and threatened night, was like a dream or a fairy-tale, so that it was at once with the pride of an emissary of justice and the rapture of a poet that I at length, my mind made up, entered the hotel. (III: 840)

The protagonist justifies his entrance into this house by figuring himself as the moral hero ("justicier") who will prevent a crime; at the same time, he recognizes how this supposedly altruistic activity satisfies his own desire to know: the "volupté de poète" (the "rapture of a poet") searching for recondite, and perhaps forbidden, experience. The quests of the poet and the hero of the earlier scenes become one. A vocabulary of desire hints at the nature of the crime whose "consummation" he wishes to frustrate, just as the dreamlike atmosphere recalls the primal lesbian scene.

The narrator drinks the cassis he has ordered,[36] but although his physical thirst has been assuaged, his curiosity has not. Instead of leaving, he climbs to the top of the building, where, "d'une chambre qui était isolée au bout d'un couloir," he hears "des plaintes étouffées" (122; "from a room situated by itself at the end of a corridor [he hears] stifled groans," III: 843). Approaching the room, he overhears a sadistic exchange in which the victim begs for mercy, but the torturer responds with insults and with the "claquement d'un martinet probablement aiguisé de clous car il fut suivi de cris de douleur" (122; "the crack of a whip, which I guessed to be reinforced with nails, for it was followed by cries of pain," III: 843). When Marcel finds a small oval window and looks into the room, he discovers M. de Charlus, "enchaîné sur un lit comme Prométhée sur son rocher, recevant les coups d'un martinet en effet planté de clous qui lui infligeait Maurice" (122; "chained to a bed like Prometheus to his rock, receiving the blows that Maurice rained upon him with a whip which was in fact studded with nails," III: 843). This time Marcel's eavesdropping reveals the haughty Charlus reveling in masochistic, verbal and physical abuse. The door to the room opens, and Jupien enters. In the ensuing conversation, which begins with Charlus's anxious question – "On ne peut pas nous entendre?" ("We can't be heard, can we?") – Marcel overhears how Jupien has indeed become the Baron's "entremetteur," providing him with a place to indulge his sadomasochism (122).

Although this eavesdropping episode exposes the depths of Charlus's sexual fantasies, its significance resides in its placing Marcel as an illicit listener and voyeur. Far from revealing the hotel as a nest of spies, it portrays the protagonist as an infiltrator of a private, secret space, the true "espion" (spy) of the episode. The continual anxious queries of the brothel's patrons about being overheard, and the male prostitutes' reminders to each other that Marcel is listening, stress not just the illicit nature of the activities of the house, but the danger of infiltration by someone who is not one of them (119, 121, 122, 124, 128, 130). Yet the language in which the narrator describes his adventure abolishes such categories, and allies his desire for knowledge with the sexual fantasies being enacted behind closed doors.[37] Jupien extends the analogy between Marcel's and Charlus's experiences by placing Marcel in a special chamber designed for the Baron, a room from which one can look and listen, but cannot be seen or overheard (130). From this special aural and visual observation post, Marcel confirms his suspicion that Charlus is a regular "habitué" of the house. By the time he leaves this specially organized space, his curiosity, his intellectual desire, has been satisfied as fully as his earlier physical thirst, his ostensible reason for entering the hotel.

After this episode, Proust continues the association of sexual pleasure with more general knowledge in explaining how the darkness during the air-raid, rather than limiting our sources of pleasure, affords us entrance into an unforeseen, profound experience. He describes how

> l'obscurité qui baigne toute chose comme un élément nouveau a pour effet... de supprimer le premier stade du plaisir et de nous faire entrer de plain-pied dans un domaine de caresses où l'on n'accède d'habitude qu'après quelque temps... Dans l'obscurité, tout ce vieux jeu [des regards] se trouve aboli... Plongés dans cet élément nouveau, les habitués de Jupien croyaient avoir voyagé, être venus assister à un phénomène naturel... et goûter au lieu d'un plaisir tout préparé et sédentaire celui d'une rencontre fortuite dans l'inconnu, célébraient, aux grondement volcaniques des bombes, au pied d'un mauvais lieu pompéien, des rites secrets dans les ténèbres des catacombes. (*TR*, 141)

> darkness, which envelops all things like a new element, has the effect... of suppressing the first halt on the road to pleasure – it permits us to enter without impediment into a region of caresses to which normally we gain access only after a certain delay... In the darkness this time-honoured ritual [of glances] is instantly abolished... Plunged into the new element, imagining that they had travelled to a distant country and were witnessing a natural phenomenon... that they were enjoying not an artificially prepared, sendentary pleasure but a chance encounter in the unknown, the men who had come away from Jupien's house celebrated, while the bombs mimicked the rumbling of a volcano, deep in the earth as in a Pompeian house of ill fame, their secret rites in the shadows of the catacombs. (III: 864)

The passage celebrates the mystery of such unexpected pleasures that life occasionally offers. It evokes, like the two prior eavesdropping episodes, a vocabulary of religious ritual, but the sacred mystery here is that of the human psyche, with all its inexplicable, contradictory, even "perverse" longings and desires. In the midst of the literal and cultural destruction of *fin-de-siècle* Paris, Proust discovers something constant in its very changeability: ever unsated, the human appetite for experience and knowledge. In the demolition of this second Pompeii, Marcel stumbles across proof of something that endures throughout the ages, inspiring reverence and a sense of mystery. Like the "habitués" of Jupien's hotel, he too experiences "au lieu d'un plaisir tout préparé et sédentaire celui d'une rencontre fortuite dans l'inconnu." Through eavesdropping, an activity that provides a shortcut to certain epistemophilic desires and a voyage to a different space and time, he witnesses "des rites secrets dans les ténèbres des catacombes," the secret underground passages of carnal and spiritual desire within the human psyche.

Eavesdropping figures the spatial position of the lover or philosopher vis-à-vis the beloved object, whether human and physical, or epistemological and metaphysical. Desire arises from the idea that there exists "quelque chose d'infranchissable" ("an insurmountable barrier") between the lover and the object of desire. Proust describes how "on se sent séparé d'elle par l'impossible. C'est ainsi que mon sentiment du mystère avait pu s'appliquer successivement à Gilberte, à la duchesse de Guermantes, à Albertine, à tant d'autres" (*TR*, 294; "one feels separated from them by the impossible. It was in this fashion that a sentiment of mystery had attached itself for me first to Gilberte, then to the Duchesse de Guermantes, then to Albertine and to so many others," III: 1038). Eavesdropping represents this separation, this distance between us and the object of our desire, and the resulting sense of mystery that surrounds it and the space it occupies. The separation between the lover and the beloved may be psychological rather than physical, but the effect remains the same. To get close requires a transgression of boundaries that threatens our own security, our own ability to remain safe from inquisitive and potentially cruel eyes and ears. In coming close, in learning secrets, we may be hurt – by finding that the beloved does not love us, or that s/he is not the idealized being we supposed him or her to be. Or, by overcoming that seemingly insurmountable barrier and reaching the beloved object, we may discover it is not worth possessing.

Thus Proust takes the exploration of public and private to a different register than that of nineteenth-century novels. His novel represents both a culmination of nineteenth-century anxieties about and delight in public and private spaces and their activities, and a recognition that such zones are cultural and psychological constructs whose boundaries are as much fictions as the narratives that represent them. A work that deliberately emphasizes those aspects of life that nineteenth-century novels tend to refer to obliquely, *A la recherche* takes as its subject the construction of public and private selves and sexualities and the fluid interplay of such categories, despite attempts to keep them separate. Just as Marcel eventually discovers the distance between the two "côtés" to be almost nonexistent, and their separation to be in his mind rather than in the physical world, so Proust indicates the arbitrary nature of the markers "public" and "private" or "masculine" and "feminine," "gay" and "straight," and the small effort required to erase such distinctions.[38]

Using a metaphor of domestic architecture, Proust makes this point in a passage that represents spatially the false security of assuming that private information or identity is inaccessible. The narrator describes

Charlus's fear that the beau monde will discover his homosexuality, and contrasts this with his false conviction that the Verdurins' "petit clan" has no inkling that he is gay, in terms of a

> petit pavillon idéal où M. de Charlus venait parfois rêver seul, quand il introduisait un instant son imagination dans l'idée que les Verdurin avaient de lui. L'atmosphère y était si sympathique, si cordiale, le repos si réconfortant, que quand M. de Charlus, avant de s'endormir, était venu s'y délasser un instant de ses soucis, il n'en sortait jamais sans un sourire. Mais, pour chacun de nous, ce genre de pavillon est double: en face de celui que nous croyons être l'unique, il y a l'autre qui nous est habituellement invisible, le vrai, symétrique avec celui que nous connaissons, mais bien différent et dont l'ornementation, où nous ne reconnaîtrions rien de ce que nous nous attendions à voir, nous épouvanterait comme faite avec les symboles odieux d'une hostilité insoupçonnée. Quelle stupeur pour M. de Charlus, s'il avait pénétré dans un de ces pavillons adverses, grâce à quelque potin comme par un de ces escaliers de service où des graffitti obscènes sont charbonnés à la porte des appartements par des fournisseurs mécontents ou des domestiques renvoyés. (*Sodome*, 435–36)

> little ideal bower to which M. de Charlus retired at times to dream, when he introduced his imagination for a moment into the idea that the Verdurins had of him. Its atmosphere was so congenial, so cordial, the repose it offered so comforting, that when M. de Charlus, before going to sleep, had withdrawn to it for a momentary relaxation from his worries, he never emerged from it without a smile. But, for each one of us, a bower of this sort is double: opposite the one which we imagine to be unique, there is the other which is normally invisible to us, the real one, symmetrical with the one we know, but very different, whose decoration, in which we should recognise nothing of what we expected to see, would horrify us as though it were composed of the odious symbols of an unsuspected hostility. What a shock it would have been for M. de Charlus if he had found his way into one of these hostile bowers, thanks to some piece of scandal, as though by one of those service staircases where obscene graffiti are scribbled outside the back doors of flats by unpaid tradesmen or dismissed servants. (II: 1082–83)

Even such an idyllic private villa contains spaces of danger such as the back staircase, where servants may reveal the secrets of the family. "Le potin" (gossip), like eavesdropping, reveals information that the inhabitants would wish to keep hidden, but that, like murder, always will out. The servants' staircase, like the corridors of a house initially built to protect the family's intimacies, also makes possible infiltrations to private space and the dissemination of its secrets. "Le petit clan," or its architectural correlative, "le petit pavillon," becomes, like the hotel that Marcel infiltrates, the site of Charlus's exposure. Far from being "un lieu sûr" (a safe place) away from the beau monde, the world of the

Verdurins constitutes a "pavillon adverse." The threat of exposure and betrayal is all the more pernicious because of the false assurance of privacy that this space provides. Proust thus exposes the fiction of separate public and private spheres and selves that many nineteenth-century novels appear to endorse. He suggests that such spheres are psychological (as well as ideological) constructs. A man's home is never his castle. If Wemmick's moated house existed in *A la recherche*, it would have, unbeknownst to its owner, a subterranean passage for secret infiltration.

The older narrator describes the interpenetration of social and psychological worlds in *Le temps retrouvé* when Mme Verdurin marries the prince de Guermantes and becomes the mistress of the Paris elite. Having returned to society after a prolonged stay in a sanitarium, the narrator marvels how,

> Ce milieu...j'avais trouvé comme un refuge matériel pour ce nom de Guermantes auquel il prêtait sa dernière réalité, ce milieu avait lui-même subi dans sa constitution intime et que j'avais cru stable, une altération profonde. La présence de gens que j'avais vus dans de tout autres sociétés et qui me semblaient ne devoir jamais pénétrer dans celle-là m'étonna moins encore que l'intime familiarité avec laquelle ils y étaient reçus, appelés par leur prénom.
> (*TR*, 262–63)

> I had found, I thought, a sort of corporeal refuge for the name of Guermantes, this coterie, which had seemed to confer upon that name its ultimate reality, had itself, in its innermost and as I had thought stable constitution, undergone a profound transformation. The presence of people whom I had seen in quite different social settings and whom I would never have expected to penetrate into this one, astonished me less than the intimate familiarity with which they were now received in it, on Christian name terms. (III: 1000)

The beau monde cannot erect barriers to keep itself aloof from the ambitious haute bourgeoisie, just as the public sphere continually encroaches on the private, denying the stability of such categories. Whereas in the three crucial eavesdropping scenes the sites of knowledge and of ignorance are represented as spatially distinct, in society such barriers – like social boundaries – no longer exist. Hence the need to develop a public disguise and thus create a psychological "appartement" – a division of self and a psychological space safe from curious ears and eyes – arises from everyone's insatiable desire to pry beneath others' social masks. *A la recherche* exposes how our desire to keep our own secrets yet learn everyone else's is a form of hypocrisy.[39] The myth of Charlus's womanizing and Saint-Loup's string of mistresses veil their less socially acceptable sexual inclinations. What Marcel concludes about artistic taste holds true as well for everyone's sexual proclivities: "Il n'y avait pas besoin qu'on eût réellement ces goûts pourvu qu'on les proclamât" (*Swann*, 241; "there was no need actually to have those tastes, as long as one proclaimed them," I: 267). Sexual identity, like other aspects of one's identity, is a performance.[40]

Eavesdropping and gossip – the subsequent dispersal of private information into an inquisitive, manipulative public realm – pervade all communities of Proust's novel. Everybody in *A la recherche* – from Françoise listening in on Marcel's amorous rendezvous, to Mme Verdurin, deliberately overhearing an exchange between one of the faithful and a newcomer to "le petit clan,"[41] to Marcel himself – is an eavesdropper. Most covert listeners at the social gatherings deliberately overhear private conversations between others, hoping to glean compromising information, to arrange someone's downfall, to advance up the social ladder, or to maintain a position at the top. The duchesse de Guermantes asks the question that floats about every social occasion, as the guests mingle and display themselves: "mais qu'est-ce qu'ils peuvent avoir à se dire?" (*Sodome*, 115; "but what can they be talking about?," II: 743). Just as everyone wishes to know the secrets of other people, so, too, do they hope, in vain, that their own private lives will remain inviolate.[42]

In situations where surreptitious listening is *de rigueur*, the set-up eavesdrop is socially transforming. It provides a means of creating or refuting an aspect of one's character, or that of someone else. By feeding others erroneous information about oneself, one convinces them of the persona one wishes to project, since the information gleaned through eavesdropping is assumed to be true. Because of the illicit manner in which it is obtained (supposedly without the speaker's knowledge), such information is believed to reveal an aspect of the speaker's authentic identity or a hidden truth. Thus, Marcel speaks to Mme de Cambremer in order to convince her daughter-in-law that Chopin is back in fashion (*Sodome*, 212), and Charlus converses with Mme de Cambremer "devant Morel ébahi et auquel à vrai dire toute cette dissertation était... destinée" (*Sodome*, 342; "in front of a flabbergasted Morel, for whose benefit the whole dissertation was intended," II: 983). Such a set-up eavesdrop can be used to cut someone, as Charlus does Mme de Saint-Euverte, by talking viciously about her when he knows she cannot help overhearing (*Sodome*, 98–99). But this attempt to disguise identity through a set-up eavesdrop can backfire when the speaker fails to convince the eavesdropper of his or her words' authenticity. When Charlus fears a passing official may have overheard his exchange with a footman, he shouts his words so that the notary will hear a different conversation. Overcompensating, "il les criait tous si fort, que tout ce jeu de scène eût suffi à décider ce qu'il cachait pour des oreilles plus averties que celles de l'officier ministériel" (*Sodome*, 377; "he shouted his words so loud, that this charade would have been enough to betray what it concealed to ears more alert than those of the legal gentleman," II: 1020). Merely setting up a scene of covert listening is not enough. In a world attuned to the subtleties of social performance, the act must be convincing. Charlus's stagy performance convinces no true connoisseur; his sexual orientation is an open secret.[43]

In his clandestine listening, Marcel is the "worst offender," yet he is also the most anxious to keep his own secrets from becoming public.[44] At the elite gatherings to which he gains access, Marcel appears as the consummate eavesdropper, rarely the person whose speech he renders for the reader. In fact, most of the conversations he relates are not between him and someone else, but between two people he has overheard. For example, he is distracted from conversing with Swann at the princess's soirée because he wants to overhear the exchange between Charlus and the young man the Baron wishes to seduce (*Sodome*, 102). Similarly, at the dinner party at La Raspalière, Marcel so intently listens to one conversation that he misses part of another. When Ski says something to Cottard, "à mi-voix, il ajouta quelque chose de confus avec un verbe, où je ne distinguai seulement les dernières syllabes 'arder', occupé que j'étais d'écouter ce que Brichot disait à M. de Charlus" (*Sodome*, 324; "in an undertone, and he added something indistinct including a word of which I caught only the last syllable, *-ast*, being engaged in listening to what Brichot was saying to M. de Charlus," II: 964).

In a narrative chronicling his entrance into society, Marcel's participation in the witty repartee around him remains singularly unrecorded. The narrator almost never presents himself speaking in extended dialogue. He relates either what others say, or his own prolonged, internal musings. His role appears to be the accepted eavesdropper, the occasional go-between in Charlus's affair with Morel,[45] the person to whom everyone allows access to their social and sexual secrets, as if they sensed that his knowledge will not harm them but, rather, foster something more profound. The narrative justifies Marcel's eavesdropping by describing how the future writer listens differently: "Il n'[é]cout[e] les autres que quand, si bêtes ou si fous qu'ils [soient], répétant comme des perroquets ce que disent les gens de caractère semblable, ils se [sont] faits par là même les oiseaux prophètes, les porte-parole d'une loi psychologique (*TR*, 207; "this has made him listen to people only when, stupid or absurd though they may have been, they have turned themselves, by repeating like parrots what other people of similar character are in the habit of saying, into birds of augury, mouthpieces of a psychological law," III: 937).

But Marcel's auditory omniscience, and hence the justification for his exceptional position as sanctioned eavesdropper, are undercut by the examples cited above. In order to hear some conversations, Marcel misses others. Unlike the omniscient third-person narrator, Marcel cannot know everything. Although by the end of the novel he is ready to write the book of all he has learned, his understanding will be as subjective, partial, changeable as all the scenarios and their revised accounts in the narrative. Although he may seem to be the seer who can interpret the songs of "les oiseaux prophètes" ("birds of augury"), Marcel's interpretations remain imperfect, as subject to revision as his other "truths." Yet, Proust intimates, the first-person voice, with its tacit admission of fallibility, offers a more authentic means of representing "reality" than the third-person omniscient voice of many nineteenth-century narratives. By admitting the factitiousness of its representation of social reality – with its intricate configurations of desire and performance – Proust concludes a century of writers whose realism resides in the effort to portray their social, political, and physical worlds in minute detail. *A la recherche* suggests that the partial, "intermittent" pieces of our world, like Vinteuil's "petite phrase" – those fragments the writer happens to overhear, and make sense of – must suffice. For Proust, "the reality effect" consists not of an exhaustive abundance of "futile" physical details, but in the admission that reality escapes attempts at such comprehensive representation.[46] However, the good writer knows how to turn even parrots' words into compelling stories, ones we wish to hear.

A la recherche also implicates its readers in this epistemophilic urge to listen secretly and to make up stories. The narrator compares reading with eavesdropping, intimating that each is an attempt to interpret information to which one is not fully privy. Infatuated with Albertine, Marcel describes how "derrière les mots de sa lettre comme derrière ceux qu'elle m'avait dits une fois au téléphone, je crus sentir la présence de plaisirs, d'êtres, qu'elle m'avait préférés. Encore une fois je fus agité tout entier par la curiosité douloureuse de savoir ce qu'elle avait pu faire" (*Sodome*, 194; "behind the words of her letter, as behind those that she had said to me once over the telephone, I thought I could detect the presence of pleasures, of people, whom she had preferred to me. Once again, my whole body was stirred by the painful longing to know what she could have been doing," II: 826).[47] During the telephone call,

Marcel had overheard other voices behind Albertine's and, because he could not hear their entire conversation, had agonized over what those half-heard utterances and their speakers signified (*Sodome*, 129–31).

The gap created between words heard (or read) and those not available produces innumerable scenarios of desire. In both reading and listening, the recipient of information is separated from anticipated pleasures and knowledge, the attainment of which is uncertain, if not impossible. Proust thus makes explicit the connection, evoked earlier in the reading of *François le Champi*, between sexual and epistemological desire. He represents the reader's appetite for both kinds of knowledge by placing him or her as an eavesdropper segregated from the desired object and its intentions. Reading becomes a "sublimated manner of obtaining mastery" over such desires. Both reading a letter and interpreting an overheard scene entail making sense of the material with which one is presented, as well as the information between or behind the lines. As *A la recherche* demonstrates, both processes are rife with misinterpretations that prolong an infatuation predicated on the impossibility of physically or psychologically "possessing" the beloved. The narrator declares, "On n'aime que ce qu'on ne possède pas tout entier" (*La prisonnière*, 98; "we love only what we do not wholly possess," III: 102). The desire to know this mystery, the "true" story of another person, compels Marcel's espionage and propels the narrative; sexual and narrative desire become inextricable from each other, both instances of the urge to know.

Proust's novel reveals an intense awareness of the reader as a second-degree eavesdropper, albeit one set up to listen. In *A la recherche*, both reading and surreptitious listening become activities that acknowledge boundaries even as they try to eliminate them, even as such oppositions as masculine and feminine, inside and outside, true and false, are abandoned as incapable of representing an ever elusive, unstable reality – elusive and unstable because the subject who conceptualizes them is also changing. Thus, in *Le temps retrouvé*, Proust asserts, "Il y a entre nous et les êtres, un liséré de contingences, comme j'avais compris dans mes lectures de Combray qu'il y en a un de perception et qui empêche la mise en contact absolue de la réalité et de l'esprit" (281; "between us and other people there exists a barrier of contingencies, just as in my hours of reading in the garden at Combray I had realised that in all perception there exists a barrier as a result of which there is never absolute contact between reality and our intelligence," III: 1023). We are separated from complete knowledge of people by a boundary that prohibits our total access to them, just as in reading we cannot surmount the gap between our minds and the represented reality. Both social encounters (such as conversation) and reading attempt to overcome this boundary, if only partially or intermittently. Eavesdropping figures this effort to conquer epistemological distance.

The writer facilitates border-crossing by bringing two different psychological spaces into contiguity, so that the reader can eavesdrop with impunity from his own space, like Marcel's "cabinet de repos," on a different world (*Swann*, 71; "sanctum," I: 78). Thus the early scene of onanism becomes a moment of readerly eavesdropping, one we recognize only after having vicariously experienced Marcel's own illicit listening. In recalling the early incident, we realize that Proust has made himself our narrative and epistemological *entremetteur*, who satisfies our desire to know, just as Jupien caters to Charlus's sexual needs. *A la recherche* obliges readers to be conscious of the project we and Proust have undertaken. Proust's novel assumes readerly involvement, even complicity, in the activity taking place within the novel: an epistemological quest in search of self and other. Such a search denies the kinds of formal, psychological, and sexual boundaries that many nineteenth-century narratives accept, yet while divulging more than before, Proust's novel creates its own "petit[s] pavillon[s]," or closets of privacy.[48] Like Charlus's, their privacy is debatable.

André Gide recalled Proust's having said to him, "Vous pouvez tout raconter... mais à condition de ne jamais dire: *Je*" ("You can tell all... provided that you never say 'I.'").[49] At first, it would seem that Proust ignores his prohibition against the first person, since his narrative is narrated by a "je" identified as *a* Marcel.[50] But the "je" of the narrative is not identical to Marcel Proust the writer. Proust's desire to keep his sexual orientation a private matter known to only his intimate friends is documented by the letters he wrote masking his homosexuality.[51] By creating a young, aspiring writer named Marcel who learns vicariously about life and love before embarking on his own amorous adventures, Proust distinguishes between actual writer and numerous characters in his work that embody various aspects of his identity. By displacing his own experience on to figures not identified as "Marcel," Proust provides a means of talking about himself safely and more analytically than would otherwise have been possible.[52]

This personal aspect of Proust's work has occasioned critical debate from the initial publication of *A la recherche* to the present. Proust's contemporaries were divided over how to judge his representation of homosexuality and lesbianism[53]. Later twentieth-century critics recognized the work as a subversive *apologia* for diverse sexual orientations and practices.[54] Proust disguises his sexual and half-Jewish identity and the identities of the people he knew, but he makes explicit that such *travestissement* (cross-dressing), like the set-up eavesdrop, is a form of self-creation.[55] In trying to define the relation between Marcel Proust the author and Marcel the character, we fall into the trap for which Proust criticized Sainte-Beuve, that of believing in a one-to-one correspondence between literature and biography.

Yet in the very construction of his work, Proust invites this activity, if only to frustrate a conclusive answer. A narrative whose form positions the reader as a listener to an autobiography,[56] this apparent confession of private thoughts, recognitions, and emotions functions instead as an act of self-construction that produces an identity – one among many possible. As early as 1888, Proust conceived of himself as composed of multiple selves.[57] Opening up a private world and a private perspective on the exclusive society of late nineteenth- and early twentieth-century Paris, *A la recherche* makes its eavesdropping readers privy to the intimate world of desire and sexual identity, to a dazzling array of social and libidinal plots. At the same time, the narrative creates the very world and personae it seems to expose and places readers of *A la recherche* in the same hermeneutic quandary as its protagonist: how to make sense of (or narrate) the often equivocal information that our reading or eavesdropping provides us.[58] By presenting his novel as a vast set-up eavesdrop, Proust obliges us to be self-conscious about the kind of project both writer and reader have undertaken. By bringing what is socially other – marginal, sometimes unacceptable – to the center of his work, Proust makes us question all kinds of received notions about human identity and desire, including our own.

Such recognitions – about self and other, about the desire to know, about sexual and social identity and their mutability – culminate at the matinée that concludes *A la recherche*. In a series of sensations that provoke the narrator's "mémoire involontaire" (involuntary memory), he relates how these recuperated moments offer an unexpected, redemptive pleasure, one that extends beyond the initial experience to "la vérité soupçonnée par chacun" ("the truth dimly apprehended by each one of us"). Through his writing the narrator will try to "elucidate" this "truth" (*TR*, 351; III: 1104). Yet despite his visual vocabulary, the crucial sensations that provoke such *aperçus* remain those of the other senses: touch, taste, smell, and, finally, sound. The ringing of the garden-gate bell becomes the most suggestive image of these last pages; the chime described at the beginning of the novel (*Swann*, 33), evoked at the matinée (*TR*, 349), now resonates within the writer. The narrator relates how, "C'était bien cette sonnette qui tintait encore en moi... pour bien l'écouter, je dus m'efforcer de ne plus entendre le son des conversations que les masques tenaient autour de moi. Pour tâcher de l'entendre de plus près, c'est en moi-même que j'étais obligé de redescendre" (*TR*, 351–52; "it was indeed this same bell which rang within me... To hear [it] properly again, I was obliged to block my ears to the conversations which were proceeding between the masked figures all round me, for in order to get nearer to the sound of the bell and to hear it better it was into my own depths that I had to re-descend," III: 1105).

Whereas earlier Marcel had been distracted from his own conversation by the desire to eavesdrop on other people's exchanges, now the only conversation that matters is internal. The "real" world of society is a mere display of masks in which he has difficulty identifying the people he once knew, whose gatherings he once frequented. Proust offers this turning inward as an "égoïsme utilisable pour autrui" (*TR*, 341; "egotism which could be put to work for the benefit of other people," III: 1093). The inverted, inwardly listening poet offers a means of eavesdropping on others that, to be fruitful, must lead us to examine ourselves. This introspection is not an evasion of society, but a means of understanding our relationship to that world. The narrator explains, "Par l'art seulement nous pouvons sortir de nous, savoir ce que voit un autre de cet univers qui n'est pas le même que le nôtre et dont les paysages nous seraient restés aussi inconnus que ceux qu'il peut y avoir dans la lune" (*TR*, 202; "through art alone are we able to emerge from ourselves to know what another person sees of a universe which is not the same as our own and of which, without art, the landscapes would remain as unknown to us as those that may exist in the moon," III: 932).

Proust does not wish us to remain eavesdroppers, vicarious readers of other people's experience, for such an enterprise will not lead to knowledge of either ourselves or others.[59] Reading is not simply a means of "engaging [the readers'] desire for vicarious experience."[60] As early as 1906, Proust expressed how reading, like eavesdropping, is a liminal activity, on the threshold to deeper understanding: "la lecture est au seuil de la vie spirituelle; elle peut nous y introduire; elle ne la constitue pas."[61] ("Reading is on the threshold of spiritual life; it can usher us into but does not constitute [this spiritual life].") Reading, "l'acte psychologique," should afford entrance into self-exploration, so that "chaque lecteur est quand il lit le propre lecteur de soi-même" ("Journées de lecture," 172; *TR*, 217; "every reader is, while he is reading, the reader of his own self," III: 949).[62] A "novelist of bad manners," Proust is not "an acutely inattentive listener," but rather one who uses impolite, covert listening to make us attend more closely to the differences and similarities *between* ourselves and others as well as the discrepancies and contradictions *within* ourselves.[63]

Proust refuses to allow us a self-congratulatory or superior stance regarding our own activity (reading or eavesdropping), just as he refuses to allow his character Marcel to label himself a hero on a quest for truth. Having deconstructed the very notion of stable truths, personalities, or identities, Proust also destabilizes the notion of hero that justified much of his earlier snooping. He first reveals how Saint-Loup, Marcel's idol and a decorated war hero, loses his "croix de guerre" at Jupien's hotel. Marcel eventually learns that the cloaked, dimly seen character he had encountered just outside the male brothel was Saint-Loup, a regular customer (*TR*, 117, 127, 147). With this discovery, Proust ironizes Marcel's self-identification as a heroic truth-seeker. The revelation unsettles the entire association of heroism and "proper" behavior; the narrative refuses to absolve Marcel – or, for that matter, us – from participation in the events being described. We, too, are situated and implicated listeners. Just as his novel makes us reflect on the changing nature of his characters and narrator, Proust makes us examine our own activities and desires, our motives and motivations. *A la recherche* entices us to eavesdrop and thereby assume a critical distance on – and tantalizing proximity to – the most fascinating, if most perplexing space for any reader: the human psyche.

Conclusion: covert listeners and secret agents

> The reader does not hear, he overhears.
> Atwood, *Negotiating with the Dead*

In his dedication of *The Secret Agent* to H. G. Wells, Joseph Conrad called his novel "a simple tale of the nineteenth century."¹ Yet although Conrad's novel is set in 1886, with its central event based on an actual attempt to blow up the Royal Observatory in 1894, it is hardly a "simple tale."² Published six years before the first volume of *A la recherche du temps perdu*, *The Secret Agent* (1907) explodes nineteenth-century assumptions about narrative, social, and psychological spaces, and about public and private identities, just as, in its experimental telling, it blows apart narrative form. The narrative space – fragmented and out of order – reflects the social world it represents. Domestic ideology, with its separate spheres for gendered activities, no longer obtains. The major eavesdropping scene in the novel stages this altered understanding of spaces and selves. Occurring late in the story and in its telling, covert listening in *The Secret Agent* is committed not by the novel's professional spies, anarchists, or police agents, but by its central female character, Winnie Verloc. She eavesdrops on her husband and Chief Inspector Heat as they stand in the Verloc parlor and discuss the botched plan to bomb the Royal Observatory at Greenwich. Her secret listening in the family shop takes place after the explosion destroys her simple-minded brother Stevie, and, with him, the fiction of domestic respectability by which she has justified her life. Her eavesdropping stands in contrast to numerous forms of professional espionage and counterespionage that preoccupy most of the male characters in the novel. *The Secret Agent* bears witness to a changing conception of space, its secrets, its bodies, their regulation and representation. It also implicates its readers in the reconstruction of plot, making them, like most of the characters, secret agents of the narrative. In contrast to Proust's *A la recherche*, Conrad's novel dwells on how acquiring secret knowledge may bring pain rather than pleasure. At the same time, Conrad reminds us of the high stakes involved in understanding our role as vicarious participants in other people's experiences.

From its opening, *The Secret Agent* merges commercial and domestic, licit and illicit, zones of activity: "Mr. Verloc, going out in the morning, left his shop nominally in charge of his brother-in-law. It could be done, because there was very little business at any time, and practically none at all before the evening. Mr. Verloc cared but little about his ostensible business. And, moreover, his wife was in charge of his brother-in-law" (45). Conrad has replaced the respectable shopkeeper of nineteenth-century fiction with a man who uses his irregular trade in pornography and anarchist literature as a cover for his even more suspect occupation as a double, even triple agent. Just as the shop, "nominally" under Stevie's supervision, is run by Verloc's wife Winnie, Verloc's "ostensible business" is a front for his compound undercover professions: Embassy agent posing as an anarchist, and informant who feeds to the British police information about his supposed allies. Verloc's real trade takes place outside the "ostensible" place of business; spaces and those who control them are not what they seem to be. Already this novel intimates that its story will be one of secrets and secret agents, of multiple identities and multiform transgressions, of ill-defined spaces and "improperly" regulated activities.

Winnie's presiding over the pornography shop exemplifies a general denial of the ideology of separate spheres that would divide the world of domesticity from the world of business. The shop itself spatially replicates this indeterminacy of spaces and their functions: the door stands "discreetly but suspiciously ajar" (45), neither fully open nor open about its business. Nor does it mark a complete separation between street and store. The layout of the shop and the home emphasizes the tenuous boundary between public and private zones and activities. The three rooms of Verloc's establishment – shop, parlor, and kitchen – are placed one directly behind the other, each linked to the next by a single door. As Stevie draws at the kitchen table, his sister can watch him as she dusts the parlor but still listen for the bell of the shop door (50).

Similarly, the narration itself connects all three spaces and their activities: "The door of the shop was the only means of entrance to the house in which Mr. Verloc carried on his business of a seller of shady wares, exercised his vocation of protector of society, and cultivated his domestic virtues. These last were pronounced. He was thoroughly domesticated" (46–47). If Dickens's Dombey is taught to appreciate his home as well as his business and to distinguish between public and private stories and selves, Verloc is too complacent about the comforts of home and about his ability to separate public and private spheres of activity. The narration and setting of *The Secret Agent* deny that such comfortable segregation is possible. The novel questions the respectable, "domestic virtues" of a household founded upon a trade in less than virtuous wares and suggests that the private and public plots cannot, in fact, be neatly walled off from each other.

In *The Secret Agent*, the word "private" more often refers to clandestine relations than to emotionally intimate ones; the distinction between public and private frequently is not one of domestic ideology but of open or secret dealings. Hence Chief Inspector Heat considers his communications with Verloc "a private affair of my own. A personal friend of mine in the French police gave me the hint that the fellow [Verloc] was an Embassy spy. Private friendship, private information, private use of it – that's how I look upon it" (136). When he comes to see Verloc about the failed bombing, he tells Winnie that he has "called to get from him a little private information" (190). Privacy here implies the concept of the secret, not the individual.

If private relations are secret ones rather than intimate ones, so are their spaces. The Embassy – with its secret passages, winding stairs, thick carpets, numerous entrances and exits – is arguably the most private space in the novel, even though an official one. Hard to decipher or to map, it remains a secret space and therefore "private." Conversely, the Verloc parlor – the Victorian space of domestic comfort and ease – functions as a political meeting place of the anarchists. We have left the parlor of Austen's or Dickens's fiction – the semipublic place where people mainly of the same class gather to discuss social, cultural, economic, or political events like the marriage of two cousins, a concert, or the possibility of Veneering's standing for Parliament.[3] The public house has come home. Public and private areas – literal and metaphoric – are indistinguishable, or barely separated, so that, as the anarchists discuss politics, on the other side of the wall Stevie draws "innumerable circles ... that by their ... confusion of intersecting lines" offer "a rendering of cosmic chaos" (76). Stevie's purposeless drawings suggest not just his mental disorder, but the contingent connections between spheres and spaces that nineteenth-century ideology tried to keep distinct. Verloc treats his house as "a public place," wearing his overcoat and hat inside (155, 176). The narrator explains how "the frequentation of foreign cafés ... was responsible for that habit, investing with a character of unceremonious impermanency Mr. Verloc's steady fidelity to his own fireside" (171). He eats with his hat on, as if ready to leave at a moment's notice, once he has paid the bill. These markers of the outside world and its "impermanency" in the place supposedly impervious to "all terror, doubt, division" suggest how little divides outside from inside, public from private, political from domestic.[4] In *The Secret Agent*, walls of all kinds no longer function according to the nineteenth-century fiction of willed impermeability.

It is not only the humble household parlor that opens its doors to political intrigue, mixed company, and unstable identities. In the lady patroness's parlor, "You never can guess who you [are] likely to come upon being received in semi-privacy within the faded blue silk and gilt frame screen, making a cosy nook for a couch and a few armchairs in the great drawing-room, with its hum of voices and the groups of people seated or standing in the light of six tall windows" (120). The parlor has changed function. It is no longer the place of Austenian conversation, nor is it a return to the eighteenth-century salon's privileged public exchange of ideas. Rather, it embodies the site of failed communication, "touching in its foredoomed futility, as the efforts at moral intercourse between the inhabitants of remote planets" (122). The collapse of boundaries – whether social or spatial – produces not understanding or social equality but incomprehension masquerading as the "lofty simplicity" and tolerance of the "great lady" who considers herself "above the play of economic conditions" (119, 122).

All spaces, in fact, in *The Secret Agent* are sites of social and psychological distance rather than concord or intimacy. The eradication of physical boundaries does little to promote affective closeness. The bedroom, the Victorian space symbolizing conjugal harmony, instead registers here the greatest emotional distance. Its very representation stresses the fact that its status as the private space *par excellence* is under reconsideration. Whereas British nineteenth-century novels might describe a bedroom and its single occupant with or without a servant, the depiction of conjugal bedrooms and their activities was more or less taboo: such intimate activities and conversations were almost never portrayed, except those exchanges among the working classes presented for comic effect.[5] *The Secret Agent*, however, represents the marriage bed to expose its occupants' emotional isolation from each other. Under pressure from Vladimir to produce a disturbance that will rouse the authorities to repress anarchist movements, Verloc cannot reach toward his wife for solace. His experience of their bedroom registers both the scanty refuge it offers from the

Conclusion: covert listeners and secret agents

cares of the outside world and the lack of emotional intimacy between them. The windowpane appears as "a fragile film of glass stretched between him and the enormity of cold, black, wet, muddy, inhospitable accumulation of bricks, slates, and stones, things in themselves unlovely and unfriendly to man" (84). Turning from this hostile vision, Verloc beholds "his wife re-enter the room and get into bed in a calm, business-like manner which made him feel hopelessly lonely in the world" (85).

While the actual partitions between the rooms of the Verloc establishment are small, its emotional barriers are enormous. When Winnie speaks to him, "it [is] as if her voice was talking on the other side of a very thick wall" (86). And if the financial stability of this household depends on the selling of pornography in the shop below, the interactions in the Verloc bedroom suggest that Winnie views their marriage as another form of "transaction," in which she provides sexual satisfaction and a neat, orderly home in return for financial security for herself, her mother, and Stevie (232). The home is an extension of the family business, as her "business-like manner" and the cashbox on the night table imply (84). Later, Winnie recalls the "seven year's security for Stevie loyally paid for on her part" (220). Private life has its debts and bonds. If little physically divides the business establishment from the household space, not much differentiates the activities of each area. More than one kind of sex is for sale in the Verloc establishment.

Indeed, the "bed of compassion," the symbolic space of comfort and love, appears in *The Secret Agent* as a nostalgic place of the past. Stevie remembers crawling as a child into Winnie's bed, as "into a haven of consoling peace." Sympathizing for a cabman and his weary horse, Stevie longs "to take them to bed with him," but even he recognizes the unfeasibility of this "supreme remedy" "on a large scale" (165, 166). Such spaces of consolation are no longer available to anyone, even on a small scale. *The Secret Agent* extends the recognition of Balzac's and Proust's texts: every "petit paradis" ("little paradise"), or "petit pavillon" ("little bower"), is actually a "pavillon adverse" ("hostile bower"). Fantasy spaces of safety and comfort either no longer exist or are not what they appear to be.[6] They represent economic or political interactions in Conrad – emotionally barren, unstable, dangerous, or deadly sites.[7] With its narrow confines, the charity cottage to which Winnie's mother moves is not a cozy retreat but "the place of training for the still more straitened circumstances of the grave" (160).

Chapter 9, where the novel's major eavesdropping scene occurs, sums up the psychologically volatile aspect of space and agency in Winnie's attitude toward her home. Alone in the house, assuming that Stevie is safe in the country and that her husband is out on business, she "glanced all round the parlour, from the corner cupboard to the good fire in the grate. Ensconced cosily behind the shop of doubtful wares, with the mysterious dim window, and its door suspiciously ajar in the obscure and narrow street, it was in all essentials of domestic propriety and domestic comfort a respectable home" (186). The ironic passage reminds us of how superficial are the "propriety" and "respectability" of this metropolitan home. Later, after a shaken Verloc has returned then left again with the Assistant Commissioner, Winnie, possessed of the family savings, "look[s] round thoughtfully, with an air of mistrust in the silence and solitude of the house. This abode of her marriage life appeared to her as lonely and unsafe as though it had been situated in the midst of the forest" (189). The house itself has not changed; rather, her situation makes the space suddenly seem isolated and insecure, so that she hides the money in the only safe place she can think of, the bodice of her dress. Winnie's body is her one possession, which she has used to purchase security for herself and Stevie. Yet very soon she learns that bodies are as fragile as the domestic spaces that house them, as she eavesdrops on her husband and Chief Inspector Heat's conversation and learns about the death of her brother.

This scene of covert listening occurs in a chapter that relates the entire day of the explosion without representing the event itself. Although the larger narrative portrays the complicated systems of visual surveillance and counter-surveillance of the police, spies, and anarchists and narrator, this chapter concentrates on aural rather than visual cues and traces Winnie's gradual understanding, by means of sound, of Stevie's untimely death. If the novel's repeated word of professional, political, narrative, and domestic supervision has been "vigilance" (from the Latin *vigilare*, "to watch"), Winnie's regulation of the Verloc household here is primarily aural (50, 51, 55).[8] It begins with the "clatter of the shop-bell" that announces Verloc's returning from the Continent (175), a discordant jangle that echoes repeatedly throughout the novel and hints at the greater discord of the establishment. If, in his capacity as spy, Verloc watches, Winnie listens. As she speaks to Verloc about Stevie, she "pause[s], attentive, her ear turned toward the door of the kitchen." But Winnie does not fear that the charwoman Mrs. Neale in the kitchen might hear the couple's conversation; rather, she listens to Mrs. Neale tell "harrowing tales about her little children" to her easily upset brother (177). Conrad inverts domestic eavesdropping: rather than having a servant eavesdrop on her employer to profit from middle-class secrets, here the mistress listens to her servant to prevent Stevie's anger. While Winnie may run a well-regulated household, this reversed covert listening suggests that the nineteenth-century rules of domestic management and domestic ideology no longer apply.

Later in the afternoon, Winnie learns of her husband's return by "recognizing his step on the pavement outside" (181); she gathers that something is amiss from the uncontrolled rattling of his teeth (182); she tries to listen to his conversation with the Assistant Commissioner (186); she reveals that Verloc has been talking in his sleep, giving her a hint of his clandestine dealings with "Embassy people" (189). Even the conjugal bed is not free from involuntary utterances and inadvertent overhearing. When Chief Inspector Heat arrives just after his superior leaves with Verloc, he gets Winnie to identify her brother as the man killed in the botched bombing that morning. Upon his return, Verloc draws Heat into the parlor, leaving Winnie, stunned, in the shop:

The door was hardly shut when Mrs. Verloc, jumping up from the chair, ran to it as if to fling it open, but instead of doing so fell on her knees, with her ear to the keyhole. The two men must have stopped directly they were through, because she heard plainly the Chief Inspector's voice, though she could not see his finger pressed against her husband's breast emphatically. (194–95)

The narrative that follows repeatedly calls attention to her listening rather than seeing. Her most finely tuned sense is that of sound, not sight; again she "presse[s] her ear to the keyhole" (196). When the Chief Inspector relates how the explosion was so strong that "they had to fetch a shovel to gather him up with" (196), Winnie can listen no longer. Springing up, she "stop[s] her ears" and then snatches up the newspaper, tearing it in half, and flinging it to the floor. She does not need to listen or read any more. If before she believed that "things [did] not stand much *looking* into," she has now *heard* too much (172, e.m.). Her frenzied tearing of the "optimistic, rosy" newspaper anticipates her more radical violence in Chapter 11, when she murders Verloc with the kitchen knife as he lies upon the family sofa. Transgressive listening in the shop leads to bloodshed at home. Political plot and domestic plot are both violent. Until now Winnie has been characterized by self-restraint: laconic speech, deliberate movements, tightly corseted bodice, and neatly coiled hair. Her covert listening, like the event she hears about, explodes that self-control. Transgressions in this twentieth-century narrative reveal and produce escalating acts of violence. The risks and rewards of eavesdropping are higher and its consequences often mortal.

If the violations of private life and its secrets in the nineteenth century centered on domestic problems and misunderstandings, in the world of *The Secret Agent*, private information and acts are simultaneously political and national concerns. Whereas *The Woman in White* ends by establishing Walter Hartright as a respectable, middle-class professional, husband, and father, leaving the "secret brotherhood" to proceed unchecked, *The Secret Agent* denies the neat division of private and public plots. Transgressive individuals cannot simply be identified, marked, and put away, relegated to the attic or the margins of society, for everyone has more than one identity, even if unknown to themselves. Verloc believes he is "loved for himself" (233) when he is merely part of a bargain that Winnie made to provide for herself and her brother. The "prudent reserve ... which had been the foundation of their respectable home life" covers the economic basis of their relations (235) and suggests that fatal assumptions about other people and their intentions may be occurring in more "respectable" households, like the Assistant Commissioner's.

Indeed, the term *domestic* acquires a double meaning in *The Secret Agent*. It no longer refers primarily to the bourgeois home, its spaces and activities, but connotes the obverse of *foreign*. Although the Assistant Commissioner reassures Sir Ethelred that the failed bombing is the consequence of a "domestic drama" (204) like one of Balzac's "drames domestiques," the Home Secretary's thoughts quickly connect the phrase with "questions of his country's *domestic* policy" (205, e.m.). If the nineteenth-century novel tends to give domestic plots priority over those of national and international affairs, *The Secret Agent* continually reiterates that such segregation of "domestic" from "Domestic" is impossible. All dramas are domestic dramas; they affect not just the domestic hearth but "*the* House *par excellence*," the House of Lords (199, Conrad's emphasis).[9] In Conrad's novel, "the Victorian angel of the hearth [can] no longer preside over a harmonious analogy between home and nation."[10] And solving domestic mysteries, regulating the bourgeois home, does not insure that the nation's problems will be resolved.

In *The Secret Agent*, the boundaries to spaces and identities are supple, sometimes inconvenient fictions. Walls no longer guarantee the semblance of privacy; the conventions of private life no longer function, so that transgressions of private and public spaces change in character. Space itself has become less physical than metaphysical or ideological. Vladimir's suggestion that Verloc blow up the

Observatory is directed less at the building than at the idea it represents: science, "the fetish of the hour" (65). Although the bombing plot was hatched in an Embassy in London's Chesham Square, the Assistant Commissioner explains that the British police "have stopped at the limits of our territory," since the Embassy is, at least "theoretically . . . foreign territory; abroad only by a fiction" (209). Individual and national territories and identities, like stories, can be redrawn, made up, made over. And threats against them take intensified symbolic as well as physical form.

The man who has the most command over his personal space is the Professor, the potential human bomb. As he walks about the city, he controls the area around him by grasping the detonator to the explosives he always carries; anyone approaching too close risks blowing himself up as well as "everything within sixty yards [of him]" (91). The anarchist makes the cost of another's trespass on his privacy too high for anyone other than another nihilist to attempt. As the Professor himself puts it, he possesses "absolutely nothing in the way of protection. What is effective is the belief [the police] have in my will to use the means. That's their impression. It is absolute. Therefore I am deadly" (93). The Professor has raised the stakes of such transgressions.

Since walls cannot prevent incursions to private life and its secrets, the means of self-protection become ever more psychological and deadly, entwined about and with the body, rather than containing it. Secrets are not locked up in closets or diaries but in "guilty breasts" (129); padlocked cupboards contain not the answers to an individual's identity but the means to produce mass destruction (89). The only capacious private spaces *per se* in the novel are mental (Heat's thoughts as he speaks to his superior), figurative, or unrepresented (the explosion, Winnie's death). Even these places are "private" only to the degree that they are unknown (Heat) or not put down in words (Stevie's and Winnie's deaths). Because every body contains such secrets and secret identities, everybody is an unwitting or deliberate secret agent, a potential instrument of transgression, even violence. Increasingly, the crimes preoccupying the novelist are not just those directed against the home and its secrets, but also those against the homeland and its institutions. Private plots and information have little to do with domestic affairs; rather, they represent political alliances or secret pacts. Both inadvertent and deliberate overhearing – with their concentration on domestic matters and intimate relations – give way to increasingly organized, politically motivated, and technologically sophisticated eavesdropping on a national and international scale.

Conrad's novel leaves its readers with a pessimistic view of subjectivity, gender, and agency, in contrast to the "optimistic, rosy sheets" of the newspaper providing its readers with reassuring answers or fabricated mysteries that sell. *The Secret Agent* stresses the perils of covert listening and other secret spying, rather than its pleasures. If Proust's narrative accentuates the aesthetic and epistemological payoff for secret listening, unstable though it may be, Conrad's novel is less sanguine and more violent. Implicating us in such acts, *The Secret Agent* refuses to give us facile solutions and instead forces us to make sense of the fragmented narrative before us. It makes us suspicious of all acts of writing and reading, yet, in its disrupted narrative form, the novel compels us to become involved, to piece it together as best we can. Conrad, not Verloc, is the true *"agent provocateur"* of *The Secret Agent*, making us all eavesdroppers on and, hence, secret agents of his narrative (209).[11]

As a distinct departure from nineteenth-century tales, Conrad's novel inaugurates a twentieth-century suspicion of master narratives, of readily identifiable criminals, of safely and securely demarcated spaces and identities. The botched explosion plot, with its numerous willing and unwitting conspirators, looks toward a century in which crimes are collective rather than single events with readily identifiable agents; global terrorist networks, rather than Colonel Mustard, in the library, with the pistol, which the boardgame Clue (or Cluedo) offers us.[12] The Watergate scandal, the failed attempt to bug the Democratic National Committee headquarters, constitutes a defining political moment of the twentieth century. It involved the covert taping of White House conversations, a United States president's participation in the plot, and his deliberate erasure of those secretly recorded dialogues. Exploiting technological innovations in eavesdropping, the Watergate conspiracy reduced Americans' confidence in the federal government as a trustworthy, law-abiding institution. If *The Secret Agent* makes us question the motives of the police as well as criminals, Watergate made us suspicious of the leaders of a nation, the foundation of democratic society, and the laws protecting its citizens and their rights to information about the operation of their government, to individual privacy, and to free expression.

As twentieth- and early twenty-first-century individuals, we experience altered and intensified nineteenth-century attitudes toward issues of privacy, publicity, and the spaces in which human interaction takes place. We are simultaneously more paranoid about incursions into private spaces and their activities, zones that seem less and less secure – as conspiracy theories and critical theories of surveillance suggest – and more willing to expose them. In our era, forms of secret looking and listening have proliferated and increased in sophistication. Technological innovations and new media – film, radio, television, cellular telephones, the internet, spy satellites, wiretapping, computer encryption, "backdoor" government programs to regulate privacy, and "reality" television shows – have made eavesdropping, with its epistemophilic drive, more pervasive in narratives about ourselves and others. Such technologies and information render situated subjectivity more complex. Our locations in space are virtual as well as literal, metaphoric, and ideological, creating psychological positions of greater variety, with access to larger and more diffuse communities of speakers and listeners. Eavesdropping in the twentieth and twenty-first centuries is markedly different from that of the preceding era: we are simultaneously closer to people on the other side of the globe, yet our proximity is virtual rather than physical. Electronic eavesdropping lacks the propinquity of nineteenth-century overhearing. Covert listening becomes impersonal, even bureaucratic. The listening or suspect body, attenuated, can be morphed, constructed, idealized, erased, and forgotten.

Yet we have not stopped eavesdropping. If our fears about others and concerns about private acts and identities are more intense, so is our curiosity about them. Even if we cannot bear to overhear more of a distressing story, and stop listening to it, we cannot totally suppress our inclination to eavesdrop. There will always be other tales that stimulate our urge to know. We return again and again to the nineteenth-century novel, where the configurations of secret listeners, speakers, and spaces may be more readily identifiable and appear in more concentrated form than those of today, but whose concerns bear on our own. Nineteenth-century eavesdropping represents a confluence of narrative form, of concerns about space, gender, and knowledge, and of ideology about public and private activities and selves. If that century's covert listening was more precisely situated and specific about its agenda than our own, it offers a model of what we must attempt on a broader scale. We cannot resign ourselves to be docile subjects, completely under panoptic control. We must overhear actively, reminding ourselves of the high personal and political stakes involved in trying to understand other people and ourselves by gathering together the scraps of ever more complex information and forming them into narratives. As the types and sources of information proliferate, the stories we are set up to hear are increasingly contradictory, imperfect, full of intentional or inadvertent gaps. If our situated listening in specific physical, psychological, and social locations is more complicated, our need to listen is all the more urgent.

Our actual and vicarious overhearing reminds us of the pleasures as well as the dangers of such transgressive activity – of its perils and moral conundrums, but also its possible rewards. Eavesdropping – both inadvertent and deliberate – stages the imperfect process of gaining knowledge about other people and ourselves. Its positioning of a secret listener in a situation of instability reminds us of how we and those around us change through our social interactions. It prompts us to make responsible connections between ourselves and other people. Through our eavesdropping, we shape our world and ourselves.

Notes

INTRODUCTION

1. The critical literature on vision and its relation to forms of knowledge and subjectivity is too vast to cite in full. Film studies and psychoanalysis are only two prominent fields that have relied on visual conceptions to discuss such important issues as subject formation, sexuality, and power. The notion of "the gaze" and Lacan's formulation of the mirror stage offer examples of influential concepts that presume the centrality of vision to human experience and its representation. Some recent work in literary, psychoanalytic, and film theory on this topic includes *Vision in Context: Historical and Contemporary Perspectives on Sight*, ed. Teresa Brennan and Martin Jay (New York and London: Routledge, 1996); Martin Jay, *Downcast Eyes: The Denigration of Vision in Twentieth-Century French Thought* (Berkeley and Los Angeles: University of California Press, 1993); *Visual Culture*, ed. Chris Jenks (London and New York: Routledge, 1995); *Visual Culture: Images and Interpretations*, ed. Norman Bryson, Michael Ann Holly, and Keith Moxey (Hanover and London: Weslyan University Press and University Press of New England, 1994); W. J. T. Mitchell, *Picture Theory: Essays in Verbal and Visual Representation* (Chicago: University of Chicago Press, 1995); Kaja Silverman, *The Threshold of the Visible World* (New York and London: Routledge, 1996). Jay notes how pervasive "the hermeneutic circle of sight" is "as perceptual experience, social practice, and discursive construct" (Jay, *Downcast Eyes*, 587). Such awareness of the centrality of sight to our experience, conception, and articulation of the modern world is not recent. For example, in 1903 Georg Simmel argued that constant bombardment by visual stimuli has changed the modern psyche. See Simmel, "The Metropolis and Mental Life," in *The Sociology of Georg Simmel*, ed., intro., and trans. Kurt H. Wolff (New York: The Free Press, 1964), 410.
2. Recent critical attention to sound in film has begun to produce analyses of eavesdropping in narrative cinema. Contending that overhearing is central to the cinematic experience, Elisabeth Weis incorporates eavesdropping into a psychoanalytic reading of film, particularly in the primal scene. See Weis, "Eavesdropping: an Aural Analogue of Voyeurism?" in *Cinesonic: The World of Sound in Film*, ed. Philip Brophy (Sydney: AFTRS, 1999), 79–107.

In *Overhearing Film Dialogue* (Berkeley: University of California Press, 2000), Sarah Kozloff examines "the double-layered aspect" of dialogue in film, in which utterances are intended for more than one audience (199). Her primary focus, however, is dialogue rather than eavesdropping.
3. Mikhail Bakhtin, "Epic and Novel," in *The Dialogic Imagination: Four Essays*, ed. Michael Holquist, trans. Caryl Emerson and Michael Holquist (Austin: University of Texas Press, 1981), 4, 5. See also Mary Poovey, who suggests that "theater has always haunted the genre of the novel, as its barely acknowledged, but inspirational twin" in "Creative Criticism and the Problem of Objectivity," *Narrative* 8.2 (May 2000): 127. Herbert F. Tucker argues that John Stuart Mill's formulation of poetry's being "overheard" does not adequately account for poetry's theatricality. See "Dramatic Monologue and the Overhearing of Lyric," *Lyric Poetry Beyond New Criticism*, ed. Chaviva Hosek and Patricia Parker (Ithaca and London: Cornell University Press, 1985), 228. In opposing the solitary activity of eavesdropping to theater's collective audience of listeners, the essay does not consider drama's repeated use of eavesdropping scenes.
4. For compelling discussions of the nineteenth-century novel's relationship to theater and theatricality, see Peter Brooks, *The Melodramatic Imagination: Balzac, Henry James, Melodrama, and the Mode of Excess* (New Haven and London: Yale University Press, 1995); and Joseph Litvak, *Caught in the Act: Theatricality in the Nineteenth-Century English Novel* (Berkeley and Los Angeles: University of California Press, 1992). Eavesdropping is melodramatic, according to Peter Brooks's definition of the term: resonant with intensified meaning. A melodramatic moment is a symbolic confrontation; it gestures toward something beyond what it presents. It represents "the effort to make the 'real' and the 'ordinary' and the 'private life' interesting through heightened dramatic utterance and gesture that lay bare the true stakes" (14).
5. Eavesdropping scenes have appeared in the novel since its inception. The early Greek romances (*Daphnis and Chloe, The Aetheopian Story*) contain such episodes, often crucial to the narrative. Miguel de Cervantes's *Don Quixote* (1605–15) and Madame de Lafayette's *La Princesse de Clèves* (1678) – each considered "the first modern novel" in the Western European tradition – present two different models of illicit listening. See Carlos Fuentes, foreword and intro., *Don Quixote de la Mancha*, by Miguel de Cervantes, trans. Tobias Smollett (London: André Deutsch Limited, 1986), xi–xii; and Nancy K. Miller, intro., *The Princess of Clèves*, trans. Walter J. Cobb (New York: New American Library, 1989), vii. In both texts an eavesdropping episode dramatizes the relationship between "reality" and its fictional representation, and the plausibility (*vraisemblance*) of the events that characters learn about in oral and written stories. Both scenes raise questions about human motivation, the nature of private and public information, and the role of covert listening in the transmission or transformation of a story. Lafayette and Cervantes construct two distinct models of eavesdropping: 1) a moment when a conversation is overheard by at least one additional person

(Lafayette); or 2) a situation where those speaking, aware of a covert listener's presence, modify or construct their exchange to feed information to him (Cervantes). In the "Tale of Ill-Advised Curiosity" within *Don Quixote*, two lovers set up an eavesdropping scene to alter the listening husband's understanding of events and cause the cuckold to act in a manner that promotes their own interests.
6. Mikhail Bakhtin, "Forms of Time and of the Chronotope in the Novel," in *The Dialogic Imagination*, 123, 124.
7. As quoted in Ian Watt, *The Rise of the Novel* (Berkeley: University of California Press, 1957), 200.
8. As noted by John Vernon in "Reading, Writing, and Eavesdropping: Some Thoughts on the Nature of Realistic Fiction," *The Kenyon Review* 4.4 (1982): 47.
9. For a discussion of how social, economic, and political formations produced the imbrication of the public world of political and literary debate with the private sphere of domestic relations, see Jürgen Habermas, *The Structural Transformation of the Public Sphere: An Inquiry into a Category of Bourgeois Society*, intro. Thomas McCarthy, trans. Thomas Burger and Frederick Lawrence (Cambridge, MA: MIT Press, 1982); and "The Public Sphere," *New German Critique* 1.3 (Fall 1974): 49–55.
10. Alexander Welsh, *George Eliot and Blackmail* (Cambridge, MA and London: Harvard University Press, 1985), vi.
11. Ibid., 73.
12. Richard Sennett notes how "When everyone has each other under surveillance, sociability decreases, silence being the only form of protection." See Sennett, *The Fall of Public Man: On the Social Psychology of Capitalism* (New York: Vintage Books, 1978), 15.
13. Michelle Perrot, ed. and intro., *From the Fires of Revolution to the Great War*, vol. IV of *A History of Private Life*, general eds. Philippe Ariès and Georges Duby (Cambridge, MA and London: Harvard University Press, 1990), 2.
14. See Karen Chase and Michael Levenson, *The Spectacle of Intimacy: A Public Life for the Victorian Family* (Princeton and Oxford: Princeton University Press, 2000). See also my Chapter 3 for a further discussion of this concept.
15. Habermas, *Structural Transformation*, 55.
16. William Makepeace Thackeray, *Vanity Fair* (1848; Oxford and New York: Oxford University Press, 1983), 591, 590.
17. Ibid., 591.
18. Patricia Meyer Spacks, *Gossip* (Chicago and London: University of Chicago Press, 1986), 228.
19. I am indebted to Peter Brooks and David Quint for calling this text to my attention.
20. For a similar argument about dishonesty, see John Kucich, *The Power of Lies: Transgression in Victorian Fiction* (Ithaca and London: Cornell University Press, 1994), especially 1–38. Brian McCuskey argues that by granting police powers to their servants, the middle classes could manage anxieties

about working-class surveillance and control more serious "professional" intrusions to the middle-class home. See McCuskey, "The Kitchen Police: Servant Surveillance and Middle-Class Transgression," *Victorian Literature and Culture* (2000): 359–75.
21. Psychoanalytic theory terms this human urge to know "epistemophilia." See Peter Brooks, *Body Work: Objects of Desire in Modern Narrative* (Cambridge, MA and London: Harvard University Press, 1993), 5–9.
22. See Walter Benjamin, "The Storyteller," in *Illuminations: Essays and Reflections*, ed. and intro. Hannah Arendt, trans. Harry Zohn (New York: Schocken Books, 1969). Benjamin notes how "the reader of a novel actually does look for human beings from whom he derives 'the meaning of life'" (101).
23. Marcel Proust, *Du côté de chez Swann*, ed. Antoine Compagnon (Paris: Editions Gallimard, 1988), 127. All subsequent references will be to this edition and will be cited parenthetically with the designation *Swann*, followed by the page number. The English translation is from Marcel Proust, *Remembrance of Things Past*, trans. C. K. Scott Moncrieiff and Terence Kilmartin, 3 vols. (London: Chatto and Windus, 1981), here I: 140. All subsequent translations will be from this edition and will be included parenthetically after the French text, followed by the volume and page number.
24. See Spacks, *Gossip*, 228.
25. Eavesdropping stages what Gérard Genette calls "narrative metalepsis" – "the transition from one narrative level to another... by narrating, the act that consists precisely of introducing into one situation, by means of discourse, the knowledge of another situation." Eavesdropping, like metalepsis, reminds us of the "shifting but sacred frontier between two worlds, the world in which one tells, the world of which one tells... The most troubling thing about metalepsis indeed lies in this unacceptable and insistent hypothesis that the extradiegetic is perhaps always diegetic, and that the narrator and his narratees – you and I – perhaps belong to some narrative." See Genette, *Narrative Discourse: An Eassy in Method*, foreword Jonathan Culler, trans. Jane E. Lewin (Ithaca: Cornell University Press, 1980), 234, 236.
26. Simmel, "The Secret Society," in *The Sociology of Georg Simmel*, 346.
27. Jürgen Habermas, *Theory of Communicative Action. Volume One: Reason and the Rationalization of Society*, trans. Thomas McCarthy (London: Heinemann, 1984), 100.
28. Graham McGregor, "Listeners' Comments on Conversation," *Language and Communication* 3.3 (1983): 271–304. McGregor states that the eavesdropper can "'interpret' the verbal behaviour of others, that is, establish a view of his own about the 'meaningfulness' ... of what is going on in some exchange" (302).
29. Graham McGregor, "Eavesdropping and the Analysis of Everyday Verbal Exchange," in *Methods in Dialectology*, ed. and pref. Alan R. Thomas, intro. Martin J. Ball (Clevedon and Philadelphia: Multilingual Matters, 1988), 368.

30. McGregor, "Listeners' Comments," 302.
31. Michel Butor, "The Novel as Research," in *Inventory: Essays by Michel Butor*, ed. and foreword Richard Howard, trans. Gerald Fabian (New York: Simon and Schuster, 1968), 26. See also Jonathan Culler, *Structuralist Poetics: Structuralism, Linguistics, and the Study of Literature* (Ithaca: Cornell University Press, 1975), 238.
32. Roland Barthes characterizes narrative as being the presentation of an enigma and the deliberate postponement of its solution. See Barthes, *S/Z*, pref. Richard Howard, trans. Richard Miller (New York: Hill and Wang, 1974).
33. Such conclusions shift critical attention from gossip to eavesdropping, an activity anterior to gossip that generates many of its relations and concerns. For analyses of the social and discursive functions of gossip, see Spacks, *Gossip*; Jan B. Gordon, *Gossip and Subversion in Nineteenth-Century British Fiction: Echo's Economies* (London: Macmillan; New York: St. Martin's Press, 1996); and Casey Finch and Peter Bowen, "'The Tittle-Tattle of Highbury': Gossip and the Free Indirect Style in *Emma*," *Representations* 31 (1990): 1–18. Occurring prior to gossip, eavesdropping provides concrete information, rather than "rumor," even if overheard information is later revealed to be incomplete. The word "hearsay" indicates the chronology and contagious quality of gossip; the sheer reiteration of a story establishes its authority. Hearsay or rumor presumes an anonymous and unauthorized origin. In contrast, eavesdropping assumes a proximity to a source that lends it authority, yet creates enough of a gap in understanding to initiate storytelling. Both eavesdropping and gossip suggest that to preserve a private identity, an individual must keep it out of language or control the kind of story that others fabricate about him or her.
34. Emily Brontë, *Wuthering Heights*, ed. William M. Sale, Jr., and Richard J. Dunn (1847; New York and London: W. W. Norton, 1990), 62.
35. See, for example, Nancy Armstrong's study of domestic ideology and its reliance on Foucauldian notions of invisible regimes of power in *Desire and Domestic Fiction: A Political History of the Novel* (New York and Oxford: Oxford University Press, 1987). I share Armstrong's belief in our need to consider fiction "as the document and as the agency of cultural history" (23). Although her book reconsiders the role that forgotten texts have in shaping the discourse of domesticity and the formation of middle-class cultural hegemony, it oversimplifies the relation between female writing and middle-class domestic ideology, granting women greater power than some of the individual texts she discusses – such as *Emma* or *Jane Eyre* – would suggest. The story of gender, class, power, and individual subjectivity is more complicated; novels represent models of human interaction in which irresolution and inconsistency become sources of both anxiety and pleasure. Due to its volatility, eavesdropping tends to register subtle fluctuations of power and agency within specific situations. For other Foucauldian readings that temper a discussion of the novel's disciplinary strategies with an

insistence on the pleasures of textuality and individual experience, see John Kucich, *Repression in Victorian Fiction: Charlotte Brontë, George Eliot, and Charles Dickens* (Berkeley and Los Angeles: University of California Press, 1987); and Mary Ann O'Farrell, *Telling Complexions: The Nineteenth-Century English Novel and the Blush* (Durham, NC and London: Duke University Press, 1997). I join both critics in stressing the fluidity of the mechanisms by which we construct and are constructed by the social, ideological, and political worlds we inhabit; my interest lies in those seductive acts of narrative and social transgression that resist disciplinary pressures. Hence I refer to the concept of identity rather than subjectivity in my analysis of eavesdropping, for it suggests a greater degree of agency in the construction of the self than does the Foucauldian term. Novelistic eavesdropping is as much about creating spaces for individual experience as it is about policing them.

36. Lacanian formulations of subjectivity such as Kaja Silverman's are predicated on the notion of loss, but intersect with my argument in emphasizing "the recognition of a distance separating self from other." See Silverman, *The Acoustic Mirror: The Female Voice in Psychoanalysis and Cinema* (Bloomington: Indiana University Press, 1988), 7.

37. *Middlemarch*'s narrator poses a similar question: "Who can know how much of his most inward life is made up of the thoughts he believes other men to have about him, until that fabric of opinion is threatened with ruin?" See George Eliot, *Middlemarch: A Tale of Provincial Life*, ed. Bert G. Hornback (1871–72; New York and London: W. W. Norton, 1977), 475.

38. The linguists Herbert H. Clark and Thomas B. Carlson note that in the set-up eavesdrop, "by designing their utterances just right, speakers can lead overhearers to form" conclusions about what they have heard, since such listeners generally do not "realize how utterances have been designed for them." See Clark and Carlson, "Hearers and Speech Acts," *Language* 58.2 (1982): 344, 345.

39. Walter Benjamin, "Louis-Philippe or the Interior," in *Charles Baudelaire: A Lyric Poet in the Era of High Capitalism*, trans. Harry Zohn (London: New Left Books, 1973), 169, 167.

40. Charles Dickens, *Dombey and Son*, ed. Peter Fairclough, intro. Raymond Williams (1848; Harmondsworth and New York: Penguin, 1986), 423.

41. Not surprisingly, psychoanalysis emerges at the end of the nineteenth century, for the model of analyst–analysand presupposes a secret part of the self that the patient cannot recognize without the help of the sanctioned listener to his or her secret fantasies and fears.

42. Walter J. Ong suggests that invoking the reader represents a nostalgic attempt to reestablish a more intimate and oral/aural relation between writer and his or her increasingly anonymous and unknown public. See Ong, *Orality and Literacy: The Technologizing of the Word* (London and New York: Methuen, 1982), 103. Patrick Brantlinger makes a similar point. Such an invocation tries to allay writers' anxieties about readers' responses, for it produces the illusion of "individual proximity and cooperation." See Brantlinger,

The Reading Lesson: The Threat of Mass Literacy in Nineteenth-Century British Fiction (Bloomington and Indianapolis: Indiana University Press, 1998), 14, 15.
43. See, for example, Susan Snaider Lanser, *Fictions of Authority: Women Writers and Narrative Voice* (Ithaca and London: Cornell University Press, 1992), 92. Lanser reminds us of the persistence of the "speakerly" terms "voice" and "teller" to signify the written (4).
44. Dickens, *Dombey and Son*, 738.
45. Frank Kermode, *The Genesis of Secrecy: On the Interpretation of Narrative* (Cambridge, MA and London: Harvard University Press, 1979), 8.
46. Peter K. Garrett also notes Dickens's association of Asmodeus and narrative omniscience and points out allusions to *Le diable boiteux* in several of his novels. See Garrett, *The Victorian Multiplot Novel: Studies in Dialogical Form* (New Haven and London: Yale University Press, 1980), 33, 34.
47. McCuskey makes a similar point about servants who spy on their employers; such surveillance confers esteem on the lives within its purview. See "The Kitchen Police," 362.
48. Eliot, *Middlemarch*, 432.
49. Michael Levenson, *A Genealogy of Modernism: A Study of English Literary Doctrine 1908–1922* (Cambridge and New York: Cambridge University Press, 1984), 8.
50. See A. J. Greimas, *Structural Semantics: An Attempt at a Method* (Lincoln: University of Nebraska Press, 1983).
51. Gérard Genette, *Figures II* (Paris: Seuil, 1969), 202; and *Narrative Discourse* 228–29.
52. See J. Hillis Miller, *The Form of Victorian Fiction* (Notre Dame and London: University of Notre Dame Press, 1968), 6.
53. Gaston Bachelard's *La poétique de l'espace* helps establish the concept of psychologically dynamic spaces, especially domestic ones (1957; Paris: Quadrige, 1989), especially 58, 77, 85, 102, 127, 130, 132, 154, 183, 191, 201.
54. Elizabeth Grosz notes how "The look is the domain of domination and mastery; it provides access to its object without necessarily being in contact with it." See Grosz, *Jacques Lacan: A Feminist Introduction* (London and New York: Routledge, 1990), 39. Literary examples of voyeurism abound. Henry James's fiction is particularly rich in voyeuristic scenes. For instance, in *The Ambassadors*, Lambert Strether glimpses from afar Chad Newsome and Madame de Vionnet on the river and realizes that they are lovers. See *The Ambassadors*, ed. S. P. Rosenbaum (New York: W. W. Norton, 1964), 307. Kaja Silverman suggests that this is a "belated" primal scene. See Silverman, *Male Subjectivity at the Margins* (New York and London: Routledge, 1992), 162–64. Christian Metz observes that voyeurism always "*concretely represents the absence of its object* in the distance at which it maintains it and which is part of its very definition." See Metz, *The Imaginary Signifier: Psychoanalysis and Cinema*, trans. Celia Britton, Annwyl Williams, Ben Brewster, and Alfred Guzzetti (Baltimore: Johns Hopkins University Press, 1982), 59. See also Silverman,

The Acoustic Mirror, 6. Although both Silverman and Metz mention listening in defining voyeurism, their analyses, like most psychoanalytic theory and film theory, center on looking and the concept of the gaze. Eavesdropping diverges from voyeurism in the greater proximity between listener and overheard conversation, and in the symbolic significance that listening offers for an account of narrative generation and transmission.

55. Bakhtin, "Forms of Time," 246, 248.
56. Michel Foucault, "Of Other Spaces," in *The Visual Culture Reader*, ed. and intro. Nicholas Mirzoeff (London and New York: Routledge, 1998), 239. In Foucault's binary, eavesdropping is "heterotopic," an activity that occurs in the "counter-sites" of culture. More precisely, eavesdropping represents the confluence of utopic and heterotopic sites. Heterotopic in its inversion of "real" space and its activities and in its juxtaposition, in a single place, of several different spaces, overhearing is also utopic in not being limited to a specific site: it is a "sit[e] with no real place" (239).
57. Peter Stallybrass and Allon White, *The Politics and Poetics of Transgression* (Ithaca: Cornell University Press, 1986), 200.
58. Erving Goffman, *Behavior in Public Places: Notes on the Social Organization of Gatherings* (New York: Free Press, 1963), 9, e.m. (emphasis mine).
59. Ibid., 151–52.
60. Donna Haraway, "The Persistence of Vision," in *The Visual Culture Reader*, ed. and intro. Nicholas Mirzoeff (London and New York: Routledge, 1998), 192, 193.
61. Such concepts appear throughout Bakhtin's writings. See Bakhtin, "Forms of Time" and "Discourse in the Novel," in *The Dialogic Imagination*, 84–258, 259–422; "From Notes Made in 1970–1971," in *Speech Genres and Other Late Essays*, trans. Vern W. McGee, ed. Caryl Emerson and Michael Holquist (Austin: University of Texas Press, 1986), 132–58; and *Toward a Philosophy of the Act*, ed. Vadim Liapunov and Michael Holquist, trans. and notes Vadim Liapunov (Austin: University of Texas Press, 1993), especially 72–73.
62. Michael Holquist, *Dialogism: Bakhtin and His World* (London and New York: Routledge, 1991), 12. For Holquist, every utterance "is a border phenomenon" since it "takes place between speakers" (61).
63. See my Chapter 2 for a discussion of how feminist critics use this expression to describe the means by which nineteenth-century women authors subtly challenged conventional expectations of gender.
64. George Levine, *The Realistic Imagination: English Fiction from Frankenstein to Lady Chatterley* (Chicago and London: University of Chicago Press, 1981), 24ff.
65. Peter Brooks, *Reading for the Plot: Design and Intention in Narrative* (New York: Vintage, 1985), 86.
66. See Sharon Marcus, *Apartment Stories: City and Home in Nineteenth-Century Paris and London* (Berkeley: University of California Press, 1999), 1–14, especially 3, and 166–98. Marcus's study offers "critical skepticism about the very hegemony of those oppositions" (7). Her work departs from my own in its

emphasis on the apartment-house (and its plots) and on French material over British.
67. For an analysis of the "privileged relation" between the discourse of sexuality and "our most prized constructs of individual identity, truth, and knowledge," see Eve Kosfsky Sedgwick, *Epistemology of the Closet* (Berkeley and Los Angeles: University of California Press, 1990), 3. Sedgwick's argument diverges from mine in its insistence on the primacy of the "homo/heterosexual definition" in "marking" all binaries in our culture (11). For a good discussion of secrecy and its location in a particular space, see 65.

1 I'M ALL EARS: *PRIDE AND PREJUDICE*

1. "Double understanding [*la double entente*] far exceeds the limited case of the play on words or the equivocation and permeates, in various forms and densities, all classic writing... The reader is an accomplice, not of this or that character, but of the discourse itself insofar as it plays on the division of reception [*l'écoute*], the impurity of communication." Roland Barthes, *S/Z*, pref. Richard Howard, trans. Richard Miller (New York: Hill and Wang, 1974), 145.
2. Emily Brontë, *Wuthering Heights*, ed. William M. Sale, Jr., and Richard J. Dunn (1847; New York and London: W. W. Norton, 1990), 62–64.
3. See Roland Barthes, *S/Z*. Barthes identifies the "hermeneutic code... whose function it is to articulate in various ways a question, its response, and the variety of chance events which can either formulate the question or delay the answer; or even, constitute an enigma and lead to its solution" (17). He notes how "an enigma leads from a question to an answer, *through a certain number of delays*" (32). The enigmas of *Pride and Prejudice* are not only how will misunderstanding be overcome, but also what conjugal pairings will allow for reconciliation and resolution.
4. D. A. Miller, *Narrative and Its Discontents: Problems of Closure in the Traditional Novel* (Princeton: Princeton University Press, 1981), ix. Miller's theory of narrative has influenced my discussion of eavesdropping. However, his progression from writers who force novelistic closure to those who advocate a "release from the tyranny of narrative control" positions Austen as a conservative author who "disapproves of" the narratable, rather than as a writer who, while signaling the limitations of narrative conventions, continues to use them (xii, xv, xiv). Austen's novels present a critique of the potentially anarchistic "narratable," rather than an imperious suppression of it.
5. We can consider eavesdropping a "narratable element" because of its capacity "to generate a story." See Miller, *Narrative and its Discontents*, 5.
6. Barthes's discussion of enigma also examines the intended double audience of such narrative devices. Narrative "snares" entrap both readers and characters (31, 32, for the reader, and throughout *S/Z* for the characters Sarrasine and Mme de Rochefide – the internal recipient of the narrator's tale).

7. Miller, *Narrative and its Discontents*, 50.
8. Graham McGregor, "Listeners' Comments on Conversation," *Language and Communication* 3.3 (1983): 271–304. McGregor asserts that the eavesdropper has "the ability to 'interpret' the verbal behaviour of others" (302).
9. McGregor, "Eavesdropping and the Analysis of Everyday Verbal Exchange," in *Methods in Dialectology*, ed. and pref. Alan R. Thomas, intro. Martin J. Ball (Clevedon and Philadelphia: Multilingual Matters, 1988), 368.
10. McGregor, "Listeners' Comments," 302.
11. Charlotte Brontë, as quoted in B. C. Southam, ed. *Jane Austen: The Critical Heritage, 1870–1940*, vol. II (London and New York: Routledge and Kegan Paul, 1987), 205. Similarly, Edith Wharton asserts in *The Writing of Fiction* (1925) that "Jane Austen has given the norm, the ideal" of "novels preeminently of character, and in which situation, dramatically viewed, is reduced to the minimum." See Southam, *The Critical Heritage*, vol. II, 284.
12. Reginald Farrer, "Jane Austen, *ob.* July 18, 1817," in Southam, *The Critical Heritage*, vol. II, 259, 262.
13. D. W. Harding, ed. and intro., *Persuasion* by Jane Austen (London and New York: Penguin, 1985), 15. Harding observes, without elaborating, that eavesdropping is inevitable in a society where privacy is rare.
14. *Emma* is the only Austen novel that does not contain some form of eavesdropping as an integral part of its narrative structure or thematic concerns. Emma is so adept at creating misunderstandings and at fabricating "riddles" to be solved that eavesdropping is unnecessary as a generator of plot. See Jane Austen, *Emma* (1816; New York and London: W. W. Norton, 1972), 193. *Emma* displaces onto its heroine the structural and dramatic conditions that create situations of "narratability."
15. Barthes, *S/Z*, 145.
16. Tony Tanner, *Jane Austen*, (London: Macmillan, 1986), 9, 36. Tanner's argument and mine converge in our discussion of communication in Austen's work but differ significantly in their conclusions. See my Chapter 2.
17. Austen's texts grapple with concerns of politics, gender, and class obliquely, through what Claudia Johnson calls "various means of indirection." See Johnson, *Jane Austen: Women, Politics, and the Novel* (Chicago and London: University of Chicago Press, 1988), xxiv.
18. See A. Walton Litz, *Jane Austen: A Study of Her Artistic Development* (New York: Oxford University Press, 1965), 100; R. W. Chapman, "*Pride and Prejudice* and *Cecilia*," in *The Novels of Jane Austen*, ed. R. W. Chapman, 3rd edn., vol. II (Oxford and New York: Oxford University Press, 1923; rptd. 1965), 408–9; Tanner, *Jane Austen*, 107–8; Marilyn Butler, *Jane Austen and the War of Ideas* (Oxford: Oxford University Press, 1975), 199, 212–13; and Kenneth Moler, *Jane Austen's Art of Allusion* (Lincoln: University of Nebraska Press, 1968). Mark M. Hennelly, Jr. notes in passing *Evelina*'s probable influence on the novel's plot; see "*Pride and Prejudice*: The Eyes Have It," in *Jane Austen: New Perspectives*, ed. and intro. Janet Todd, Women and Literature, n.s., 3 (New York and London: Holmes and Meier, 1983), 193.

19. Moler terms Darcy's remarks about Elizabeth a "parody of Lord Orville's unfavorable first impression of Evelina," but does not stress that both episodes are based on overhearing. See *Jane Austen's Art of Allusion*, 90.
20. Frances Burney, *Evelina* (1778; Oxford and New York: Oxford University Press, 1990), 35, 36. All subsequent references will be to this edition.
21. Jane Austen, *Pride and Prejudice* (1813; London and New York: Penguin, 1972), 69. All subsequent references will be to this edition.
22. See Franco Moretti's discussion of *Pride and Prejudice* as a *Bildungsroman* in *The Way of the World: The* Bildungsroman *in European Culture* (London: Verso, 1987), especially Chapter 1.
23. Tanner analyzes the association between the words "property" and "propriety" in Austen, noting how "the ideal marriage at the end of a Jane Austen novel... offers itself as an emblem of the ideal union of property and propriety... on which the future of her society depends" (19). He asserts that "the ultimate propriety on which all other proprieties depended was true propriety of language" (20). Hence a transgression of conversational proprieties is a serious offence indeed.
24. Moretti, *The Way of the World*, 60.
25. Barthes, *S/Z*, 32, 38.
26. Bakhtin, *The Dialogic Imagination: Four Essays*, ed. Michael Holquist, trans. Caryl Emerson and Michael Holquist (Austin: University of Texas Press, 1981), 338. Noting the prevalence of gossip in everyday life, Bakhtin describes how "people talk most of all about what others talk about – they transmit, recall, weigh and pass judgment on other people's words, opinions, assertions, information... Reflect how enormous is the weight of 'everyone says' and 'it is said' in public opinion, public rumor, gossip, slander, and so forth."
27. In *Mansfield Park*, Edmund asks Fanny to evaluate Mary Crawford through her conversation; both cousins conclude that there is something morally "not quite right" about this attractive, playful Londoner. See Jane Austen, *Mansfield Park* (1814; London: Penguin, 1985), 94. That Mary considers Henry's seduction of a married woman as mere "folly" provokes Edmund's recognition that between the two of them, nothing could "be understood" (441).
28. See, for example, Tanner, *Jane Austen*, 25, 41; Ian Watt, "Introduction," in *Jane Austen: A Collection of Critical Essays* (Englewood Cliffs: Prentice-Hall, 1963); and Lloyd W. Brown, *Bits of Ivory: Narrative Techniques in Jane Austen's Fiction* (Baton Rouge: Louisiana State University Press, 1973), especially Chapters 5 and 7.
29. Bakhtin, *The Dialogic Imagination*, 353.
30. Several critics focus on visual rather than aural means of perception in *Pride and Prejudice* and emphasize the metaphoric import of words such as "insight" or "observation." See Hennelly, "The Eyes Have It," 187–207; Lesley H. Willis, "Eyes and the Imagery of Sight in *Pride and Prejudice*," *English Studies in Canada* 2 (1976): 156–62. In her introduction to *Jane Austen: New Perspectives*, Janet Todd notes how "looking" is "much the subject of these essays" (8).

31. See also Willis, "Eyes and the Imagery of Sight," 159.
32. Moretti, *The Way of the World*, 57. He also notes the second "semantic field" that the word "prejudice" evokes: "partisanship, partiality." This second meaning characterizes Elizabeth's initial willingness to listen to Wickham's story, which confirms her good opinion of him and her disparaging one of Darcy.
33. David Monaghan identifies the initial antagonism between Darcy and Elizabeth as one of social class: "Elizabeth's view of Darcy is obscured by the middle-class prejudice that all aristocrats are snobs, and he is blinded by the aristocratic conviction that to be middle-class is to be automatically vulgar." See Monaghan, "The Complexity of Jane Austen's Novels," in Todd, *Jane Austen: New Perspectives*, 90.
34. John Milton, "Doctrine and Discipline of Divorce," in *John Milton: Complete Poems and Major Prose*, ed. Merritt Y. Hughes (New York: Odyssey Press, 1957), 707.
35. Stanley Cavell, *Pursuits of Happiness: The Hollywood Comedy of Remarriage* (Cambridge, MA: Harvard University Press, 1981), 87. For all the meanings of "conversation," see *The Compact Edition of the Oxford English Dictionary*, 2 vols. (Oxford: Oxford University Press, 1984) 1: 545–46.
36. Lawrence Stone, *The Road to Divorce: England 1530–1987* (Oxford: Oxford University Press, 1990), 233. Stone states that the number of suits brought for "crim. con." reached its height during the years 1790–1829 (255).
37. See Stone, *Divorce*, 7, 13, 30.
38. The *Oxford English Dictionary* states that the term "eavesdrop" is "chiefly used with reference to the ancient custom or law which prohibited a proprietor from building at a less distance than two feet from the boundary of the land, lest he should injure his neighbor's land by 'eavesdrop'". See *OED*, 1: 829.
39. *OED* 1: 545. Samuel Johnson's 1755 *Dictionary of the English Language* (New York: Arno Press, 1979 reprint), n.p., defines "conversation" as "commerce; intercourse; familiarity" or "behaviour; manner of acting in common life" It defines "to converse" as "to cohabit with; to hold intercourse with; to be a companion to." All of these definitions imply a broader and more sustained interaction of individuals than does the modern meaning.
40. In this, my discussion of the word "conversation" approaches Bakhtin's notion of "dialogue," which stresses the very particularity and situatedness of individuals that becomes part of the activity or process of communication. See, for example, Bakhtin, *Speech Genres and Other Late Essays*, ed. Caryl Emerson and Michael Holquist, trans. Vern W. McGee. (Austin: University of Texas Press, 1986), 143–44, 148.
41. Cavell, *Pursuits of Happiness*, 87.
42. Anonymous reviewer, *The North British Review* lii (April 1870): 129–52, as quoted in Lionel Trilling, *Sincerity and Authenticity* (Cambridge, MA: Harvard University Press, 1972), 81.
43. Barthes, *S/Z*, 132. See also 145, 149, 151, 160.

44. Austen extends the story of privacy beyond the conclusion of the novel. After describing her visit to an exhibition of fictional portraits that included one of Jane but not of Elizabeth, Austen concludes, "I can only imagine that Mr. D. prizes any Picture of her too much to like it should be exposed to the public eye. – I can imagine he wd have that sort of feeling – that mixture of Love, Pride & Delicacy." See Austen to Cassandra Austen, 24 May 1813, *Jane Austen's Letters to Her Sister Cassandra and Others*, vol. II: 1811–1817, coll. and ed. R. W. Chapman (Oxford: Clarendon Press, 1932), 312.
45. Tanner, *Jane Austen*, 207.
46. *Emma*, 297.
47. See also Tanner, *Jane Austen*, 211, 212.

2 EAVESDROPPING AND THE GENTLE ART OF *PERSUASION*

1. Jane Austen, to Cassandra, 4 February, 1813. See *Letters to Her Sister Cassandra and Others*, vol. II: 1811–17, ed. R. W. Chapman (Oxford: Clarendon Press, 1932), 299.
2. Park Honan assesses the role of "happiness" in Austen's *Weltanschauung* as a "growth of awareness" or "a spiritual pursuit with rewards." See *Jane Austen: Her Life* (London: Weidenfeld and Nicolson, 1987), 253.
3. Barthes, *S/Z*, pref. Richard Howard, trans. Richard Miller (New York: Hill and Wang, 1974), 75.
4. Walter Benjamin, "The Storyteller," in *Illuminations: Essays and Reflections*, ed. and intro. Hannah Arendt, trans. Harry Zohn (New York: Schocken Books, 1969), 92.
5. Many critics mention that the scene involves overhearing, but do not dwell on its implications. See Richard Whately's unsigned review of *Northanger Abbey* and *Persuasion* in the *Quarterly Review* 24 (January 1821), rptd. in B. C. Southam, ed., *Jane Austen: The Critical Heritage*, vol. I (London: Routledge and Kegan Paul; New York: Barnes and Noble, 1968), 103; Richard Simpson's unsigned review of *A Memoir of Jane Austen* by her nephew in *The North British Review* 52 (April 1870), 129–52, rptd. in Southam, 241–265, especially 256. D. W. Harding acknowledges the importance of "overhearing" in Austen's novels but only comments that it creates "the sense of compressed social milieu" in which privacy is a luxury. See Harding "Introduction," *Persuasion*, by Jane Austen (1818; London and New York: Penguin, 1985), 15. Frank O'Connor notes in passing how "Almost everything in this...book is overheard." See "Jane Austen: The Flight from Fancy," in *Discussions of Jane Austen*, ed. and intro. William Heath (Boston: D. C. Heath and Co., 1961), 74. Marylea Meyersohn refers to *Persuasion* as "a novel as much about overhearing as about hearing" in the final sentence of "Jane Austen's Garrulous Speakers: Social Criticism in *Sense and Sensibility, Emma,* and *Persuasion,*" in *Reading and Writing Women's Lives: A Study of the*

Novel of Manners, ed. Bege K. Bowers and Barbara Brothers (Ann Arbor and London: UMI Research Press, 1990), 47.

6. Barbara Hardy, *A Reading of Jane Austen* (London: Peter Owen, 1975), 96; and Stuart Tave, *Some Words of Jane Austen* (Chicago and London: University of Chicago Press, 1973), 264.
7. Tony Tanner, *Jane Austen* (Cambridge, MA: Harvard University Press, 1986), 209. Tanner's general observations about communication, gender, and narrative in *Persuasion* are similar to mine. However, he does not consider eavesdropping's centrality in representing the difficulty of communication and women's agency. Although Tanner, like Hugh Hennedy, notes "the indirect mode of communication" in the last eavesdropping scene, he says little about mediation in Anne's and Wentworth's communication until then. See Tanner, *Jane Austen*, 215; and Hugh L. Hennedy, "Acts of Perception in Jane Austen's Novels," *Studies in the Novel* 5 (1973): 35.
8. Tave notes how Anne continually "stand[s] between opposed forces" but he focuses on the moral implications of this position. See Tave, *Some Words of Jane Austen*, 274.
9. Hennedy, "Acts of Perception," 24. See also Hardy, *A Reading of Jane Austen*, 67, 96.
10. Tave, *Some Words of Jane Austen*, 256. Karen Newman makes a similar point in "Can This Marriage Be Saved? Jane Austen Makes Sense of an Ending," *ELH* 50.4 (1983): 707.
11. Jane Austen, *Emma* (1816; New York and London: W. W. Norton, 1972), 228.
12. Meyersohn's description of Fanny could also apply to Anne: she calls Fanny "the moral presence who watches and listens, especially listens." See "What Fanny Knew: 'A Quiet Auditor of the Whole,'" in *Jane Austen: New Perspectives*, ed. and intro. Janet Todd, Women and Literature, n. s., 3 (New York and London: Holmes and Meier, 1983), 225.
13. Jane Austen, *Persuasion* (1818; New York: Signet Classic, 1980), 48. All subsequent references will be to this edition.
14. Hardy, *A Reading of Jane Austen*, 67. Alistair M. Duckworth notes how Anne substitutes quiet helpfulness for the verbal power she lacks. See *The Improvement of the Estate: A Study of Jane Austen's Novels* (Baltimore and London: Johns Hopkins University Press, 1971), 188, 197. Tave contrasts Anne's quiet activity with the rest of her family's inaction. See Tave, *Some Words of Jane Austen*, 284–85.
15. She "long[s] for the power of representing to them all what they were about, and of pointing out some of the evils they were exposing themselves to" (80).
16. For a discussion of the novel's narrative technique, see Michael Orange, "Aspects of Narration in *Persuasion*," *Sydney Studies in English* 15 (1989–90): 63–71.
17. Often our understanding of Anne comes from reported dialogue or free indirect discourse. Susan Snaider Lanser analyzes how *Persuasion* continues eighteenth-century women writers' use of free indirect discourse "to

authorize intelligent and morally superior woman [*sic*] as critics and interpreters of their society," and extends that purpose "to authorize not characters but the narrator herself." See Susan Snaider Lanser, *Fictions of Authority: Women Writers and Narrative Voice* (Ithaca and London: Cornell University Press, 1992), 74.
18. See Mary Poovey, *The Proper Lady and the Woman Writer: Ideology as Style in the Works of Mary Wollstonecraft, Mary Shelley, and Jane Austen* (Chicago and London: University of Chicago Press, 1984), 28; Claudia Johnson, *Jane Austen: Women, Politics, and the Novel* (Chicago and London: University of Chicago Press, 1988), xxiv; and Janis P. Stout, *Strategies of Reticence: Silence and Meaning in the Works of Jane Austen, Willa Cather, Katherine Anne Porter, and Joan Didion* (Charlottesville and London: University Press of Virginia, 1990), viii–ix. Lanser notes how forms of indirection (free indirect discourse, irony, ellipsis, euphemism, and ambiguity) are characteristic of Austen's style. See Lanser, *Fictions of Authority*, 62. For an analysis of the formal differences in gendered rhetoric, see Thomas J. Farrell's "The Female and Male Modes of Rhetoric," *College English* 40.8 (1979): 909–21. Farrell considers the masculine mode of rhetoric as controlled, filled with "strong, implicit assertions" and "assertive antagonism" (915, 917); he categorizes as feminine a mode of rhetoric that avoids "unnecessary antagonism," and is characterized by "indirection" (916, 909). Anne's and her creator's linguistic strategies typify the latter mode.
19. "He meant to avoid hearing her thanks, and rather sought to testify that her conversation was the last of his wants" (79). Even in his return to the sea, Wentworth associates curtailed speech with separation from Anne, so that he commands the ship *Laconia*. In the novel's second half, Austen replaces this disinclination to listen to Anne with a desire to hear and speak directly to her.
20. Lloyd W. Brown notes how Austen's dialogue often "dramatizes all the psychological and moral barriers to meaningful human relationships," See Brown, *Bits of Ivory: Narrative Technique in Jane Austen's Fiction* (Baton Rouge: Louisiana State University Press, 1973), 169. Tave discusses the former lovers' physical proximity and separation primarily in terms of Wentworth's character. See Tave, *Some Words of Jane Austen*, 262.
21. See Earl Miner's discussion of the reader's additional "object of attention" in *Comparative Poetics: An Intercultural Essay on Theories of Literature* (Princeton: Princeton University Press, 1990), 193–94.
22. Mary Poovey, "*Persuasion* and the Promises of Love," in *The Representation of Women in Fiction*, ed. and intro. Carolyn G. Heilbrun and Margaret R. Higonnet, Selected Papers from the English Institute, 1981, n.s., 7 (Baltimore: Johns Hopkins University Press, 1983), 167; also *The Proper Lady*, 232. Poovey discusses how Wentworth's having to wait for Louisa to release him from their tacit engagement places him in the position usually occupied by women. However, as Poovey notes, a great difference exists between the Captain's temporary passivity and his general mobility: he could still leave

Lyme at will, whereas a woman, dependent upon others for transportation and accompaniment, could not.
23. Mary Lascelles criticizes this scene as "an oversight," because of its failure to present Anne's perspective and hence maintain "a consistent point of view." See Lascelles, *Jane Austen and Her Art* (Oxford: Clarendon Press, 1939), 205, 204. However, Austen's deviation from Anne's point of view in fact serves to stress the repositioning of listeners that occurs in the novel's second half.
24. For a discussion of this "difficulty" in Austen, see, among others, A. Walton Litz, *Jane Austen: A Study of Her Artistic Development* (New York: Oxford University Press, 1965), 159; and Tanner, *Jane Austen*, 41.
25. Marvin Mudrick also notes this inconsistency. See Mudrick, *Jane Austen: Irony as Defense and Discovery* (Princeton: Princeton University Press, 1952), 217.
26. Jane Austen, *The Manuscript Chapters of* Persuasion, ed. R. W. Chapman (London: Oxford University Press, 1926; rptd. London and Dover, NH: Athlone Press, 1985), 9. All subsequent references will be to this edition.
27. Harding also notes Anne's passivity and compares her to Fanny in *Mansfield Park*. See Harding, "Introduction," 11. He characterizes both heroines as being "involved with [other people] (as spectator or overhearer) but left out of account by them" (15). Tave notes the parallel between the original ending and the scene at the hedgerow, as well as this ending's failure to present Anne speaking. See Tave, *Some Words of Jane Austen*, 265, 266.
28. "It was a silent, but a very powerful Dialogue; – on his side, Supplication, on her's [*sic*] acceptance. – Still, a little nearer – and a hand taken and pressed – and 'Anne, my own dear Anne!' – bursting forth in the fullness of exquisite feeling... – They were re-united. They were restored to all that had been lost" (16).
29. Janice Bowman Swanson discusses how the revisions develop Anne's "voice." See "Toward a Rhetoric of Self: The Art of *Persuasion*," *Nineteenth-Century Fiction* 36.1 (1981): 15, 19.
30. See Tanner, *Jane Austen*, 236.
31. Hennedy perceives the symbolic significance of setting this attempt at a concert, a performance of the harmony of voices or instruments. See Hennedy, "Acts of Perception," 38. Austen also compares social and musical concord in *Mansfield Park*, where music "helped conceal the want of real harmony" (207).
32. Harding notes how Anne plays an "active part in bringing her lover back." See Harding, "Introduction," 11. The revisions to the novel also include a new Chapter 10, which rehearses Anne's speech to a third person (in order to address Wentworth) that occurs in the final eavesdropping scene. See *Persuasion*, 213.
33. Several critics note this role reversal. See Hennedy, "Acts of Perception," 36; Hardy, *A Reading of Jane Austen*, 96; Poovey, "Promises of Love," 167; and Stout, *Strategies of Reticence*, 12.

34. Poovey, *The Proper Lady*, 232.
35. Anne's invalid friend Mrs. Smith is a rare exception. Despite her forced physical inactivity, she finds two outlets: her "work" provides her with an income; and she relates the tale of her misfortunes, so that, even if no one rectifies Mr. Elliot's mistreatment of her, she has "at least the comfort of telling the whole story her own way" (200).
36. Sandra Gilbert and Sandra Gubar were among the first critics to note the symbolic importance of Wentworth's dropping his pen. See *The Madwoman in the Attic: The Woman Writer and the Nineteenth-Century Literary Imagination* (New Haven and London: Yale University Press, 1984), 179.
37. Even their discussion inverts the conventional assumption that men are better at generalities than women, who supposedly stick to the specific and personal. In her exchange with Captain Harville, Anne bases her argument upon general statements, whereas his emotional rebuttals continually refer to personal experience. Howard S. Babb notes the difference in their rhetoric but does not relate it to issues of gender. See *Jane Austen's Novels: The Fabric of Dialogue* (Columbus: Ohio State University Press, 1962), 228, 230.
38. Stout asserts that in Austen, "much of the deepest feeling is conveyed... by what is omitted." See Stout, *Strategies of Reticence*, 57. See also Alice Chandler, "'A Pair of Fine Eyes': Jane Austen's Treatment of Sex," *Studies in the Novel* 7 (1985): 88–103, especially 100; Tave, *Some Words of Jane Austen*, 275; and James Thompson, "Jane Austen and the Limits of Language," *Journal of English and Germanic Philology* 85.4 (1986): 510–31.
39. For example, Marilyn Butler, *Jane Austen and the War of Ideas* (Oxford: Oxford University Press, 1975); and David Monaghan, "The Complexity of Jane Austen's Novels," 88–97, in Todd, *Jane Austen: New Perspectives*, especially 90.
40. Margaret Kirkham, "Feminist Irony and the Priceless Heroine of *Mansfield Park*," 231–47, in Todd, *Jane Austen: New Perspectives*, although she resists making the novel into "a piece of feminist propaganda" (246); and Julia Prewitt Brown, *Jane Austen's Novels: Social Change and Literary Form* (Cambridge, MA and London: Harvard University Press, 1979), 154.
41. For balanced discussions of Austen's gender politics, see Newman, "Can This Marriage Be Saved?," 706; Hardy, *A Reading of Jane Austen*, 133; Johnson, *Women, Politics, and the Novel*, especially 163–66; and Deborah Kaplan, *Jane Austen Among Women* (Baltimore and London: Johns Hopkins University Press, 1992).
42. Immediately before the climactic eavesdropping scene, Anne and Captain Wentworth overhear Mrs. Croft and Mrs. Musgrove's conversation about the inadvisability of a long engagement (219–22); the episode concludes with the lovers' gazing at each other.
43. Austen also retains the portion of the original Chapter 10 that contains direct dialogue between Anne and Wentworth. Compare 22 in the first draft with 231 in the final version.
44. See Duckworth's different formulation of this rejection as a "physical emblem of a cultural heritage" that her earlier novels maintained. See

Duckworth, *The Improvement of the Estate*, 184. In *Persuasion* cultural values reside in individuals, not places.

45. Stanley Cavell, *Pursuits of Happiness: The Hollywood Comedy of Remarriage* (Cambridge, MA and London: Harvard University Press, 1981), 208.
46. The German word *heimlich*, adjectival form of *Heim*, from which our word "home" derives, means "secret, private," but also "snug, cozy."
47. The symbolism of this substitution is obvious: Wentworth replaces Charles in escorting Anne home, just as Wentworth supplants Charles as Anne's suitor.
48. For a contrasting reading of the relation between public and private in Austen's fiction, see Duckworth, *The Improvement of the Estate*, 201.
49. Poovey identifies "the gradual emergence of the private plot into the public sphere and its eventual triumph" (*The Proper Lady*, 228). See also Hardy, *A Reading of Jane Austen*, 67, 69; Poovey, "Promises of Love," 162; and Poovey, *The Proper Lady*, 228–29.
50. Prewitt Brown, *Jane Austen's Novels*, 20. Poovey asserts that "women of the landed gentry and professional classes... envision the defense of their class in terms of individual moral efforts," although she determines that "the fairytale quality of her novels' conclusions suggest that Austen senses... the futility of this 'solution'" (*The Proper Lady*, 28).
51. See Raymond Williams, *The Country and the City* (New York: Oxford University Press, 1973), 166. For a discussion of the distinction between public and private spheres, see Jürgen Habermas, "The Public Sphere," *New German Critique* 1.3 (Fall 1974): 49–55.
52. We might thus consider Anne and Wentworth's story as a "comed[y] of remarriage." See Cavell, *Pursuits of Happiness*, 217.
53. See Monaghan's discussion of the difference between the ideal, individual moment and the imperfect, "realistic" norm in Austen's fiction in "The Complexity of Jane Austen's Novels," 93.
54. Tanner, *Jane Austen*, 42.
55. See *Pride and Prejudice*, 381; and *Emma*, 241.
56. Gilbert and Gubar, *The Madwoman in the Attic*, 166. Louisa's lack of verbal and physical self-control leads to her fall on the Cobb, whereas Anne's firmness in crisis proves the value of her blend of strength and reticence. For a discussion of the "abuse of linguistic power," see Meyersohn, "Jane Austen's Garrulous Speakers," 36.
57. *Pride and Prejudice* (1813), *Mansfield Park* (1814), *Emma* (1816), and *Persuasion* (1818). Even *Sense and Sensibility* (1811) demonstrates Austen's concern with female expression and with balancing two extremes that, singly, create misunderstanding and unhappiness.
58. For a reading favoring openness over reserve, see David Monaghan, *Jane Austen: Structure and Social Vision* (London and Basingstoke: Macmillan, 1980), 145.
59. Stout, *Strategies of Reticence*, 28.

60. I hardly support Arnold Kettle's and H. W. Garrod's readings of Austen as artistically limited. See Kettle, "*Emma*," in Heath, *Discussions of Jane Austen*, 104–13; and Garrod, "Jane Austen: A Depreciation," in Heath, *Discussions*, 32–40. Rather, her texts display an awareness of the restrictions under which she wrote and lived. For different arguments that refute Kettle's and Garrod's perspective, see, among others, Donald Greene, "The Myth of Limitation," in *Jane Austen Today*, ed. Joel Weinsheimer (Athens, GA: University of Georgia Press, 1975), 142–75; and Babb, *Jane Austen's Novels*, Chapter 1.
61. Mikhail Bakhtin discusses "situatedness" as the condition in which every utterance is located in a specific space/time and involves interlocutors who engage in multiple discourses. See *The Dialogic Imagination: Four Essays*, ed. Michael Holquist, trans. Caryl Emerson and Michael Holquist (Austin: University of Texas Press, 1981), 84–258, 259–422; *Speech Genres and Other Late Essays*, ed. Caryl Emerson and Michael Holquist, trans. Vern W. McGee (Austin: University of Texas Press, 1986), 132–58; and *Toward a Philosophy of the Act*, ed. Vadim Liapunov and Michael Holquist, trans. and notes Vadim Liapunov (Austin: University of Texas Press, 1993), especially 72–73.
62. See Gilbert and Gubar, *The Madwoman in the Attic*, especially 109, 121, 144. They stress Austen's "ambivalent" attitude toward "the confinement of the female writer" and "the power of patriarchy" (121).
63. See Newman, "Can This Marriage Be Saved?," 705.
64. See Tave's discussion of spatio-temporal limitation in Austen in Tave, *Some Words of Jane Austen*, especially 6–13.
65. Joyce Quiring Erickson, "Public and Private in Jane Austen's Novels," *Midwest Quarterly: A Journal of Contemporary Thought* 25.2 (1984): 205–6. In contrast, Poovey reads in Austen an attempt to separate public and private spheres (*The Proper Lady*, 236–40; and "*Persuasion* and the Promises of Love," 172–77).
66. Erickson, "Public and Private," 216.
67. See Francis R. Hart, "The Spaces of Privacy: Jane Austen," *Nineteenth-Century Fiction* 30 (1975): 305–33, especially 308. Hardy speaks of Austen's "fusion of private and public worlds" in *A Reading of Jane Austen*, 15.
68. Williams, *The Country and the City*, 166.

3 HOUSEHOLD WORDS: BALZAC'S AND DICKENS'S DOMESTIC SPACES

1. Guadet: "A turn of the key or a push of the bolt, and the intimate life of the family ought to be impregnable in its fortress: the bedroom and its adjoining rooms." Translations, unless otherwise noted, are my own. Balzac, *La Fausse Maîtresse*: "Architecture is the expression of mores." Balzac, *Le Cousin Pons*: "In Paris the very paving-stones have ears, and doorways have tongues, the window-bars have eyes: there is no greater danger than gossiping at front entrances. The tail-end of a conversation, like the postscript of a letter, may

be as dangerously indiscreet both for those who let themselves be overheard as for those who overhear it." Herbert J. Hunt, trans., *Cousin Pons*, by Honoré de Balzac (London: The Folio Society, 1984), 100–1. All subsequent translations will be from this edition and will be included parenthetically after the French text, followed by the relevant page number.

2. Michelle Perrot, ed. and intro., *From the Fires of Revolution to the Great War*, vol. IV of *A History of Private Life*, general eds. Philippe Ariès and Georges Duby (Cambridge, MA: and London: Harvard University Press, 1990), 2.

3. See Jürgen Habermas, "The Public Sphere," *New German Critique* 1.3 (Fall 1974): 49–55; and Richard Sennett, *The Fall of Public Man: On the Social Psychology of Capitalism* (New York: Vintage Books, 1978). For a discussion of the development of the ideology of separate spheres in France and its roots in industrialization and the Revolution, see Lynn Hunt, "The Unstable Boundaries of the French Revolution," in Perrot, *Fires of Revolution*, especially 44–45. Catherine Hall analyzes the emergence of domestic ideology in nineteenth-century England and France in "The Sweet Delights of Home," in Perrot, *Fires of Revolution*, 47–97.

4. For diverse approaches to the history and ideology of the concept of "home," see *Home: A Place in the World*, ed. Arien Mack (New York and London: New York University Press, 1993). For an account of the evolving meaning of "comfort" from "to strengthen or console" to physical and mental well-being, see Witold Rybczynski, *Home: A Short History of an Idea* (New York and London: Penguin, 1987), 19–22. The *Oxford English Dictionary* dates this second meaning to the late eighteenth century. It defines the first occurrence of comfort, from Wordsworth's *Excursion*, as "a state of physical and material well-being, with freedom from pain and trouble, and satisfaction of bodily needs; the condition of being comfortable." The first use of "comfortable" as meaning "in a state of tranquil enjoyment and content; free from pain and trouble; at ease" occurs in Walpole's letter to G. Montague of 1 July 1770. See *The Compact OED*, vol. I (Oxford: Oxford University Press, 1971), 476. Although the word comfort is of Old French origin, it acquired this modern meaning in England, and was reimported to France at the end of the eighteenth century (Rybczynski, *Home*, 121).

5. John Ruskin, *Sesame and Lilies* (1865; London: Merrill and Baker, 1888), 102.

6. Henri Lefebvre, *The Production of Space*, trans. Donald Nicholson-Smith (Cambridge, MA and Oxford: Blackwell, 1991), 27, 42.

7. Karen Chase and Michael Levenson, *The Spectacle of Intimacy: A Public Life for the Victorian Family* (Princeton and Oxford: Princeton University Press, 2000), 143.

8. Raymond Williams, *The English Novel from Dickens to Lawrence* (London: Chatto and Windus, 1970), 34; and Honoré de Balzac, *La Cousine Bette* (1846; Paris: Garnier-Flammarion, 1977), 203, 425. All subsequent references will be to this edition.

9. Chase and Levenson, *The Spectacle of Intimacy*, 13.

10. Tim Farrant notes how it is impossible to speak of the latent or private in Balzac without referring to its opposite, the obvious or public. See "Le Privé: Espace menacé? Des premières 'Scènes de la vie privée' aux 'Secrets de la Princesse de Cadignan,'" *L'Année balzacienne* 15 (1994): 121.
11. See Chase and Levenson, *The Spectacle of Intimacy*, especially, 143–78. As Jean-Pierre Richard observes, "L'indiscretion suprême, n'est-ce-pas finalement le fait même de raconter, d'écrire?... Toute narration peut presque apparaître comme la trahison expressive du narré, comme sa mise au jour." See Richard, *Etudes sur le romantisme* (Paris: Editions du Seuil, 1971), 97.
12. Christopher Prendergast, "Introduction: Realism, God's Secret, and the Body," in *Spectacles of Realism: Body, Gender, and Genre*, eds. Margaret Cohen and Christopher Prendergast (Minneapolis and London: University of Minnesota Press, 1995), 4–5.
13. Chase and Levenson, *The Spectacle of Intimacy*, 7.
14. Sharon Marcus, *Apartment Stories: City and Home in Nineteenth-Century Paris and London* (Berkeley: University of California Press, 1999), especially 32–38.
15. Marcus, *Apartment Stories*, 36–38; and François Loyer, *Paris, Nineteenth-Century: Architecture and Urbanism*, trans. Charles Lynn Clark (New York: Abbeville Press, 1988), 94, 136.
16. See Philippe Hamon, *Expositions: Literature and Architecture in Nineteenth-Century France*, intro. Richard Sieburth, trans. Katia Sainson-Frank and Lisa Maguire (Berkeley: University of California Press, 1992), 27. Focusing on literature and architecture produced after 1850, Hamon's semiotic analysis emphasizes visual experience rather than aurality or the psychological dynamism of dwelling space. For social histories of space indebted to Foucault, see Jacques Donzelot, *The Policing of Families*, trans. R. Hurley (New York: Pantheon, 1979), especially 40–47; and Thomas A. Markus, *Buildings and Power: Freedom and Control in the Origin of Modern Building Types* (New York and London: Routledge, 1993), especially 113–18, 123–45. Markus focuses on the interaction between people and large, public buildings. For other investigations into the treatment of space in literature, see Ellen Frank, *Literary Architecture: Essays Toward a Tradition* (Berkeley: University of California Press, 1979); Marilyn R. Chandler, *Dwelling in the Text: Houses in American Fiction* (Berkeley: University of California Press, 1991); Christina Marsden Gillis, "Private Room and Public Space: The Paradox of Form in *Clarissa*," *Studies in Voltaire and the Eighteenth Century* 176 (1979): 153–68; Philippa Tristram, *Living Space in Fact and Fiction* (London and New York: Routledge, 1989); and Simon Varey, *Space and the Eighteenth-Century English Novel* (Cambridge: Cambridge University Press, 1990).
17. Max Milner analyzes the hidden observer throughout Balzac's oeuvre; André Vanoncini discusses relations between observer and observed, and decoding secrets in Balzac. See Milner, "Les dispositifs voyeuristes dans le récit balzacien," in Stéphan Vachon, ed., *Balzac: Une poétique du roman* (Montreal: XYZ Editeur, 1996), 157–71; and Vanoncini, "Quête et enquête dans le roman balzacien," in Vachon, 173–80. See also Farrant, "Le Privé:

Espace menacé?," 121–38; Danielle Dupuis, "Spécificité et rôle du décor dans les 'Scènes de la vie privée,'" *L'Année balzacienne* 15 (1994): 139–53; and Nathalie Preiss, "Les 'Scènes de la vie privée': Scènes originaires? Autour du lexique de la vie privée," *L'Année balzacienne* 17 (1996): 355–66.

18. Dioramas and panoramas in Paris and in London presented realistic tableaux, complete with people, animals, and objects, accompanied by music. Dioramas replicated the experience of the voyeur: the spectator looked through a peephole while the impresario created the illusion of change by varying the light cast upon semitransparent sets. The inventor of the diorama, which drew huge crowds from 1822 until it closed in 1839, was Jacques Daguerre, famous today for his role in the development of photography. For an analysis of visual culture and its technological developments in the nineteenth century, as well as a theory of the observing subject, see Jonathan Crary, *Techniques of the Observer* (Cambridge, MA and London: MIT Press, 1991), 5.

19. Chase and Levenson mention this. See *The Spectacle of Intimacy*, 152. See also Erving Goffman, *Behavior in Public Places: Notes on the Social Organization of Gatherings* (New York: Free Press, 1963), 151–52; and Lefebvre, *The Production of Space*, 87.

20. See Donald Fanger's classic *Dostoevsky and Romantic Realism: A Study of Dostoevsky in Relation to Balzac, Dickens, and Gogol* (Cambridge, MA: Harvard University Press, 1965). More recent studies include Kevin McLaughlin, *Writing in Parts: Imitation and Exchange in Nineteenth-Century Literature* (Stanford: Stanford University Press, 1995); and Efraim Sicher, "The Boundaries of Space in the Modern Literary Text: Balzac, Dostoevsky, Dickens," in Roger Bauer and Douwe Fokkema, eds., *Proceedings of the XIIth Congress of the International Comparative Literature Association, Volume III: Space and Boundaries in Literature*, 5 vols. (Munich: Iudicium, 1990), 306–09.

21. See Charles Dickens, *Oliver Twist*, ed. Kathleen Tillotson, intro. Stephen Gill (1837–38; Oxford and New York: Oxford University Press, 1999), 273.

22. Ibid., Chapter 46 (367–77); Chapter 26 (206), Chapter 39 (316).

23. George Eliot, *Middlemarch: A Tale of Provincial Life*, ed. Bert G. Hornback (1871–72; New York and London: W. W. Norton, 1977), 474.

24. See his explanation of the project's structure in a letter dated 26 October, 1834 to Eveline Hanska: "Les moeurs sont le *spectacle*, les causes sont les *coulisses* et les *machines*. Les principes, c'est l'*auteur*," (Balzac's emphasis). Honoré de Balzac, *Lettres à Madame Hanska*, 2 vols., ed. Roger Pierrot (Paris: Editions Robert Laffont, 1990), I: 204. Every generation of Balzac scholars has discussed the significance of theatrical vocabulary in his novels. Peter Brooks's important study of melodrama explores Balzac's complicated use of the genre and its devices. See Brooks, *The Melodramatic Imagination: Balzac, Henry James, Melodrama, and the Mode of Excess* (New Haven and London: Yale University Press, 1976; reprinted, with new preface, 1995), especially 110–52. Recent works include Jacques Neefs, "L'Intensité dramatique des scènes balzaciennes," in *Balzac: Une poétique du roman*, ed.

Stéphan Vachon (Montreal: XYZ Editeur, 1996), 143–52; Catherine Nesci, *La femme, mode d'emploi: Balzac, de* la Physiologie du mariage *à* La Comédie humaine (Lexington, KY: French Forum, 1992), 206; Linzy Erika Dickinson, *Theater in Balzac's* La comédie humaine (Amsterdam and Atlanta: Rodopi, 2000). Recalling that Balzac's first career choice was dramatist, Anne-Marie Baron discusses the importance of the "mise en scène" and theatrical metaphors in his work. See Baron, "Artifices de mise en scène et art de l'illusion," *L'Année balzacienne* 17 (1996): 23–35.

25. See Marcus, *Apartment Stories*, 29; and Crary, *Techniques of the Observer*, 112–13.
26. See Frédéric Soulié, "Les drames invisibles," in *Le diable à Paris* (1845; Paris: Hetzel), I: 85–120. Of course, conceptualizing narrative possibilities or social worlds within a single house or "domestic drama" is not unique to Balzac but continues through the modernist writers influenced by nineteenth-century European novelists, as Henry James's famous phrase, "the house of fiction" (1908), and Edith Wharton's title, *The House of Mirth* (1905), suggest. Georges Perec's novel *La vie: Mode d'emploi* (Paris: Hachette, 1978) offers a late twentieth-century reworking of this concept.
27. See Philippe Ariès and Georges Duby, general eds., *A History of Private Life*, 5 vols. (Cambridge, MA and London: Harvard University Press, 1987–91); Sennett, *The Fall of Public Man*, especially 16–21; Mark Girouard, *Life in the English Country House* (New Haven and London: Yale University Press, 1978); and Robin Evans, "Figures, Doors and Passages," *Architectural Design* 4 (1978): 267–78.
28. Robert Morris, Preface, *Rural Architecture* (1750), as quoted in Gillis, "Private Room and Public Space," 164.
29. Gillis, "Private Room and Public Space," 161. Her article discusses the correlation between privacy in eighteenth-century epistolary fiction and the spaces in which letter-writing occurs.
30. Rybczynski, *Home*, 104.
31. As quoted in Rybczynski, *Home*, 105.
32. Ibid., 105–6, 109.
33. Hall, "The Sweet Delights of Home," 72.
34. Evans, "Figures, Doors and Passages," 270–73.
35. As quoted by Michelle Perrot, "Introduction: les secrets de la maison," in Monique Eleb-Vidal and Anne Debarre-Blanchard, *Architectures de la vie privée: maisons et mentalités XVIIe–XIXe siècles* (Brussels: Archives d'Architecture Moderne, 1989), 5.
36. Rybczynski, *Home*, 86; Perrot, "Introduction," *Architectures de la vie privée*, 7.
37. Rybczynski, *Home*, 87.
38. Girouard, *Life in the English Country House*, 219, 276. A notable exception to this was the lady's maid. Through the mid-nineteenth century, her room was next to her mistress's, so that she might always be nearby. See Chase and Levenson, *The Spectacle of Intimacy*, 166.
39. Hall, "The Sweet Delights of Home," 89.

40. Girouard, *Life in the English Country House*, 279.
41. Robert Kerr, *The Gentleman's House* (1864; London: John Murray, 1871), 67.
42. For a discussion of how an increasing desire for family privacy affects the representation of servants in mid and late nineteenth-century narratives, see Anthea Trodd, "Household Spies: The Servant and the Plot in Victorian Fiction," *Literature and History* 13.2 (1987): 175–87. Conversely, Brian W. McCuskey argues that the novel, by granting the power of surveillance to servants, manages anxieties about working-class eyes and ears in the middle-class home and exerts a disciplinary pressure on the professional elites. See McCuskey, "The Kitchen Police: Servant Surveillance and Middle-Class Transgression," *Victorian Literature and Culture* (2000): 359–75.
43. Robert Neuman, "French Domestic Architecture in the Early 18th Century: The Town Houses of Robert de Cotte," *Journal of the Society of Architectural Historians* 39.2 (1990): 129.
44. Ibid., 130, 131.
45. Eleb-Vidal and Debarre-Blanchard, *Architectures de la vie privée*, 58, 236.
46. Ibid., 231.
47. Ibid., 11, 187, 238, 284.
48. According to Michelle Perrot, the parental bedroom, with its double bed, did not become a permanent fixture in the French bourgeois home until the Third Republic. See Perrot, "Introduction," *Architectures de la vie privée*, 7.
49. Ibid., 13.
50. See Chase and Levenson, *The Spectacle of Intimacy*, 149–51; and Roy Porter, *London: A Social History* (Cambridge, MA: Harvard University Press, 1994), 266–69.
51. James Waring, trans., *Cousin Bette*, by Honoré de Balzac (London: Everyman's Library, 1991), 466. All subsequent translations will be from this edition and will be included parenthetically after the French text, followed by the page number.
52. Loyer, *Paris, Nineteenth Century*, 106–7.
53. François Loyer, *Paris, XIXe siècle. L'immeuble et l'espace urbain* (Paris: APUR, 1981) II: 7, 20–21, as quoted in Eleb-Vidal and Debarre-Blanchard, *Architectures de la vie privée*, 84–85.
54. His families are generally more middle class than those in Balzac's fiction, who often come from or aspire to join the aristocracy.
55. Evans, "Figures, Doors and Passages," 270–71.
56. See Erich Auerbach's classic discussion of the opening to *Le Père Goriot*, with its minute description of the Maison Vauquer and its proprietor; each "implies" the other. Auerbach, *Mimesis: The Representation of Reality in Western Literature*, trans. Willard R. Trask (Princeton: Princeton University Press, 1953), 468–73.
57. Honoré de Balzac, *Le Cousin Pons* (1847; Paris: Gallimard, 1973), 192. All subsequent references will be to this edition.
58. Hamon, *Expositions*, 4, 5.

59. Honoré de Balzac, *Le Père Goriot* (1834–35; Paris: Gallimard, 1971), 21. All subsequent references will be to this edition. Burton Raffel, trans., *Père Goriot (Old Goriot)*, by Honoré de Balzac, ed. Peter Brooks (New York and London: W. W. Norton, 1994), 4. All subsequent translations, unless otherwise noted will be from this edition and will be included parenthetically after the French text, followed by the page number. My emendations will appear in brackets.
60. "Elle a l'oeil vitreux, l'air innocent d'une entremetteuse qui va se gendarmer pour se faire payer plus cher, mais d'ailleurs prête à tout pour adoucir son sort, à livrer George ou Pichegru, si Georges ou Pichegru étaient encore à livrer" (29; "she has the hard, brittle eyes and artless expression of a female pimp, ready to do anything to make herself a profit, prepared to sell out or inform on anyone she can find to sell or inform on," 11). The comparison of Mme Vauquer to a procuress suggests she would sell the most intimate aspects of her boarders' lives if the opportunity arose.
61. Victorine, who "found herself, year after year, stopped by her father's barred door, shut inexorably against her" (17). Dickens uses the same image to describe Florence Dombey's relationship with her father.
62. These stories correspond to the American second, third, and fourth floors, respectively.
63. The word "méfiance" ("distrust, suspicion") recurs continually in the novel. Balzac uses it here to establish the atmosphere of speculation and rumor pervading the *pension*.
64. In a narrative in which Rastignac must choose between two paternal models, Janet Beizer reads this as an Oedipal moment, where a "primal mystery" is revealed. See Beizer, *Family Plots: Balzac's Narrative Generations* (New Haven and London: Yale University Press, 1986), 122.
65. On visual observation in Balzac, see Anne-Marie Baron, "Statut et fonctions de l'observateur balzacien," *L'Année balzacienne* 10 (1989): 301–16.
66. Similarly, Bianchon overhears fragments of the two confidential conversations between Poiret, la Michonneau, and the chief of the police; had he mentioned these clandestine rendezvous to Vautrin, the archcriminal would have escaped capture, and the "family" of the boarding-house would have remained intact.
67. See, for example, 282.
68. The Raffel edition translates "Trompe-la-Mort" as "Death-Dodger."
69. Ariès and Duby, *A History of Private Life*, IV: 3.
70. See David Bell, "Marque, trace, pistes: Balzac à la recherche d'une science des indices," in *Balzac ou la tentation de l'impossible*, eds. Robert Mahieu and Franc Schuerewegen (Paris: SEDES, 1998), 107–12.
71. Florence Terrasse-Riou considers the threshold in relation to time in Balzac's fiction. See Terrasse-Riou, "Les enjeux de la représentation d'un seuil: l'hôtel de Chaulieu," in *Balzac ou la tentation de l'impossible*, eds. Robert Mahieu and Franc Schuerewegen (Pains: SEDES, 1998), 47–55.

72. Marcus makes a similar point. See Marcus, *Apartment Stories*, 53.
73. Marcus also notes how *Le Cousin Pons* "makes kin into strangers" (12).
74. Graham Robb, *Balzac: A Biography* (London: Picador, 1994), 365. André Lorant notes reflections of Balzac's personal life in *La Cousine Bette*, particularly his relationship with his housekeeper, Louise Breugniot. See "Introduction," *La Cousine Bette* (Paris: Garnier-Flammarion, 1977), 20.
75. Most of the characters in *Bette* move at least once; some maintain more than one home or identity at the same time. Bette moves three times, as does the baroness, while Valérie presides over at least four separate establishments. Only Victorin and Célestine steadfastly maintain one home in "un des plus beaux immeubles de Paris" ("one of the most beautiful buildings in Paris"), which the young lawyer bought in 1834, when prices were low (397). His father, in contrast, inhabits a succession of apartments and identities with a string of mistresses – at least five – plus the increasingly threadbare accommodations he provides for his wife. See 127, 203, 393, 464, 476, 487.
76. Just as Valérie's body circulates among the men, so, too, does knowledge of its circulation. But in both the information and sexual economies, Valérie controls who knows and gets what when.
77. As Joséphina declares to the baroness while preparing to coax Hulot's whereabouts from Mme Bijou, "Elle ne lâcherait rien en devinant que vous êtes intéressée à ses confidences, laissez-moi la confesser! Cachez-vous là, vous entendrez tout. Cette scène se joue aussi souvent dans la vie qu'au théâtre" (415; "She would let nothing out if she suspected that you were interested in the information. Leave me to catechise her. Hide there, and you will hear everything. It is a scene that is played quite as often in real life as on the stage," 400).
78. See, among others, 128, 150, 174, 224, 225, 233, 239, 246, 285, 303, 307, 309, 314, 317, 331, 375, 379, 393, 406, 441, 458, 486, 487.
79. Frank Kermode, *The Genesis of Secrecy: On the Interpretation of Narrative* (Cambridge, MA and London: Harvard University Press, 1979), 1–2.
80. See, for example, 239, 246, 285, 286, 303, 307, 308, 309, 314, 316, 317.
81. Balzac uses the phrase in his first preface to *Le Père Goriot* (395).
82. A wily administration takes advantage of the press's power. By manipulating the news of the Algerian embezzlement, the government convinces the opposition newspapers that it publicizes state secrets, when it actually covers them up (383).
83. In Balzac's novels, such unpremeditated overhearing provides the irrefutable evidence to good, naïve individuals that domestic bliss is a fiction. Their secret listening brings not power but chagrin and death. In *Le Colonel Chabert*, inadvertent eavesdropping confirms the Colonel's betrayal by his wife and leaves him devastated; long presumed dead, Chabert "dies" again by renouncing his claims to his identity (and wealth), and ends up in a "home" for indigent men, leaving his wife to continue a luxurious life with her second husband. See *Le Colonel Chabert* (1832; Paris: Gallimard, 1974), 108ff.

84. For historical accounts of the concierge, her management of space, and her dealings with the police, see Ariès and Duby, *A History of Private Life*, IV: 229–30, 364; Jean-Louis Deaucourt, *Premières loges: Paris et ses concierges au XIXe siècle* (Paris: Aubier, 1992); and Jean-Louis Deaucourt, "Une police des sentiments: les concierges et les portiers," *Romantisme* 68.2 (1990): 49–60.
85. The French expression "vivre en bonne intelligence avec quelqu'un" means "to live or be on good terms with someone." It also suggests the idea of "being in cahoots with someone." Other expressions with the word "intelligence" have this sinister slant: "être d'intelligence avec quelqu'un" ("to have a secret understanding with someone"); "avoir des intelligences dans la place" ("to have secret relations or contacts there").
86. My translation; the Hunt edition translates the passage in less dramatic terms: "That's how Nature made me – to take on a mother's cares" (164).
87. "To put an inheritance in probate one closes all the doors." The French chapter title plays with the opposition between putting an inheritance in probate ("ouvrir une succession": literally, to "open" [ouvrir] a "succession" or "inheritance"), and closing ("fermer") doors.
88. Marcus, *Apartment Stories*, 53.
89. James McGuire suggests that lesbiansim is the other crime against the patriarchal family for which these women are punished. See McGuire, "The Feminine Conspiracy in Balzac's *La Cousine Bette*," *Nineteenth-Century French Studies* 20.3–4 (1992): 295–304.
90. I use this word deliberately, since the word *scot* means "tax." Although the ambitious male writers of *tableaux, physiologies*, or novels pay nothing for the secrets of private life from which they earn a living, they insure that their fictional female counterparts do.
91. No wonder the vicomtesse Popinot and her mother rewrite the story of Pons's gift to Mme Camusot of Mme de Pompadour's fan. Their version of how Pons turned a symbol of aristocratic decadence into one of bourgeois morality transforms a story of underhanded plotting into a legacy of familial affection; a false "vertu" (virtue) replaces "le vice" (vice) in a troubling, double sense (366).
92. In May 1846, Dickens moved his entire family to Lausanne, where they stayed until November, and where he began the composition of the novel. From November until spring of the following year, the Dickenses rented a small house in Paris's rue de Courcelles. They returned to England to nurse their son who had caught scarlet fever in London. There, Dickens finished writing *Dombey and Son*, in March 1848. See Peter Ackroyd, *Dickens* (New York: HarperCollins, 1990), 497–545. Balzac's diptych of poor relations appeared serially in *Le Constitutionnel* between 1846 and 1847; *La Cousine Bette* and *Le Cousin Pons* were published in book form in 1847 and 1848 respectively.
93. Frances Armstrong's study *Dickens and the Concept of Home* traces the development of the idea of home from its beginnings in the late seventeenth

century to its formulation in the nineteenth century. See Armstrong, *Dickens and the Concept of Home* (Ann Arbor and London: UMI Research Press, 1990), 4. She analyzes Florence's "creative process of homemaking" (62) and Dickens's representation of the interaction between home and the larger world (61–69, 91–93).

94. Among others, Kathleen Tillotson notes how the changing state of the physical house in *Dombey and Son* parallels the family narrative. See Tillotson, *Novels of the Eighteen-Forties* (Oxford: Clarendon Press, 1956), 197.
95. Charles Dickens, *Dombey and Son*, ed. Peter Fairclough, intro. Raymond Williams (1848; Harmondsworth and New York: Penguin, 1986), 738, 653. All subsequent references will be to this edition.
96. In taking the "freedom of peering in, and listening, through the skylight in the roof" of the shop, Rob presents the evil double of this "good spirit" (415). Jonathan Arac discusses the unsettling quality of what he terms this "position of overview" in several nineteenth-century authors, including Dickens. See *Commissioned Spirits: The Shaping of Social Motion in Dickens, Carlyle, Melville, and Hawthorne* (New Brunswick: Rutgers University Press, 1979), 2–3.
97. Ackroyd, *Dickens*, 93.
98. See also Tristram, *Living Space in Fact and Fiction*, 213. Henri Talon notes that, "what a house ought to be we learn through... the poor." See "*Dombey and Son*: A Closer Look at the Text," *Dickens Studies Annual* 1 (1970): 148.
99. Dickens, *Great Expectations*, ed. Angus Calder (1860–61; London and New York: Penguin, 1985), 405. See also 231, 310, 382.
100. Rybczynski, *Home*, 62.
101. Tristram notes that tasteful decor is no longer the index of morality it was in eighteenth-century England; the humblest dwelling with vulgar furnishings could be considered a proper home if it displayed a concern for domestic harmony and security. See Tristram, *Living Space in Fact and Fiction*, 214, 23.
102. Carker has access to the most intimate spaces in the Dombey house, a familiarity that carries sexual implications as well. At one point, Florence sees Carker leaving her stepmother's private rooms alone: "No bell was rung to announce his departure, no servant in attendance. He... opened the door for himself, glided out, and shut it softly after him" (752).
103. For other instances, see 385, 509, 587–88.
104. Carker also warns Rob, "[T]ake care you talk about affairs of mine to nobody but me" (386).
105. Generally, the domestic spaces in *Dombey and Son*, as in most of Dickens's fiction, reveal as much about their occupants as they hope to conceal. Alice bitterly remarks about Mrs. Brown, "She's as much a mother, as her dwelling is a home" (565).
106. See Patricia Meyer Spacks's discussion of this kind of community-building in *Gossip* (Chicago and London: University of Chicago Press, 1986), 5ff.

107. Dickens relates corporate, physical, and spiritual houses in *Dombey and Son* through the metaphor of the body. See, for example, the "carcasses of houses" littering the landscape of the former Staggs's Gardens (289).
108. Dickens makes this point implicitly by describing Alice's dead body as "the ruin of the mortal house" (923). This description immediately precedes the dismantling of the Dombey household in the next chapter.

4 THE MADWOMAN OUTSIDE THE ATTIC

1. Reproduced courtesy of the Tate Gallery, London/Art Resource, New York.
2. Jonathan Loesberg, among others, notes "the concern with identity and its loss" as a recurrent preoccupation of sensation fiction. See Loesberg, "The Ideology of Form in Sensation Fiction," *Representations* 13 (1986): 117. Ronald R. Thomas reads identity as being socially constructed through "some conspiracy of law and medicine." See "Wilkie Collins and the Sensation Novel," in *The Columbia History of the British Novel*, ed. John Richetti (New York: Columbia University Press, 1994), 492. See also Winifred Hughes, *The Maniac in the Cellar: Sensation Novels of the 1860s* (Princeton: Princeton University Press, 1980), 21; Tamar Heller, *Dead Secrets: Wilkie Collins and the Female Gothic* (New Haven and London: Yale University Press, 1992), 139; and Andrew Gasson, *Wilkie Collins: An Illustrated Guide*, consultant ed. Catherine Peters (Oxford and New York: Oxford University Press, 1998), 83–84.
3. For a summary of critical interpretations of sensation fiction's stance toward gender issues not mentioned here, see Loesberg, "The Ideology of Form," 136. Critics tend to fall into two camps: those who believe Collins's representation of women offers an unqualified subversion of dominant ideology, and those who believe his narratives evince a sympathetic, if ambivalent, attitude toward the situation of women and the need for their greater empowerment. For the former reading, see Sally Shuttleworth, "Demonic Motherhood: Ideologies of Bourgeois Motherhood in the Mid-Victorian Era," in *Rewriting the Victorians: Theory, History, and the Politics of Gender*, ed. Linda M. Shires (New York and London: Routledge, 1992), 31–51; and Susan Balée, "Wilkie Collins and Surplus Women: The Case of Marian Halcombe," *Victorian Literature and Culture* 20 (1992): 197–215. For the latter, see Richard Barickman, Susan MacDonald, and Myra Stark, *Corrupt Relations: Dickens, Thackeray, Trollope, Collins, and the Victorian Sexual System* (New York: Columbia University Press, 1982), 18; Sue Lonoff, *Wilkie Collins and His Victorian Readers* (New York: AMS Press, 1982); Ann Cvetkovich, *Mixed Feelings: Feminisim, Mass Culture, and Victorian Sensationalism* (New Brunswick, NJ: Rutgers University Press, 1992), who argues that "the figure of the middle-class woman in the sensation novel is... alternately privileged and oppressed, in ways that challenge the binary oppositions between these categories" (203); and Heller, *Dead Secrets*. My reading falls into this second category of analyses.

4. Peter Thoms, *The Windings of the Labyrinth: Quest and Structure in the Major Novels of Wilkie Collins* (Athens, OH: University of Ohio Press, 1992), 4–5.
5. Heller, *Dead Secrets*, 11; also 110–41.
6. Contemporary reviewers censured Collins's use of eavesdropping. Andrew Lang wrote of *Armadale*, "We are vexed by the number of persons who spy, listen, and overhear what was not meant for them." See "Mr. Wilkie Collins's Novels," *Contemporary Review*, January 1890, in *Wilkie Collins: The Critical Heritage*, ed. Norman Page (London and Boston: Routledge and Kegan Paul, 1974), 270–71. Describing *No Name*, Alexander Smith deplored the "monstrosities" of a plot dependent on such activities, in an unsigned review, *The North British Review*, February 1863, in *Wilkie Collins: The Critical Heritage*, ed. Norman Page, 141. Both express a concern about transgressions of seemly behavior and suggest the immorality of literature that stoops to present such acts.
7. D. A. Miller discusses how Collins's novel "is profoundly about enclosing and secluding the woman in male 'bodies,' among them institutions like marriage and madhouses," but his argument subsumes the "sequestration of the woman" into an investigation of the disciplining of non-normative sexual inclinations. He thus turns away from examining female narrative agency. See *The Novel and the Police* (Berkeley: University of California Press, 1988), 155–56.
8. Heller argues that woman's transgression is the "dead secret" of Collins's novels. See *Dead Secrets*, 2.
9. Wilkie Collins, *The Woman in White*, ed. and intro. Julian Symons (London and New York: Penguin, 1974), 33. All subsequent references will be to this edition. Where it is necessary to distinguish among editions, it will be cited as *WW*. *The Woman in White* was first published serially in 1859–60 in Dickens's *All the Year Round*. The Penguin text, based on the 1861 edition of the novel, contains minor changes that Collins made when it was first published in book form in 1860, and again in 1861. The Riverside edition, eds. Kathleen Tillotson and Anthea Trodd (Boston: Houghton Mifflin, 1969) is based on the serial text as it appeared in *All the Year Round*, but adopts the chronology corrections of 1860 and 1861; it will henceforth be cited as *Riverside*, with references incorporated within the text. Discrepancies among editions relevant to my argument will be discussed below.
10. Walter Kendrick points out that the preamble was subsumed under the heading of Walter Hartright's first narrative after serial publication. See "The Sensationalism of *The Woman in White*," *Nineteenth-Century Fiction* 32.1 (1977): 24. However, the manner in which the preamble refers to Walter in the third person continues to suggest an initial difference between this narrator and Walter. Most current editions (Penguin, Oxford, and Riverside, for example) continue to treat the preamble as separate from Walter's first narrative.
11. U. C. Knoepflmacher notes the "artificiality of this return to convention." See "The Counterworld of Victorian Fiction and *The Woman in White*," in

The Worlds of Victorian Fiction, ed. Jerome H. Buckley (Cambridge, MA and London: Harvard University Press, 1975), 365.
12. Several critics examine the double valence of the word "asylum" in *The Woman in White*. See, for example, Jenny Bourne Taylor, *In the Secret Theatre of Home: Wilkie Collins, Sensation Narrative, and Nineteenth-Century Psychology* (New York and London: Routledge, 1988), 112; and Miller, *The Novel and the Police*, 171–72.
13. See Pamela Perkins and Mary Donaghy, "A Man's Resolution: Narrative Strategies in Wilkie Collins's *The Woman in White*," *Studies in the Novel* 22.2 (1990): 392. They consider Collins's criticism of Victorian gender norms as unambiguous. See also Kendrick, "The Sensationalism of *The Woman in White*," 34.
14. John Sutherland notes "the analogy of *The Woman in White*'s narrative to the process of *law*, as it is ritually played out in the English criminal court." See "Wilkie Collins and the Origins of the Sensation Novel," *Dickens Studies Annual* 20 (1991): 248.
15. Miller notes the association between reader and judge. See *The Novel and the Police*, 158. Knoepflmacher identifies the "participatory quality" of Victorian fiction in general. See *Laughter and Despair: Readings in Ten Novels of the Victorian Era* (Berkeley: University of California Press, 1971), ix.
16. See Franco Moretti's discussion of the relation between literature and the law in *The Way of the World: The* Bildungsroman *in European Culture* (London: Verso, 1987), 212. Leila Silvana May focuses on the law's role in disciplining illicit, often homosexual loves. See May, "Sensational Sisters: Wilkie Collins's *The Woman in White*," *Pacific Coast Philology* 30.1 (1995): 82–102.
17. For a discussion of how written statements acquire the weight of evidence, see Philip O'Neill, *Wilkie Collins: Women, Property and Propriety* (London: Macmillan, 1988), 121.
18. Wilkie Collins, "How I Write My Books: Related in a Letter to a Friend," *The Globe* (26 November, 1887), in *The Woman in White*, ed. Harvey Peter Sucksmith (Oxford and New York: Oxford University Press, 1989), 596.
19. Elaine Showalter, *The Female Malady: Women, Madness, and English Culture, 1830–1980* (New York: Pantheon Books, 1985), 29. Showalter explains how "the domestication of insanity and its assimilation by the Victorian institution coincide with its feminization" (52). She argues that the madwoman must be "purged from the plot" for the Victorian novel to reach a happy ending (68).
20. Ibid., 78.
21. Taylor also notes how Walter hides his position of "general editor." See Taylor, *In the Secret Theatre of Home*, 110. Taylor's reading stresses the usurpation of individuals' cognitive "perceptions" rather than their aural acquisition and linguistic presentation (109).
22. Miller, *The Novel and the Police*, 146ff., 160. For a discussion of the origins and characteristics of the sensation novel, see Hughes, *The Maniac in the Cellar*; Walter C. Phillips, *Dickens, Reade, and Collins: Sensation Novelists* (New York:

Columbia University Press, 1919); and Cvetkovich, *Mixed Feelings*. Cvetkovich relates nineteenth-century sensationalism to the politics and discourse of affect.
23. Miller, *The Novel and the Police*, 180, 176. See also his larger discussion of Karl Ulrich's formulation of male homosexuality and its incarceration of the sexually "deviant" (154ff.).
24. Ibid., 165, 153, 163.
25. Ibid., 156.
26. For a similar criticism of Miller's argument, see Laurie Langbauer, "Women in White, Men in Feminism," *Yale Journal of Criticism* 2.2 (1989): 219–43. She asserts that his essay "shares the attitudes it may also be critiquing" (232).
27. O'Neill notes how "The semes which traditionally allow us to identify certain traits as either masculine or feminine exist in a state of flux in *The Woman in White*." See *Wilkie Collins*, 115. See also Loesberg, "The Ideology of Form," 131.
28. Taylor discusses the different familial oppositions in the novel and their implications. See Taylor, *In the Secret Theatre of Home*, 107–8. Balée analyzes female subversion of traditional gender binaries in the novel. See Balée, "Wilkie Collins and Surplus Women," 201–4.
29. In *The Physiology and Pathology of the Mind* (1867), Henry Maudsley asserts, "Insanity descends more often from the mother than the father, and from the mother to the daughters more often than to the sons" (Henry Maudsley, as quoted in Shuttleworth, "Demonic Motherhood," 36–37).
30. Many critics note the obvious doublings in the novel. See Symons, "Introduction," in *The Woman in White*, 13. Hughes identifies the doubling of character and incident as integral to the sensation novel. See Hughes, *The Maniac in the Cellar*, 20–21. Some scholars indicate the complex and contradictory nature of these juxtapositions. See, for example, Mark Hennelly, Jr., "Reading Detection in *The Woman in White*," *Texas Studies in Literature and Language* 22.4 (1980): 461.
31. Knoepflmacher points out this attraction between the novel's most socially deviant characters. See Knoepflmacher, "The Counterworld," 366. Marian, however, is both attracted and repelled by Fosco only when she is an active, writing subject (*WW*, 240, 310). Once he writes in her diary, she feels nothing but "loathing" for him; she no longer stands as a desiring subject, but only as desired object (566). In contrast, she loses none of her attraction for him, because he maintains his position of active subjectivity (568).
32. Taylor considers Walter as a "male governess figure." See Taylor, *In the Secret Theatre of Home*, 108. Balée describes him as "safely emasculated." See Balée, "Wilkie Collins and Surplus Women," 203.
33. Miller, *The Novel and the Police*, 152.
34. As Barickman, MacDonald, and Stark observe, "it is often the very blatancy of sexual stereotypes... that alerts us to the complex, psychologically and socially accurate material that the novel is trying both to suppress

and to explore." See Barickman, MacDonald, and Stark, *Corrupt Relations*, 19.
35. Nina Auerbach also notes "Marian's abandonment of stays" and indicates how this "defiant assertion of new space and scope for herself" threatens Walter. See *Woman and the Demon: The Life of a Victorian Myth* (Cambridge, MA and London: Harvard University Press, 1982), 136.
36. The word "resolute" in *The Woman in White* usually signals the amount of power a character wields at a given moment. Perkins and Donaghy note the "collapse" of gender stereotypes in the novel's use of the word "resolute." See Perkins and Donaghy, "A Man's Resolution," 394–95.
37. Auerbach, *Woman and the Demon*, 135.
38. For Victorian constructions of the "angel of the house" and the "strong-minded woman," see Elizabeth Helsinger, Robin Lauterbach Sheets, and William Veeder, *The Woman Question: Society and Literature in Britain and America, 1837–1888*, vol. III, *Literary Issues* (Chicago and London: University of Chicago Press, 1983), 79–110.
39. Moreover, as narrator, she mediates between the reader and the story; her narrative appears between those of the "irresolute" and "resolute" Walter. See also Miller, *The Novel and the Police*, 174.
40. Edmund Yates relates Collins's account of having received, after the publication of *The Woman in White*, "a number of letters from single gentlemen, stating... their wish to marry the original of Marian Halcombe." One wonders whether their attraction, however, is to the early, powerful Marian, or the domesticated angel at the novel's end (Collins as quoted by Yates, *Celebrities at Home*, 1879; reprinted in Sucksmith, *The Woman in White*, 592).
41. Roland Barthes, *The Pleasure of the Text*, trans. Richard Miller (London: Basil Blackwell, 1975), 9–10.
42. See Miller's discussion of the act of reading as the "definitive fantasy of the liberal subject, who imagines himself free from the surveillance that he nonetheless sees operating everywhere around him" (*The Novel and the Police*, 162). I would, however, take issue with Miller's conclusion about the novel's coercion of readers, and emphasize instead its ability to engender identification with and readerly pleasure from the novel's transgressive characters.
43. However, whereas Sir Percival's illicit writing authorizes his identity as gentleman of title, to prove that "Sir Percival" is guilty of forgery, Walter must produce the authentic document that records the *absence* of writing: the space between entries that confirms that his parents' marriage is a later addition to the register.
44. Michel Foucault, *Discipline and Punish: The Birth of the Prison*, trans. Alan Sheridan (New York: Vintage Books, 1979), 317 n.3.
45. Kendrick presents this double violation simply as a two-step process of reading and writing. See Kendrick, "The Sensationalism of *The Woman in White*," 29.

46. Miller, *The Novel and the Police*, 160. Balée considers it a "psychic rape." See Balée, "Wilkie Collins and Surplus Women," 203.
47. See Helsinger, Sheets, and Veeder, *The Woman Question*, 26–78.
48. Discussing epistolary fiction, Terry Castle notes how fictional acts of reading reflect our own. See *Clarissa's Ciphers: Meaning and Disruption in Richardson's "Clarissa"* (Ithaca and London: Cornell University Press, 1982), 46.
49. My discussion here is indebted to Sandra Gilbert and Susan Gubar's groundbreaking study of female authorship, *The Madwoman in the Attic: The Woman Writer and the Nineteenth-Century Literary Imagination* (New Haven and London: Yale University Press, 1984). For a discussion of Collins's transformation of Gothic elements and ideology, see Stephen Bernstein, "Reading Blackwater Park: Gothicism, Narrative, and Ideology in *The Woman in White*," *Studies in the Novel* 25.3 (1993): 291–305.
50. Kendrick points out that two moral codes operate in the novel, so that the rhetorical deceptions Fosco commits are considered crimes, while those of Walter are "forgivable" because they are necessary for the narrative's "sensational" aspects. See Kendrick, "The Sensationalism of *The Woman in White*," 34.
51. Although Walter does not control Marian completely (she reads only portions of her journal to him, selecting what he will know), he decides what should be included in the larger narrative (456) and boasts of being "in possession of all that Marian could tell" (457). By the end of the novel, women's power resides in their ability to withhold information.
52. *The Compact Oxford English Dictionary* (Oxford: Oxford University Press, 1984), II: 2075. English definitions of "flourish" include "to thrive, display vigour in;" "to be at the height of fame or excellence;" "to adorn, decorate, embellish, ornament;" "to display ostentatiously;" "to wave [a weapon] about by way of show or triumph;" and "to boast" (*Compact OED*, I: 1031–32).
53. Kendrick notes the "reinscription" that takes place on Fosco's body. See Kendrick, "The Sensationalism of *The Woman in White*," 29.
54. William M. Clarke, *The Secret Life of Wilkie Collins* (London: W. H. Allen, 1988), 7.
55. Heller, *Dead Secrets*, 8.
56. See Gaye Tuchman with Nina E. Fortin, *Edging Women Out: Victorian Novelists, Publishers, and Social Change* (New Haven: Yale University Press, 1989); and Julia Swindells, *Victorian Writing and Working Women: The Other Side of Silence* (Minneapolis: University of Minnesota Press, 1985).
57. I am indebted to U. C. Knoepflmacher for pointing out the uncanny similarity of names and the parallels it suggests between fictional and real-world competition among male and female writers. Catherine Peters mentions the physical resemblance between Marian and George Eliot but does not develop the implications of this similarity. See Peters, *The King of Inventors: A Life of Wilkie Collins* (London: Secker and Warburg, 1991), 217.
58. See Dickens's letters to George Henry Lewes, dated 14 November 1859, and to Gaskell, dated 20 December 1859, in *The Letters of Charles Dickens*, ed. Walter Dexter (Bloomsbury: Nonesuch Press, 1938), III: 136, 139.

59. Leo Bersani, "Death and Literary Authority," in *A New History of French Literature*, ed. Denis Hollier (Cambridge, MA and London: Harvard University Press, 1989), 863.

5 LA DOUBLE ENTENTE

1. "Our wisdom begins where the author's ends, and we would like him to give us answers, when all he can do is give us desires" (my translation).
2. For critical work tracing Proust's debt to Ruskin, see Ronald Hayman, *Proust: A Biography* (London: Heinemann, 1990), 138. For critical studies concentrating on visual perception and Proust's visual sensibility, see Roger Shattuck, *Proust's Binoculars: A Study of Memory, Time, and Recognition* (New York: Knopf, 1963; Princeton: Princeton University Press, 1983); Howard Moss, "The Windows," in Harold Bloom, ed. and intro., *Marcel Proust: Modern Critical Views* (New York, New Haven, and Philadelphia: Chelsea House, 1987), 97–108; and Margaret E. Gray, *Postmodern Proust* (Philadelphia: University of Pennsylvania Press, 1992), 7–8.
3. In a letter to his childhood friend Robert Dreyfus, alluded to by Louis de Robert in his *De l'amour à la sagesse* (Paris: Eugène Figuière, 1930), rptd. in Leighton Hodson, ed., *Marcel Proust: The Critical Heritage* (London and New York: Routledge, 1989), 391.
4. Marcel Proust, *Du côté de chez Swann*, ed. Antoine Compagnon (Paris: Editions Gallimard, 1988), 321. All subsequent references will be to this edition and will be cited parenthetically with the designation *Swann*, followed by the page number. English translations are taken from Marcel Proust, *Remembrance of Things Past*, trans. C. K. Scott Moncrieff and Terence Kilmartin, 3 vols. (London: Chatto and Windus, 1981), I: 356. All subsequent translations will be included parenthetically after the French text, followed by the volume and page number.
5. *La prisonnière*, ed. Pierre-Edmond Robert (Paris: Editions Gallimard, 1989), 19. All subsequent references will be to this edition. Shattuck's study devoted to Proust's "optics" exemplifies the critical treatment of sound in *A la recherche*; he mentions in passing how "it is equally meaningful to speak of the hypersensitivity of his olfactory sense or of his hearing" (20).
6. He subscribed and listened regularly to the telephone performance service, or Théâtrophone, which enabled him to hear performances of the Opéra, Opéra-Comique, the Comédie Française, etc. via the telephone; he maintained an enduring passion for music; he continually complained about noises from disturbing neighbors, and eventually had his room lined in cork in 1910; he tested what he had written by reading it aloud. See Hayman, *Proust*, 343, 89, 366, 369, 381, 279, 337, 422.
7. See, for example, the long passage in *Le côté de Guermantes I*, where the narrator muses on what it would be like to be deaf, and on the role that sound plays in our everyday experience. Similarly, the description of his grandmother's telephone call to him at Doncières emphasizes the telephone's

ability to isolate the voice and to make us aware of its singular role in the revelation of character. See Proust, *Le côté de Guermantes I*, ed. Thierry Laget (Paris: Editions Gallimard, 1988), 68–71, 125–26. All subsequent references will be to this edition and will be cited parenthetically with the designation *Guermantes I*, followed by the page number.

8. See, for example, E. M. Forster's discussion of Vinteuil's "petite phrase" in *Aspects of the Novel* (London: Harcourt, Brace and World, 1927; New York and London: Harcourt Brace Jovanovich, 1974), 167. Benjamin Crémieux notes the centrality of "oral language" to Proust's style. See Crémieux, "Nouveauté d'*Albertine disparue*," *La nouvelle revue française*, 1 February 1926, rptd. in Hodson, *Marcel Proust*, 314–19. Jean-Pierre Richard considers the "petite phrase" one of the many "hermeneutic objects" that the various senses evoke and that call for interpretation. See Jean-Pierre Richard, *Proust et le monde sensible* (Paris: Editions du Seuil, 1974), 133.

9. I borrow this term from Luce Irigaray's critique of male oculocentrism in *Speculum of the Other Woman*, trans. Gillian C. Gill (Ithaca: Cornell University Press, 1985), 48. Referring to the "ocularcentric discourse" of Western culture, Martin Jay characterizes twentieth-century French cultural theorists and philosophers as "antiocularcentric." See *Downcast Eyes: The Denigration of Vision in Twentieth-Century French Thought* (Berkeley and Los Angeles: University of California Press, 1993).

10. Marcel Proust, *Le temps retrouvé*, ed. and pref. Pierre-Louis Rey and Brian Rogers (Paris: Editions Gallimard, 1990), 336. All subsequent references will be to this edition and will be cited parenthetically text with the designation *TR*, followed by the page number.

11. See Eve Kosfsky Sedgwick's discussion of the binary hetero/homosexuality in twentieth-century culture and its importance in Proust in *Epistemology of the Closet* (Berkeley and Los Angeles: University of California Press, 1990), 213–51.

12. See, for example, Peter Brooks, *Body Work: Objects of Desire in Modern Narrative* (Cambridge, MA and London: Harvard University Press, 1993), 5.

13. Gregorio Kohon, "Reflections on Dora: The Case of Hysteria," in *The British School of Psychoanalysis: The Independent Tradition*, ed. Gregorio Kohon (New Haven and London: Yale University Press, 1986), 371.

14. See, for example, *Swann*, 50, 78.

15. See Moss's discussion of windows and discovery in Proust in "The Windows," 97–108.

16. Proust joins a long tradition associating the pleasures of reading with sexual pleasure. The fifth canto of Dante's *Inferno*, which describes how Paolo and Francesca fell in love while reading the "Galeotto" – a story about the adulterous love of Lancelot and Guinevere – is considered the *locus classicus* linking reading and illicit love.

17. Antoine Compagnon notes that in 1906 Proust was planning to write a melodrama in which a sadistic man who adores his wife would sleep with prostitutes and defile her name by speaking to them of her (*Swann*, 490). Through

eavesdropping, the wife discovers her husband's infidelity and leaves him, in consequence of which he kills himself. Proust, like Collins, was thus fully aware of the possibilities that such scenes offer to melodrama. See Hayman, *Proust*, 246. See also Proust's letter to Reynaldo Hahn in *Correspondance générale de Marcel Proust*, ed. Robert Proust, Paul Brach, and Suzy Mante-Proust, 6 vols. (Paris: Plon, 1930–36), III: 70–71.

18. See Joseph Litvak's discussion of the interdependence of the "sophisticated and the vulgar, of the refined and the excremental" in Proustian desire in *Strange Gourmets: Sophistication, Theory, and the Novel* (Durham and London: Duke University Press, 1997), 83. In Litvak's account, the lover's relation to the beloved object undergoes a series of shifts. Once "tantalizingly proscribed," the beloved loses its desirability when deidealized, only to regain its attraction "in its contemptability" (93). Vinteuil's daughter's love represents the first stage of this process; her object choice depends upon the forbidden, "méchant" quality of the lover and the kind of love (lesbianism) chosen.
19. Germaine Brée also notes this world's inaccessibility for Marcel. See "The Closed Door," in Bloom, *Marcel Proust*, 52.
20. Roland Barthes notes the convergence of the two "routes" in Gilberte Swann's marriage to Robert de Saint-Loup. See Barthes, "Une idée de recherche," in *Recherche de Proust*, ed. Gérard Genette and Tzvetan Todorov (Paris: Editions du Seuil, 1980), 38.
21. See, among others, Shattuck, *Proust's Binoculars*, 98.
22. Marcel only later recognizes the futility of trying to capture the essence, or "truth" of another person; see *Sodome et Gomorrhe*, ed. and pref. Antoine Compagnon (Paris: Editions Gallimard, 1989), 131. All subsequent references will be to this edition and will be cited parenthetically with the designation *Sodome*, followed by the page number.
23. This is the first of several confluences of "ways" – psychological spaces, social worlds, and identities – that initially seem far apart in *A la recherche*. Albertine reveals how the woman who raised her is Mlle Vinteuil's friend; Gilberte, representing "le côté de chez Swann," eventually marries Saint-Loup, a scion of the Guermantes way; Morel provides the point of intersection between Charlus and "le petit clan;" Mme Verdurin finally becomes a Guermante through marriage, just as Odette enters the elite world by marrying Fourcheville.
24. *Rapporter* can mean "moucharder" (to tattle on) or it can signify "répéter pour dénoncer"; "un rapporteur" (or "mouchard") is a talebearer.
25. From cahier 51, in "Documents," in *Sodome*, 532. My translation. My emendations are within brackets, the editor's interpretations of the unpublished manuscript within arrowheads.
26. See *Swann*, 82–87, and Paul de Man's discussion of the "allegory" of reading in Proust, "Reading (Proust)," in Bloom, *Marcel Proust*, 183–200.
27. These critics analyze the kinds of orality in the novel: eating, kissing, oral sex, etc. See Leo Bersani, *Marcel Proust: The Fictions of Life and Art* (New York: Oxford University Press, 1965), 35–37; Litvak, *Strange Gourmets*, 77–111

passim; Richard, *Proust et le monde sensible*, 14–34; Serge Doubrovsky, *Writing and Fantasy in Proust: La place de la madeleine*, trans. Carol Mastrangelo Bové, with Paul A. Bové, pref. Carol Mastrangelo Bové, afterword Paul A. Bové (Lincoln and London: University of Nebraska Press, 1986); and Kaja Silverman, *Male Subjectivity at the Margins* (New York and London: Routledge, 1992), 373–88.

28. See Bersani, *Marcel Proust*, 6. For a reading subsuming all binaries in Proust's novel under the opposition of homo/heterosexuality, see Sedgwick, *Epistemology of the Closet*.
29. Freud wrote his "Three Essays on the Theory of Sexuality" in 1905, but added the section on sexual theories relating to children and the pregenital organization of the libido only in 1915, when Proust was working on the preliminary version of *Sodome* (1912–16), which was in complete manuscript form as of 1916. See James Strachey, "Editor's Note," *The Standard Edition of the Complete Psychological Works of Sigmund Freud*, trans. and ed. James Strachey, assisted by Alix Strachey and Alan Tyson, 24 vols., vol. VII: 1901–5 (London: Hogarth Press, 1953), 126; and Compagnon, "Préface," in *Sodome*, xxvii–xxviii. See also Malcolm Bowie's comparison of Proust's and Freud's epistemological projects in *Freud, Proust, and Lacan: Theory as Fiction* (Cambridge: Cambridge University Press, 1987), especially 68–97.
30. Although corroborating Freud's assertions that humans are inherently curious, recent studies of child development have found that this urge manifests itself far earlier than Freud suggested. Infants begin gathering information as early as the first few weeks of life, through various sensory stimuli. Although visual curiosity develops first, touching and listening quickly follow. See Burton L. White, *The First Three Years of Life* (New York and London: Prentice-Hall, 1990), 32, 36, 40–41, 52, 68, 120–21, 162–63, 219–20, 232; and White, *Educating the Infant and Toddler* (Lexington, MA and Toronto: Lexington Books, 1990), especially 47–49. White notes that the period from eight to fourteen months is a "period of life virtually dominated by curiosity" (*The First Three Years of Life*, 232).
31. Brooks, *Body Work*, 7.
32. Although Freud refers to an adolescent's fantasy of "overhearing" his parents engaging in sexual intercourse in "Three Essays," the psychoanalyst emphasizes the visual component of the activity, as his term "scopophilia" suggests (226). Not until 1925 does he revise this theory to suggest that "the fact of a child at a very early age *listening* to his parents copulating may set up his first sexual excitation." See Freud, "Some Psychical Consequences of the Anatomical Distinction Between the Sexes," in *The Standard Edition*, 24 vols., (London: Hogarth Press, 1961), XIX: 250 (e.m.).
33. Freud, "Three Essays on the Theory of Sexuality," 168.
34. Significantly, the second eavesdropping scene serves as the prelude to "La Race des Tantes" the section of *A la recherche* that discusses the secret life of "invertis," a life of continuous subterfuge, where one "imprudent" act can have disastrous consequences. Although Proust concludes this episode with

a visual metaphor (15; II: 635), he reiterates the importance of sound in revealing someone's sexual identity. What gives the invert away is a certain quality of his voice, an intonation that, once recognized, makes disguise almost impossible (*Sodome*, 63).

35. Roland Barthes also signals the "proximité (identité) de la jouissance et de la peur." See *Le plaisir du texte* (Paris: Editions du Seuil, 1973), 77.
36. The cassis recalls the plant of the same name outside Marcel's room in the scene of onanism.
37. The description of the young Russians who appear "partagés entre le désir, la tentation et une extrême frousse" (129; "torn between desire, temptation and extreme fright," III: 851) continues to connect Marcel's activities with those of the hotel patrons.
38. One could extend Litvak's analysis of how theatricality "is directed against a stable subjectivity" to eavesdropping, particularly the "set-up" eavesdrop. A highly theatrical moment, it complicates simple identifications and truths. See Litvak, *Caught in the Act: Theatricality in the Nineteenth-Century English Novel* (Berkeley and Los Angeles: University of California Press, 1992), xii.
39. Moss notes that "the secrecy of the homosexual and the hypocrisy of society are twin mirrors." See Moss, "The Windows," 100.
40. Proust's work thus anticipates theories of gender performativity. See Judith Butler, *Gender Trouble: Feminisim and the Subversion of Identity* (New York and London: Routledge, 1990).
41. *Le temps retrouvé*, 56; *La prisonnière*, 218.
42. Characters repeatedly fear being overheard. For examples, see *Sodome*, 96, 459.
43. For an alternative formulation that privileges vision and the homo/heterosexual binary, see Sedgwick's discussion of "the spectacle of the closet" in *Epistemology of the Closet*, especially 223–31. By focusing on *Sodome et Gomorrhe*, Sedgwick overemphasizes Charlus's functioning as spectacle to conclude that the display of his homosexuality prevents reading Albertine's sexuality as anything but straight; she dismisses the possibility of understanding Albertine's sexuality in more fluid terms. See 230–51.
44. For example, he asks the elevator boy to come to his room to make arrangements for Albertine to visit him. But "[a]vant de lui faire mes recommandations, je vis qu'il avait laissé la porte ouverte; je le lui fis remarquer, j'avais peur qu'on ne nous entendît; il condescendit à mon désir et revint ayant diminué l'ouverture. 'C'est pour vous faire plaisir. Mais il n'y a plus personne à l'étage.' Aussitôt j'entendis passer une, puis deux, puis trois personnes" (*Sodome*, 188; "[b]efore giving him my instructions, I saw that he had left the door open; I pointed this out to him, for I was afraid that people might hear us; he acceded to my request and returned, having reduced the gap. 'Anything to oblige. But there's nobody on this floor except us two.' Immediately I heard one, then a second, then a third person go by," II: 820). Similarly, when Albertine visits him in his room, he cautions her to whisper, so that his mother will not hear them (*Sodome*, 502; II, 1155).

45. See *Sodome*, 451 ff., 461.
46. See Roland Barthes, "The Reality Effect," in *The Rustle of Language*, trans. Richard Howard (Oxford: Basil Blackwell, 1986), 148, 141.
47. This passage recalls the moment when Albertine telephones Marcel to cancel a rendezvous. Listening to the sounds behind her voice over the wire, he realizes that she inhabits a world he neither knows completely nor controls, one separate from the part of her life that joins his (*Sodome*, 129–31).
48. Litvak also notes the "whole range of closet effects" throughout Proust's novel. See Litvak, *Strange Gourmets*, 91.
49. André Gide, *Journal*, 14 May 1921; cited in "Documents," in *Sodome*, 542.
50. On the controversy of identifying the first-person narrator as "Marcel," see Genette, *Narrative Discourse*, 249.
51. See, for example, letters to Robert Dreyfus and Georges de Lauris from, respectively, June 28 or 29, and 27 November 1909. *Correspondance*, ed. Philip Kolb, 21 vols. (Paris: Librairie Plon, 1970–93), IX: 119, 216.
52. See also Hayman, *Proust*, 311; and Genette, *Narrative Discourse*, 249, 251.
53. Some criticized him for immorality in his depiction of such a "perverse" world. Others, like Jacques Rivière, wrote approvingly of his "negative" portrayal of this world. See Compagnon's summary of the range of critical responses to Proust's depiction of "inversion" in "Préface," *Sodome*, vii–xxxiii. For an extensive array of early twentieth-century criticism, see Hodson, *Marcel Proust*.
54. See Gilles Deleuze, *Proust et les signes* (Paris: Presses Universitaires de France, 1983), 98, 161, 163–66, 213; Litvak, *Strange Gourmets*, 77–111; Sedgwick, *Epistemology of the Closet*, 213–51; and Silverman, *Male Subjectivity*, 373–88.
55. Proust makes an analogy several times between Jews and homosexuals as individuals who must hide their identity as members of marginalized social groups. See *Sodome*, 16, 17, 18, 66. However, as Litvak points out, the "two closets" are not interchangeable. See Litvak, *Strange Gourmets*, 91.
56. Proust figures the reader as "un ami à qui on ne se rappelle plus, après tant d'entretiens, si on a pensé ou trouvé l'occasion de le mettre au courant d'une certaine chose" (*La prisonnière*, 224; "a friend with regard to whom one has forgotten, after so many conversations, whether one has remembered or had a chance to tell him something," III: 236).
57. See his letter to Robert Dreyfus, 7 September 1888, where he speaks of "les différents Messieurs dont je me compose" ("the different men who comprise me") *Correspondance*, I: 113.
58. In an aside between an imagined reader and the narrator, *A la recherche* admits the possible, facile identification of first-person narrator and author. See *Sodome*, 51 (II: 675). See also Gray's discussion of the difficulty of "any critical act" in a work that "scrambl[es] confession, autobiography, and fiction," in *Postmodern Proust*, 9.
59. For example: "Personne ne sait tout d'abord qu'il est inverti, ou poète, ou snob, ou méchant. Tel collégien qui apprenait des vers d'amour ou regardait des images obscènes, s'il se serrait alors contre un camarade, s'imaginait seulement communier avec lui dans un même désir de la femme. Comment

croirait-il n'être pas pareil à tous, quand ce qu'il éprouve il en reconnaît la substance en lisant Mme de Lafayette, Racine, Baudelaire, Walter Scott, alors qu'il est encore trop peu capable de s'observer soi-même pour se rendre compte de ce qu'il ajoute de son cru, et que si le sentiment est le même l'objet diffère? (*Sodome*, 25; "No one can tell at first that he is an invert, or a poet, or a snob, or a scoundrel. The boy who has been reading erotic poetry or looking at obscene pictures, if he then presses his body against a schoolfellow's, imagines himself only to be communing with him in an identical desire for a woman. How should he suppose that he is not like everybody else when he recognises the substance of what he feels in reading Mme de La Fayette [*sic*], Racine, Baudelaire, Walter Scott, at a time when he is still too little capable of observing himself to take into account what he has added from his own store to the picture, and to realise that if the sentiment be the same the object differs?," II: 646–47). A comparison of our lives and desires with those of literary characters is insufficient, for it can disguise rather than reveal aspects of our identity. Reading, like eavesdropping, is only a preliminary step toward self-understanding.

60. Thomas M. Leicht, "For (Against) a Theory of Rereading," *Modern Fiction Studies* 33.3 (1987): 500.
61. "Journées de lecture," in *Contre Sainte-Beuve, Précédé de* pastiches et mélanges *et suivi de* Essais et articles, ed. Pierre Clarac and Yues Sandre (Paris: Editions Gallimard, 1971), 178.
62. Proust repeats this idea toward the end of the final volume: "ils ne seraient pas, selon moi, mes lecteurs, mais les propres lecteurs d'eux-mêmes" (*TR*, 338; "it seemed to me that they would not be 'my' readers, but the readers of their own selves," III: 1089).
63. Litvak, *Strange Gourmets*, 107.

CONCLUSION: COVERT LISTENERS AND SECRET AGENTS

1. Joseph Conrad, *The Secret Agent: A Simple Tale*, ed. and intro. Martin Seymour-Smith (1907; London: Penguin, 1984), 5. All subsequent references will be to this edition.
2. Ronald R. Thomas also notes Conrad's disingenuous reference to his story as a "simple" one, although he reads *The Secret Agent* as "the culmination of the rise of detective fiction and forensic science in the nineteenth century." See Thomas, *Detective Fiction and the Rise of Forensic Science* (Cambridge and New York: Cambridge University Press, 1999), 276.
3. See Charles Dickens, *Our Mutual Friend*, ed. Stephen Gill (1865; London: Penguin, 1997), 792.
4. John Ruskin, *Sesame and Lilies* (1865; London: Merrill and Baker, 1888), 102.
5. For example, in *Bleak House*, Inspector Bucket waits until bedtime to tell his wife about his plan to catch a murderess; although he trusts Mrs. Bucket, he takes the precaution of "stuff[ing] the sheet into Mrs. Bucket's mouth

that she shouldn't say a word of surprise." See Charles Dickens, *Bleak House*, ed. and intro. Nicola Bradbury (1853; London: Penguin, 1996), 833. Although the interaction takes place in the bedroom, the only object that places the scene in that intimate space is the sheet, used not to suggest the covering up of sensual bodies but the suppression of secrets. Intimacy is verbal rather than sexual, and the matter-of-fact, humorous tone expels any sense of impropriety from the brief exposure of the conjugal bedroom. French nineteenth-century fiction depicts the bedrooms of extramarital affairs frequently, but rarely sanctified unions with both husband and wife together in bed. Even Balzac, who spares few intimate details of the tale of adulterous passion, murder, and excess in *La fille aux yeux d'or*, describes the chastely separate bedrooms of the economical Grandets in *Eugénie Grandet*. *Madame Bovary* is one of the few exceptions; it not only portrays Emma's sexual escapades with Léon, but also conveys Charles's initial happiness and Emma's dissatisfaction with their marriage by describing each considering the other in the conjugal bed. See Gustave Flaubert, *Madame Bovary* (Paris: Garnier-Flammarion, 1986), 337–38, 92–93, 264–65.

6. Honoré de Balzac, *La Cousine Bette*, ed. André Lorant (Paris: Garnier-Flammarion, 1977), 251; *Cousin Bette*, trans. James Waring (London: Everyman's Library, 1991), 217; Marcel Proust, *Sodome et Gomorrhe*, ed. Antoine Compagnon (Paris: Gallimard, 1989), 435–36; *Remembrance of Things Past*, trans C. K. Scott Moncrieff and Terence Kilmartin, 3 vols. (London: Chatto and Windus, 1981), II: 1083.

7. In *Under Western Eyes*, the revolutionary Haldin hides in Razumov's room, lying in the student's bed while he waits for an opportunity to escape. Haldin's assumption of Razumov's most private place implicates Razumov in a larger conspiracy of plots and counterplots; it changes the course of his life. No space is free from political or economic associations. Since all places are under surveillance, all activities are public ones. See Joseph Conrad, *Under Western Eyes* (1911; London: Penguin, 1986), 71.

8. Other words and expressions include "watchfulness" (58), "under my eye" (64), "glance" (82), "vision" (84), "unwinking orbs" (90), "searchlights" (97), "watching" (113), "round and habitually roving eyes" (134), "eyed" (210), etc.

9. *The Secret Agent* refuses to separate its own metaphoric, narrative spaces and subjects. The figurative language of descriptive passages steals the topic of a dialogue between Toodles and the Assistant Commissioner, the Fisheries bill (149). Thus the Assistant Commissioner's descent into the streets is likened to a plunge "into a slimy aquarium... He might have been but one more of the queer foreign fish that can be seen of an evening about there flitting round the dark corners" (151).

10. Rishona Zimring, "Conrad's Pornography Shop," *Modern Fiction Studies* 43.2 (1997): 340.

11. Even less overtly political modernist fiction stresses the perils of remaining mere eavesdroppers on other people's lives. Edith Wharton's *The Age of Innocence* explores the psychological costs of remaining a "looker-on" of life.

See Wharton, *The Age of Innocence* (1920; New York: Penguin, 1996), 161. Refusing to transgress social boundaries and to risk scandal, Newland Archer passes up opportunities for awareness, intimacy, and self-transformation. Figures such as Lambert Strether in *The Ambassadors* (1903) and Dowell of *The Good Soldier* (1915) also learn belatedly the experiential costs of that safe position.

12. Clue (or Cluedo) renders concrete the essential elements of conventional detective fiction. The game reiterates the fact that, in contrast to spy fiction, detective fiction identifies a single culprit and places him with the murder weapon at the scene of the crime. The genre and its conventions "exis[t] expressly to dispel the doubt that guilt might be impersonal, and therefore collective and social." See Franco Moretti, *Signs Taken for Wonders: Essays in the Sociology of Literary Forms*, trans. Susan Fischer, David Forgacs, and David Miller (London and New York: Verso, 1988), 135.

Select bibliography

Ackroyd, Peter. *Dickens*. New York: HarperCollins, 1990.
Apter, Emily. *Feminizing the Fetish: Psychoanalysis and Narrative Obsession in Turn-of-the-Century France*. Ithaca and London: Cornell University Press, 1991.
Ariès, Philippe, and Georges Duby, general eds. *A History of Private Life*. 5 vols. Cambridge, MA and London: Harvard University Press, 1987–91. Trans. of *Histoire de la vie privée*. Paris: Seuil, 1985–87.
Armstrong, Frances. *Dickens and the Concept of Home*. Ann Arbor and London: UMI Research Press, 1990.
Armstrong, Nancy. *Desire and Domestic Fiction: A Political History of the Novel*. New York and Oxford: Oxford University Press, 1987.
Auerbach, Erich. *The Representation of Reality in Western Literature*. Trans. Willard R. Trask. Princeton: Princeton University Press, 1953.
Auerbach, Nina. *Woman and the Demon: The Life of a Victorian Myth*. Cambridge, MA and London: Harvard University Press, 1982.
Austen, Jane. *Emma*. 1816. Ed. Stephen M. Parrish. New York and London: W. W. Norton, 1972.
  Jane Austen's Letters to Her Sister Cassandra and Others. Coll. and ed. R. W. Chapman. 2 vols. Oxford: Clarendon Press, 1932.
  Mansfield Park. 1814. Ed. Tony Tanner. London: Penguin, 1985.
  Persuasion. 1818. Afterword Marvin Mudrick. New York: Signet Classic, 1980.
  Pride and Prejudice. 1813. Ed. and intro. Tony Tanner. London and New York: Penguin, 1972.
Babb, Howard S. *Jane Austen's Novels: The Fabric of Dialogue*. Columbus: Ohio State University Press, 1962.
Bachelard, Gaston. *La poétique de l'espace*. Paris: Presses Universitaires de France, 1957. Paris: Quadrige, 1989.
Bakhtin, Mikhail. *The Dialogic Imagination: Four Essays*. Ed. Michael Holquist. Trans. Caryl Emerson and Michael Holquist. Austin: University of Texas Press, 1981.
  Speech Genres and Other Late Essays. Ed. Caryl Emerson and Michael Holquist. Trans. Vern W. McGee. Austin: University of Texas Press, 1986.
  Toward a Philosophy of the Act. Ed. Vadim Liapunov and Michael Holquist. Trans. and notes Vadim Liapunov. Austin: University of Texas Press, 1993.

Balée, Susan. "Wilkie Collins and Surplus Women: The Case of Marian Halcombe." *Victorian Literature and Culture* 20 (1992): 197–215.
Balzac, Honoré de. "Avant-Propos." 1842. *La comédie humaine*. 12 vols. Vol. I. Paris: Gallimard, Bibliothèque de la Pléïade, 1976.
Le Colonel Chabert. 1832. *La comédie humaine*. 12 vols. Vol. III. Paris: Gallimard, Bibliothèque de la Pléïade, 1976.
La Cousine Bette. 1846. Ed. André Lorant. Paris: Garnier-Flammarion, 1977.
Le Cousin Pons. 1847. Ed. and postface André Lorant. Pref. Jacques Thuillier. Paris: Gallimard, 1973.
Lettres à Madame Hanska, 1832–1850. Ed. Roger Pierrot. 2 vols. Paris: Robert Laffont, 1990.
Le Père Goriot. 1834–35. Ed. Thierry Bodrin. Préf. Félicien Marceau. Paris: Gallimard, 1971.
Bander, Elaine. "Jane Austen and the Uses of Silence." *Literature and Ethics: Essays Presented to A. E. Malloch*. Ed. Gary Wihl and David Williams. Kingston and Montreal: McGill-Queen's University Press, 1988, 46–61.
Banfield, Ann. "The Influence of Place: Jane Austen and the Novel of Social Consciousness." Monaghan, ed., *Jane Austen in a Social Context*, 28–48.
Barickman, Richard, Susan MacDonald, and Myra Stark. *Corrupt Relations: Dickens, Thackeray, Trollope, Collins, and the Victorian Sexual System*. New York: Columbia University Press, 1982.
Baron, Anne-Marie. "Artifices de mise en scène et art de l'illusion." *L'Année balzacienne* 17 (1996): 23–35.
"Statut et fonctions de l'observateur balzacien." *L'Année balzacienne* 10 (1989): 301–16.
Barthes, Roland. "Une idée de recherche." *Recherche de Proust*. Ed. Gérard Genette and Tzvetan Todorov. Paris: Editions du Seuil, 1980, 34–39.
Le Plaisir du texte. Paris: Editions du Seuil, 1973.
The Pleasure of the Text. Trans. Richard Miller. London: Basil Blackwell, 1975.
"The Reality Effect." *The Rustle of Language*. Trans. Richard Howard. Oxford: Basil Blackwell, 1986, 141–48.
The Responsibility of Forms: Critical Essays on Music, Art, and Representation. New York: Hill and Wang, 1985. Trans. of *L'Obvie et l'obtus*. Paris: Seuil, 1982.
S/Z. Pref. Richard Howard. Trans. Richard Miller. New York: Hill and Wang, 1974.
Beizer, Janet. *Family Plots: Balzac's Narrative Generations*. New Haven and London: Yale University Press, 1986.
Bell, David. "Marque, trace, pistes: Balzac à la recherche d'une science des indices." Mahieu and Schuerewegen, eds., *Balzac*, 107–12.
Benjamin, Walter. "Louis-Philippe or the Interior." *Charles Baudelaire: A Lyric Poet in the Era of High Capitalism*. Trans. Harry Zohn. London: New Left Books, 1973, 167–69.

"The Storyteller." *Illuminations: Essays and Reflections.* Trans. Harry Zohn. Ed. and intro. Hannah Arendt. New York: Schocken Books, 1969, 83–109.
Bernstein, Stephen. "Reading Blackwater Park: Gothicism, Narrative, and Ideology in *The Woman in White.*" *Studies in the Novel* 25.3 (1993): 291–305.
Bersani, Leo. *Marcel Proust: The Fictions of Life and Art.* New York: Oxford University Press, 1965.
Bloom, Harold, ed. and intro. *Marcel Proust: Modern Critical Views.* New York, New Haven, and Philadelphia: Chelsea House, 1987.
Bowers, Bege K., and Brothers, Barbara, eds. *Reading and Writing Women's Lives: A Study of the Novel of Manners.* Ann Arbor and London: UMI Research Press, 1990.
Bowie, Malcolm. *Freud, Proust, and Lacan: Theory as Fiction.* Cambridge: Cambridge University Press, 1987.
Brantlinger, Patrick. *The Reading Lesson: The Threat of Mass Literacy in Nineteenth-Century British Fiction.* Bloomington and Indianapolis: Indiana University Press, 1998.
Brée, Germaine. "The Closed Door." Bloom, ed., *Marcel Proust*, 37–58.
Brennan, Teresa, and Martin Jay, eds. *Vision in Context: Historical and Contemporary Perspectives on Sight.* New York and London: Routledge, 1996.
Brontë, Emily. *Wuthering Heights.* 1847. Ed. William M. Sale, Jr., and Richard J. Dunn. New York and London: W. W. Norton, 1990.
Brooks, Peter. *Body Work: Objects of Desire in Modern Narrative.* Cambridge, MA and London: Harvard University Press, 1993.
  The Melodramatic Imagination: Balzac, Henry James, Melodrama, and the Mode of Excess. New Haven and London: Yale University Press, 1976; rptd. with new preface, 1995.
  Reading for the Plot: Design and Intention in Narrative. New York: Vintage, 1985.
Brower, Reuben A. "Light and Bright and Sparkling: Irony and Fiction in *Pride and Prejudice.*" Watt, ed., *Jane Austen*, 62–75.
Brown, Julia Prewitt. *Jane Austen's Novels: Social Change and Literary Form.* Cambridge, MA and London: Harvard University Press, 1979.
Brown, Lloyd W. *Bits of Ivory: Narrative Techniques in Jane Austen's Fiction.* Baton Rouge: Louisiana State University Press, 1973.
Bryson, Norman, Michael Ann Holly, and Keith Moxey, eds. *Visual Culture: Images and Interpretations.* Hanover and London: Wesleyan University Press and University Press of New England, 1994.
Burney, Frances. *Evelina.* 1778. Oxford and New York: Oxford University Press, 1990.
Butler, Judith. *Gender Trouble: Feminisim and the Subversion of Identity.* New York and London: Routledge, 1990.
Butler, Marilyn. *Jane Austen and the War of Ideas.* Oxford: Oxford University Press, 1975.

Butor, Michel. "The Novel as Research." *Inventory: Essays by Michel Butor*. Ed. and foreword Richard Howard. Trans. Gerald Fabian. New York: Simon and Schuster, 1968, 26–30.
Castle, Terry. *Clarissa's Ciphers: Meaning and Disruption in Richardson's "Clarissa."* Ithaca and London: Cornell University Press, 1982.
Cavell, Stanley. *Pursuits of Happiness: The Hollywood Comedy of Remarriage*. Cambridge, MA and London: Harvard University Press, 1981.
Chandler, Alice. "'A Pair of Fine Eyes': Jane Austen's Treatment of Sex." *Studies in the Novel* 7 (1985): 88–103.
Chandler, Marilyn R. *Dwelling in the Text: Houses in American Fiction*. Berkeley: University of California Press, 1991.
Chapman, R. W., ed. *The Manuscript Chapters of* Persuasion. London: Oxford University Press, 1926; rptd. London and Dover, NH: Athlore Press, 1985.
  "*Pride and Prejudice* and *Cecilia*." *The Novels of Jane Austen*. 3rd edn. 5 vols. Vol. II. Oxford and New York: Oxford University Press, 1923; rptd. 1965, 408–09.
Chase, Karen and Michael Levenson. *The Spectacle of Intimacy: A Public Life for the Victorian Family*. Princeton and Oxford: Princeton University Press, 2000.
Clarke, William M. *The Secret Life of Wilkie Collins*. London: W. H. Allen, 1988.
Collins, W. Wilkie. *Armadale*. 1866. Ed. Catherine Peters. Oxford and New York: Oxford University Press, 1989.
  The Law and the Lady. 1875. Ed. Jenny Bourne Taylor. Oxford and New York: Oxford University Press, 1992.
  No Name. 1862. Ed. Virginia Blain. Oxford and New York: Oxford University Press, 1989.
  The Woman in White. 1860–61. Eds. Kathleen Tillotson and Anthea Trodd. Riverside Edition. Boston: Houghton Mifflin, 1969.
  The Woman in White. 1860–61. Ed. and intro. Julian Symons. London and New York: Penguin, 1974.
Conrad, Joseph. *The Secret Agent: A Simple Tale*. 1907. Ed. and intro. Martin Seymour-Smith. London: Penguin, 1984.
Crary, Jonathan. *Techniques of the Observer*. Cambridge, MA and London: MIT Press, 1991.
Culler, Jonathan. *Structuralist Poetics: Structuralism, Linguistics, and the Study of Literature*. Ithaca: Cornell University Press, 1975.
Cvetkovich, Ann. *Mixed Feelings: Feminism, Mass Culture, and Victorian Sensationalism*. New Brunswick: Rutgers University Press, 1992.
Deaucourt, Jean-Louis. "Une police des sentiments: les concierges et les portiers." *Romantisme* 68.2 (1990): 49–60.
  Premières loges: Paris et ses concierges au XIXe siècle. Paris: Aubier, 1992.
Deleuze, Gilles. *Proust et les signes*. 1964. Paris: Presses Universitaires de France, 1983.
De Man, Paul. "Reading (Proust)." Bloom, ed., *Marcel Proust*, 183–200.
Dickens, Charles. *Dombey and Son*. 1848. Ed. Peter Fairclough. Intro. Raymond Williams. Harmondsworth and New York: Penguin, 1986.

Bleak House. 1853. Ed. and intro. Nicola Bradbury. London: Penguin, 1996.
Great Expectations. 1860–61. Ed. Angus Calder. London and New York: Penguin, 1985.
Oliver Twist. 1837–38. Ed. Kathleen Tillotson. Intro. Stephen Gill. Oxford and New York: Oxford University Press, 1999.
Our Mutual Friend. 1865. Ed. Stephen Gill, London: Penguin, 1997.
Donzelot, Jacques. *The Policing of Families*. Trans. R. Hurley. New York: Pantheon, 1979. Trans. of *La police des familles*. Paris: Minuit, 1977.
Doubrovsky, Serge. *Writing and Fantasy in Proust: La place de la madeleine*. Pref. Carol Mastrangelo Bové. Afterword Paul A. Bové. Trans. Carol Mastrangelo Bové with Paul A. Bové. Lincoln and London: University of Nebraska Press, 1986.
Duckworth, Alistair M. *The Improvement of the Estate: A Study of Jane Austen's Novels*. Baltimore and London: Johns Hopkins University Press, 1971.
Elam, Diane. "White Narratology: Gender and Reference in Wilkie Collins's *The Woman in White*." *Virginal Sexuality and Textuality in Victorian Literature*. Ed. Lloyd Davis. Albany: State University Press of New York, 1993, 49–63.
Eleb-Vidal, Monique, and Anne Debarre-Blanchard. *Architectures de la vie privée: maisons et mentalités XVIIe–XIXe siècles*. Intro. Michelle Perrot. Brussels: Archives d'Architecture Moderne, 1989.
Eliot, George. *Middlemarch: A Tale of Provincial Life*. 1871–72. Ed. Bert G. Hornback. New York and London: W. W. Norton, 1977.
Erickson, Joyce Quiring. "Public and Private in Jane Austen's Novels." *Midwest Quarterly: A Journal of Contemporary Thought* 25.2 (1984): 201–19.
Evans, Robin. "Figures, Doors and Passages." *Architectural Design* 4 (1978): 267–78.
Fanger, Donald. *Dostoevsky and Romantic Realism: A Study of Dostoevsky in Relation to Balzac, Dickens, and Gogol*. Cambridge, MA: Harvard University Press, 1965.
Farrant, Tim. "Le Privé: Espace menacé? Des premières 'Scènes de la vie privée' aux 'Secrets de la Princesse de Cadignan.'" *L'Année balzacienne* 15 (1994): 121–38.
Farrell, Thomas J. "The Female and Male Modes of Rhetoric." *College English* 40.8 (1979): 909–21.
Farrer, Reginald. "Jane Austen, ob. July 18, 1817." *Quarterly Review* July 1917; rptd. in Southam, ed., *Jane Austen*, vol. II, 245–72.
Ferris, Ina. "From Trope to Code: The Novel and the Rhetoric of Gender in Nineteenth-Century Critical Discourse." Shires, ed., *Rewriting the Victorians*, 18–30.
Finch, Casey, and Peter Bowen. "'The Tittle-Tattle of Highbury': Gossip and the Free Indirect Style in *Emma*." *Representations* 31 (1990): 1–18.
Forster, E. M. *Aspects of the Novel*. London: Harcourt, Brace and World, 1927. New York and London: Harcourt Brace Jovanovich, 1974.
Foucault, Michel. *Discipline and Punish: The Birth of the Prison*. Trans. Alan Sheridan. New York: Vintage Books, 1979. Trans. of *Surveiller et punir: Naissance de la prison*. Paris: Gallimard, 1975.

The History of Sexuality. Volume One: An Introduction. Trans. Robert Hurley. New York: Vintage Books, 1990. Trans. of *La volenté de savoir.* 3 vols. Paris: Gallimard, 1976.

"Of Other Spaces." Mirzoeff, ed., *Visual Culture Reader,* 237–44.

Frank, Ellen. *Literary Architecture: Essays Toward a Tradition.* Berkeley: University of California Press, 1979.

Freud, Sigmund. "Three Essays on the Theory of Sexuality." *The Standard Edition of the Complete Psychological Works of Sigmund Freud.* Trans. and ed. James Strachey. 24 vols. Vol. VII. London: Hogarth Press, 1953, 135–245.

"Some Psychical Consequences of the Anatomical Distinction Between the Sexes." *The Standard Edition of the Complete Psychological Works of Sigmund Freud.* Trans. and ed. James Strachey. 24 vols. Vol. XIX. London: Hogarth Press, 1961, 248–58.

Fuentes, Carlos, foreword and intro. *Don Quixote de la Mancha.* By Miguel de Cervantes. Trans. Tobias Smollett. London: André Deutsch Limited, 1986.

Garrett, Peter K. *The Victorian Multiplot Novel: Studies in Dialogical Form.* New Haven and London: Yale University Press, 1980.

Genette, Gérard. *Figures II.* Paris: Seuil, 1969.

Narrative Discourse: An Essay in Method. Foreword Jonathan Culler. Trans. Jane E. Lewin. Ithaca: Cornell University Press, 1980.

Gilbert, Sandra M., and Susan Gubar. *The Madwoman in the Attic: The Woman Writer and the Nineteenth-Century Literary Imagination.* New Haven and London: Yale University Press, 1984.

Gillis, Christina Marsden. "Private Room and Public Space: The Paradox of Form in *Clarissa.*" *Studies in Voltaire and the Eighteenth Century* 176 (1979): 153–68.

Girouard, Mark. *Life in the English Country House: A Social and Architectural History.* New Haven and London: Yale University Press, 1978.

Goffman, Erving. *Behavior in Public Places: Notes on the Social Organization of Gatherings.* New York: Free Press, 1963.

Gordon, Jan B. *Gossip and Subversion in Nineteenth-Century British Fiction: Echo's Economies.* London: Macmillan; New York: St. Martin's Press, 1996.

Gray, Margaret E. *Postmodern Proust.* Philadelphia: University of Pennsylvania Press, 1992.

Greimas, A. J. *Structural Semantics: An Attempt at a Method.* Intro. Ronald Schleifer. Lincoln: University of Nebraska Press, 1983.

Grosz, Elizabeth. *Jacques Lacan: A Feminist Introduction.* London and New York: Routledge, 1990.

Habermas, Jürgen. "The Public Sphere." *New German Critique* 1.3 (Fall 1974): 49–55.

The Structural Transformation of the Public Sphere: An Inquiry into a Category of Bourgeois Society. Intro. Thomas McCarthy. Trans. Thomas Burger and Frederick Lawrence. Cambridge, MA: MIT Press, 1982.

Hall, Catherine. "The Sweet Delights of Home." Perrot, ed., *Fires of Revolution,* 47–97.

Hamon, Philippe. *Expositions: Literature and Architecture in Nineteenth-Century France*. Intro. Richard Sieburth. Trans. Katia Sainson-Frank and Lisa Maguire. Berkeley: University of California Press, 1992.

Haraway, Donna. "The Persistence of Vision." Mirzoeff, ed., *The Visual Culture Reader*, 191–98.

Harding, D. W. "Regulated Hatred: An Aspect of the Work of Jane Austen." Watt, ed., *Jane Austen*, 166–79.

  Intro. *Persuasion*. By Jane Austen. London and New York: Penguin, 1985, 7–26.

Hardy, Barbara. *A Reading of Jane Austen*. London: Peter Owen, 1975.

Hart, Francis R. "The Spaces of Privacy: Jane Austen." *Nineteenth-Century Fiction* 30 (1975): 305–33.

Hayman, Ronald. *Proust: A Biography*. London: Heinemann, 1990.

Heath, William, ed. and intro. *Discussions of Jane Austen*. Boston: D. C. Heath and Co., 1961.

Heller, Tamar. *Dead Secrets: Wilkie Collins and the Female Gothic*. New Haven and London: Yale University Press, 1992.

Helsinger, Elizabeth, Robin Lauterbach Sheets, and William Veeder. *Literary Issues*. Vol. III of *The Woman Question: Society and Literature in Britain and America, 1837–1883*. 3 vols. Chicago and London: University of Chicago Press, 1983.

Hennedy, Hugh L. "Acts of Perception in Jane Austen's Novels." *Studies in the Novel* 5 (1973): 22–38.

Hennelly, Mark, Jr. "*Pride and Prejudice:* The Eyes Have It." Todd, ed., *Jane Austen*, 187–207.

  "Reading Detection in *The Woman in White*." *Texas Studies in Literature and Language* 22.4 (1980): 449–67.

Hodson, Leighton, ed. *Marcel Proust: The Critical Heritage*. London and New York: Routledge, 1989.

Holquist, Michael. *Dialogism: Bakhtin and His World*. London and New York: Routledge, 1991.

Honan, Park. *Jane Austen: Her Life*. London: Weidenfeld and Nicolson, 1987.

Hughes, Winifred. *The Maniac in the Cellar: Sensation Novels of the 1860s*. Princeton: Princeton University Press, 1980.

Hunt, Herbert J., trans. *Cousin Pons*. By Honoré de Balzac. London: The Folio Society, 1984.

Irigaray, Luce. *Speculum of the Other Woman*. Trans. Gillian C. Gill. Ithaca: Cornell University Press, 1985. Trans. of *Speculum de l'autre femme*. Paris: Editions de Minuit, 1974.

James, Henry. "Miss Braddon." Page, ed., *Wilkie Collins*, 122–24.

Jay, Martin. *Downcast Eyes: The Denigration of Vision in Twentieth-Century French Thought*. Berkeley and Los Angeles: University of California Press, 1993.

Jenks, Chris. "The Centrality of the Eye in Western Culture: An Introduction." *Visual Culture*. Ed. Chris Jenks. London and New York: Routledge, 1995, 1–25.

Johnson, Claudia. *Jane Austen: Women, Politics, and the Novel*. Chicago and London: University of Chicago Press, 1988.
Johnson, Samuel. *Dictionary of the English Language*. 1755. New York: Arno Press, 1979.
Kendrick, Walter M. "The Sensationalism of *The Woman in White*." *Nineteenth-Century Fiction* 32.1 (1977): 18–35.
Kent, Christopher. "'Real Solemn History' and Social History." Monaghan, ed., *Jane Austen in a Social Context*, 86–104.
Kermode, Frank. *The Genesis of Secrecy: On the Interpretation of Narrative*. Cambridge, MA and London: Harvard University Press, 1979.
Kerr, Robert. *The Gentleman's House*. 1864. London: John Murray, 1871.
Knoepflmacher, U. C. "The Counterworld of Victorian Fiction and *The Woman in White*." *The Worlds of Victorian Fiction*. Ed. Jerome H. Buckley. Cambridge, MA and London: Harvard University Press, 1975, 351–69.
  Laughter and Despair: Readings in Ten Novels of the Victorian Era. Berkeley: University of California Press, 1971.
Kohon, Gregorio. "Reflections on Dora: The Case of Hysteria." *The British School of Psychoanalysis: The Independent Tradition*. Ed. Gregorio Kohon. New Haven and London: Yale University Press, 1986, 97–108.
Kucich, John. *The Power of Lies: Transgression in Victorian Fiction*. Ithaca and London: Cornell University Press, 1994.
  Repression in Victorian Fiction: Charlotte Brontë, George Eliot, and Charles Dickens. Berkeley and Los Angeles: University of California Press, 1987.
Langbauer, Laurie. "Women in White, Men in Feminism." *Yale Journal of Criticism* 2.2 (1989): 219–43.
Lanser, Susan Snaider. *Fictions of Authority: Women Writers and Narrative Voice*. Ithaca and London: Cornell University Press, 1992.
Lefebvre, Henri. *The Production of Space*. Trans. Donald Nicholson-Smith. Cambridge, MA and Oxford: Blackwell, 1991.
Leicht, Thomas M. "For (Against) a Theory of Rereading." *Modern Fiction Studies* 33.3 (1987): 491–508.
Levenson, Michael. *A Genealogy of Modernism: A Study of English Literary Doctrine 1908–1922*. Cambridge and New York: Cambridge University Press, 1984.
Levine, George. *The Realistic Imagination: English Fiction from Frankenstein to Lady Chatterley*. Chicago and London: University of Chicago Press, 1981.
Litvak, Joseph. *Caught in the Act: Theatricality in the Nineteenth-Century English Novel*. Berkeley and Los Angeles: University of California Press, 1992.
  Strange Gourmets: Sophistication, Theory, and the Novel. Durham, NC and London: Duke University Press, 1997.
Litz, A. Walton. *Jane Austen: A Study of Her Artistic Development*. New York: Oxford University Press, 1965.
Loesberg, Jonathan. "The Ideology of Form in Sensation Fiction." *Representations* 13 (1986): 115–38.

Lonoff, Sue. "Multiple Narratives and Relative Truths: A Study of *The Ring and the Book*, *The Woman in White*, and *The Moonstone*." *Browning Institute Studies* 10 (1982): 143–61.
Wilkie Collins and His Victorian Readers: A Study in the Rhetoric of Authorship. New York: AMS Press, 1982.
Loyer, François. *Paris, Nineteenth Century: Architecture and Urbanism*. Trans. Charles Lynn Clark. New York: Abbeville Press, 1988.
Mack, Arien, ed. *Home: A Place in the World*. New York and London: New York University Press, 1993.
Mahieu, Robert and Franc Schuerewegen, eds. *Balzac ou la tentation de l'impossible*. Paris: SEDES, 1998.
Marcus, Sharon. *Apartment Stories: City and Home in Nineteenth-Century Paris and London*. Berkeley: University of California Press, 1999.
Markus, Thomas A. *Buildings and Power: Freedom and Control in the Origin of Modern Building Types*. New York and London: Routledge, 1993.
Maxwell, Richard. *The Mysteries of Paris and London*. Charlottesville and London: University Press of Virginia, 1992.
May, Leila Silvana. "Sensational Sisters: Wilkie Collins's *The Woman in White*." *Pacific Coast Philology* 30.1 (1995): 82–102.
McCuskey, Brian W. "The Kitchen Police: Servant Surveillance and Middle-Class Transgression." *Victorian Literature and Culture* (2000): 359–75.
McGregor, Graham. "Eavesdropping and the Analysis of Everyday Verbal Exchange." Ed. and pref. Alan R. Thomas. Intro. Martin J. Ball. *Methods in Dialectology*. Clevedon and Philadelphia: Multilingual Matters, 1988, 362–72.
"Listeners' Comments on Conversation." *Language and Communication: An Interdisciplinary Journal* 3.3 (1983): 271–304.
McGuire, James R. "The Feminine Conspiracy in Balzac's *La Cousine Bette*." *Nineteenth-Century French Studies* 20.3–4 (1992): 295–304.
McLaughlin, Kevin. *Writing in Parts: Imitation and Exchange in Nineteenth-Century Literature*. Stanford: Stanford University Press, 1995.
Metz, Christian. *The Imaginary Signifier: Psychoanalysis and Cinema*. Trans. Celia Britton, Annwyl Williams, Ben Brewster, and Alfred Guzzetti. Baltimore: Johns Hopkins University Press, 1982.
Meyersohn, Marylea. "Jane Austen's Garrulous Speakers: Social Criticism in *Sense and Sensibility*, *Emma*, and *Persuasion*." Bowers and Brothers, eds., *Reading and Writing Women's Lives*, 35–48.
"What Fanny Knew: 'A Quiet Auditor of the Whole.'" Todd, ed., *Jane Austen*, 224–30.
Miller, D. A. *Narrative and Its Discontents: Problems of Closure in the Traditional Novel*. Princeton: Princeton University Press, 1981.
The Novel and the Police. Berkeley: University of California Press, 1988.
Miller, J. Hillis. *Charles Dickens: The World of His Novels*. Cambridge, MA: Harvard University Press, 1959.

The Form of Victorian Fiction: Thackeray, Dickens, Trollope, George Eliot, Meredith, and Hardy. Notre Dame and London: University of Notre Dame Press, 1968.

Miller, Nancy K., intro. *The Princess of Clèves.* By Madame de Lafayette. Trans. Walter J. Cobb. New York: New American Library, 1989.

Milner, Max. "Les dispositifs voyeuristes dans le récit balzacien." Vachon, ed., *Balzac,* 157–71.

Milton, John. "Doctrine and Discipline of Divorce." 1643. *John Milton: Complete Poems and Major Prose.* Ed. Merritt Y. Hughes. New York: Odyssey Press, 1957, 696–715.

Mimouni, Isabelle. "Écriture et architecture: Une question de langue." *L'Année balzacienne* 19 (1998): 303–22.

Miner, Earl. *Comparative Poetics: An Intercultural Essay on Theories of Literature.* Princeton: Princeton University Press, 1990.

Mirzoeff, Nicholas, ed. and intro. *The Visual Culture Reader.* London and New York: Routledge, 1998.

Mitchell, W. J. T. *Picture Theory: Essays in Verbal and Visual Representation.* Chicago: University of Chicago Press, 1995.

Moler, Kenneth L. *Jane Austen's Art of Allusion.* Lincoln: University of Nebraska Press, 1968.

Monaghan, David. "The Complexity of Jane Austen's Novels." Todd, ed., *Jane Austen,* 88–97.

Jane Austen: Structure and Social Vision. London and Basingstoke: Macmillan, 1980.

Monaghan, David, ed. *Jane Austen in a Social Context.* London: Macmillan; Totowa: Barnes and Noble, 1981.

Moncrieff, C. K. Scott, and Terence Kilmartin, trans. *Remembrance of Things Past.* By Marcel Proust. 3 vols. London: Chatto and Windus, 1981.

Moretti, Franco. *The Way of the World: The* Bildungsroman *in European Culture.* London: Verso, 1987.

Signs Taken for Wonders: Essays in the Sociology of Literary Forms. Trans. Susan Fischer, David Forgacs, and David Miller. London and New York: Verso, 1988.

Moss, Howard. "The Windows." Bloom, ed., *Marcel Proust,* 97–108.

Mudrick, Marvin. *Jane Austen: Irony as Defense and Discovery.* Princeton: Princeton University Press, 1952.

"Irony as Discrimination: *Pride and Prejudice.*" Watt, ed., *Jane Austen,* 76–97.

Neuman, Robert. "French Domestic Architecture in the Early 18th Century: The Town Houses of Robert de Cotte." *Journal of the Society of Architectural Historians* 39.2 (1990): 128–44.

Newman, Karen. "Can This Marriage Be Saved? Jane Austen Makes Sense of an Ending." *ELH* 50.4 (1983): 693–710.

O'Connor, Frank. "Jane Austen: The Flight from Fancy." Heath, ed., *Discussions of Jane Austen,* 65–74.

O'Farrell, Mary Ann. *Telling Complexions: The Nineteenth-Century English Novel and the Blush.* Durham, NC and London: Duke University Press, 1997.

O'Neill, Philip. *Wilkie Collins: Women, Property and Propriety*. London: Macmillan, 1988.
Ong, Walter J. *Orality and Literacy: The Technologizing of the Word*. London and New York: Methuen, 1982.
Orange, Michael. "Aspects of Narration in Persuasion." *Sydney Studies in English* 15 (1989–90): 63–71.
Page, Norman, ed. *Wilkie Collins: The Critical Heritage*. London and Boston: Routledge and Kegan Paul, 1974.
Perkins, Pamela, and Mary Donaghy. "A Man's Resolution: Narrative Strategies in Wilkie Collins's *The Woman in White*." *Studies in the Novel* 22.2 (1990): 392–402.
Perrot, Michelle, ed. and intro. *From the Fires of Revolution to the Great War*. Vol. IV of *A History of Private Life*. General eds. Philippe Ariès and Georges Duby. 5 vols. Cambridge, MA and London: Harvard University Press, 1990.
 Intro. "Les secrets de la maison." *Architectures de la vie privée: maisons et mentalités XVIIe–XIXe siècles*. By Monique Eleb-Vidal and Anne Debarre-Blanchard. Brussels: Archives d'Architecture Moderne, 1989, 5–8.
Phillips, Walter C. *Dickens, Reade, and Collins: Sensation Novelists*. New York: Columbia University Press, 1919.
Poovey, Mary. "Creative Criticism and the Problem of Objectivity." *Narrative* 8.2 (May 2000): 109–33.
 "*Persuasion* and the Promises of Love." *The Representation of Women in Fiction*. Ed. Carolyn G. Heilbrun and Margaret R. Higonnet. Selected Papers from the English Institute, n.s., 7. Baltimore and London: Johns Hopkins University Press, 1983, 152–79.
 The Proper Lady and the Woman Writer: Ideology as Style in the Works of Mary Wollstonecraft, Mary Shelley, and Jane Austen. Chicago and London: University of Chicago Press, 1984.
Porter, Roy. *London: A Social History*. Cambridge, MA: Harvard University Press, 1994.
Preiss, Nathalie. "Les 'Scènes de la vie privée': Scènes originaires? Autour du lexique de la vie privée." *L'Année balzacienne* 17 (1996): 355–66.
Prendergast, Christopher. "Introduction: Realism, God's Secret, and the Body." *Spectacles of Realism: Body, Gender, and Genre*. Eds. Margaret Cohen and Christopher Prendergast. Minneapolis and London: University of Minnesota Press, 1995, 1–10.
Proust, Marcel. *Albertine disparue*. Ed. Anne Chevalier. Paris: Editions Gallimard, 1990.
 Contre Sainte-Beuve. Précédé de Pastiches et mélanges *et suivi de* Essais et articles. Ed. Pierre Clarac and Yves Sandre. Paris: Editions Gallimard, 1971.
 Correspondance. Ed. Philip Kolb. 21 vols. Paris: Librairie Plon, 1970–93.
 Correspondance générale de Marcel Proust. Ed. Robert Proust, Paul Brach, and Suzy Mante-Proust. 6 vols. Paris: Plon, 1930–36.

Du côté de chez Swann. Ed. Antoine Compagnon. Paris: Editions Gallimard, 1988.
Le côté de Guermantes I. Ed. Thierry Laget. Paris: Editions Gallimard, 1988.
Le côté de Guermantes II. Ed. Thierry Laget and Brian Rogers. Paris: Editions Gallimard, 1988.
A l'ombre des jeunes filles en fleurs. Ed. Pierre-Louis Rey. Paris: Editions Gallimard, 1988.
On Reading Ruskin: Prefaces to La Bible d'Amiens *and* Sésame et les lys *with Selections from the Notes to the Translated Texts*. Trans. and eds. Jean Autret, William Burford, and Phillip J. Wolfe. Intro. Richard Macksey. New Haven and London: Yale University Press, 1987.
La prisonnière. Ed. Pierre-Edmond Robert. Paris: Editions Gallimard, 1989.
Sodome et Gomorrhe. Ed. Antoine Compagnon. Paris: Editions Gallimard, 1989.
Sur la lecture. 1906. Ed. Jacques Antoine. Paris: Le Vice Impuni, 1985.
Le temps retrouvé. Ed. Pierre-Louis Rey and Brian Rogers. Paris: Editions Gallimard, 1990.
Raffel, Burton, trans. *Père Goriot (Old Goriot)*. By Honoré de Balzac. Ed. Peter Brooks. New York and London: W. W. Norton, 1994.
Richard, Jean-Pierre. *Etudes sur le romantisme*. Paris: Editions du Seuil, 1971.
Proust et le monde sensible. Paris: Editions du Seuil, 1974.
Robb, Graham. *Balzac: A Biography*. London: Picador, 1994.
Robinson, Kenneth. *Wilkie Collins: A Biography*. London: The Bodley Head, 1951.
Ruskin, John. *Complete Works*. Ed. E. T. Cook and Alexander Wedderburn. Library Edition. 39 vols. Vol. V. London: George Allen. New York: Longman, 1904.
Sesame and Lilies. 1865. London: Merrill and Baker, 1888.
Rybczynski, Witold. *Home: A Short History of an Idea*. New York and London: Penguin, 1987.
Scott, Sir Walter. Review of *Emma*. By Jane Austen. *Quarterly Review* (1816), 188–201; rptd. Southam, ed., *Jane Austen*, vol. I, 58–69.
Sedgwick, Eve Kosfsky. *Epistemology of the Closet*. Berkeley and Los Angeles: University of California Press, 1990.
Sennett, Richard. *The Fall of Public Man: On the Social Psychology of Capitalism*. New York: Vintage Books, 1978.
Shattuck, Roger. *Proust's Binoculars: A Study of Memory, Time, and Recognition in* A la recherche du temps perdu. New York: Knopf, 1963; Princeton: Princeton University Press, 1983.
Shires, Linda M., ed. *Rewriting the Victorians: Theory, History, and the Politics of Gender*. New York and London: Routledge, 1992.
Showalter, Elaine. *The Female Malady: Women, Madness, and English Culture 1830–1980*. New York: Pantheon Books, 1985.

Shuttleworth, Sally. "Demonic Motherhood: Ideologies of Bourgeois Motherhood in the Mid-Victorian Era." Shires, ed., *Rewriting the Victorians*, 31–51.

Sicher, Efraim. "The Boundaries of Space in the Modern Literary Text: Balzac, Dostoevsky, Dickens." Eds. Roger Bauer and Douwe Fokkema. *Proceedings of the XIIth Congress of the International Comparative Literature Association. Volume III: Space and Boundaries in Literature*. 5 vols. Munich: Iudicium, 1990, 306–09.

Silverman, Kaja. *The Acoustic Mirror: The Female Voice in Psychoanalysis and Cinema*. Bloomington: Indiana University Press, 1988.

  Male Subjectivity at the Margins. New York and London: Routledge, 1992.

  The Threshold of the Visible World. New York and London: Routledge, 1996.

Simmel, Georg. *The Sociology of Georg Simmel*. Trans., ed., and intro. Kurt H. Wolff. New York: Free Press, 1964.

Simpson, Richard. Unsigned review of *A Memoir of Jane Austen* by James Edward Austen-Leigh. *The North British Review* 52 (April 1870): 129–421; rptd. Southam, ed., *Jane Austen*, vol. I, 241–65.

Southam, B. C., ed. *Jane Austen: The Critical Heritage*. 2 vols. Vol. I. London: Routledge and Kegan Paul; New York: Barnes and Noble, 1968.

  Jane Austen: The Critical Heritage, 1870–1940. 2 vols. Vol. II. London and New York: Routledge and Kegan Paul, 1987.

Spacks, Patricia Meyer. *Gossip*. Chicago and London: University of Chicago Press, 1986.

  "Muted Discord: Conflict in Jane Austen." Monaghan, ed., *Jane Austen in a Social Context*, 159–79.

Stallybrass, Peter, and Allon White. *The Politics and Poetics of Transgression*. Ithaca: Cornell University Press, 1986.

Stewart, J. L. "Wilkie Collins as Novelist." Page, ed., *Wilkie Collins*, 224–29.

Stone, Lawrence. *The Road to Divorce: England 1530–87*. Oxford: Oxford University Press, 1990.

Stout, Janis P. *Strategies of Reticence: Silence and Meaning in the Works of Jane Austen, Willa Cather, Katherine Anne Porter, and Joan Didion*. Charlottesville and London: University Press of Virginia, 1990.

Stowe, William W. *Balzac, James, and the Realistic Novel*. Princeton: Princeton University Press, 1983.

Strachey, James, trans. and ed. "Editor's Note." *The Standard Edition of the Complete Psychological Works of Sigmund Freud*. 24 vols. Vol. VII. London: The Hogarth Press, 1953, 125–29.

Sucksmith, Harvey Peter, ed. "Introduction." *The Woman in White*. By Wilkie Collins. Oxford and New York: Oxford University Press, 1989.

Sutherland, John. "Wilkie Collins and the Origins of the Sensation Novel." *Dickens Studies Annual* 20 (1991): 243–58.

Swanson, Janice Bowman. "Toward a Rhetoric of Self: The Art of *Persuasion*." *Nineteenth-Century Fiction* 36.1 (1981): 1–21.

Talon, Henri. "*Dombey and Son*: A Closer Look at the Text." *Dickens Studies Annual* 1 (1970): 147–60.
Tanner, Tony. *Jane Austen*. Cambridge, MA: Harvard University Press, 1986.
  "In Between: Anne Elliot Marries a Sailor and Charlotte Heywood Goes to the Seaside." Monaghan, ed., *Jane Austen in a Social Context*, 180–94.
Tave, Stuart. *Some Words of Jane Austen*. Chicago and London: University of Chicago Press, 1973.
Taylor, Jenny Bourne. *In the Secret Theatre of Home: Wilkie Collins, Sensation Narrative, and Nineteenth-Century Psychology*. New York and London: Routledge, 1988.
Terrasse-Riou, Florence. "Les enjeux de la représentation d'un seuil: l'hôtel de Chaulieu." Mahieu and Schuerewegen, eds., *Balzac*, 47–55.
Thackeray, William Makepeace. *Vanity Fair*. 1847–48. Oxford and New York: Oxford University Press, 1983.
Thomas, Ronald R. *Detective Fiction and the Rise of Forensic Science*. Cambridge and New York: Cambridge University Press, 1999.
  "Wilkie Collins and the Sensation Novel." *The Columbia History of the British Novel*. Ed. John Richetti. New York: Columbia University Press, 1994.
Thompson, James. "Jane Austen and the Limits of Language." *Journal of English and Germanic Philology* 85.4 (1986): 510–31.
Thoms, Peter. *The Windings of the Labyrinth: Quest and Structure in the Major Novels of Wilkie Collins*. Athens, OH: University of Ohio Press, 1992.
Tillotson, Kathleen. *Novels of the Eighteen-Forties*. Oxford: Clarendon Press, 1956.
Todd, Janet, ed. and intro. *Jane Austen: New Perspectives*. Women and Literature, n.s., 3. New York and London: Holmes and Meier, 1983.
Todorov, Tzvetan. *The Poetics of Prose*. Foreword Jonathan Culler. Trans. Richard Howard. Ithaca: Cornell University Press, 1977.
Trilling, Lionel. *Sincerity and Authenticity*. Cambridge, MA: Harvard University Press, 1972.
Tristram, Philippa. *Living Space in Fact and Fiction*. New York and London: Routledge, 1989.
Trodd, Anthea. "Household Spies: The Servant and the Plot in Victorian Fiction." *Literature and History* 13.2 (1987): 175–87.
Tucker, Herbert F. "Dramatic Monologue and the Overhearing of Lyric." *Lyric Poetry Beyond New Criticism*. Ed. Chaviva Hosek and Patricia Parker. Ithaca and London: Cornell University Press, 1985, 21–36.
Vachon, Stéphan, ed. *Balzac: Une poétique du roman*. Montreal: XYZ Editeur, 1996.
Vanoncini, André. "Quête et enquête dans le roman balzacien." Vachon, ed., *Balzac*, 173–80.
Varey, Simon. *Space and the Eighteenth-Century English Novel*. Cambridge and New York: Cambridge University Press, 1990.
Vernon, John. "Reading, Writing, and Eavesdropping: Some Thoughts on the Nature of Realistic Fiction." *The Kenyon Review* 4.4 (1982): 44–54.
Waring, James, trans. *Cousin Bette*. By Honoré de Balzac. London: Everyman's Library, 1991.

Watt, Ian. *The Rise of the Novel*. Berkeley: University of California Press, 1957.
Watt, Ian, ed. and intro. *Jane Austen: A Collection of Critical Essays. Twentieth-Century Views*. Englewood Cliffs: Prentice-Hall, 1963.
Welsh, Alexander. *George Eliot and Blackmail*. Cambridge, MA: Harvard University Press, 1985.
Whately, Richard. Unsigned review of *Northanger Abbey* and *Persuasion*. *Quarterly Review* 24 (January 1821): 352–76; rptd. Southam, ed., *Jane Austen*, vol. I, 87–105.
Williams, Raymond. *The English Novel from Dickens to Lawrence*. London: Chatto and Windus, 1970.
  The Country and the City. New York: Oxford University Press, 1973.
Willis, Lesley H. "Eyes and the Imagery of Sight in *Pride and Prejudice*." *English Studies in Canada* 2 (1976): 156–62.
Wright, Andrew H. "*Persuasion*." Watt, ed., *Jane Austen*, 145–53.
Zimring, Rishona. "Conrad's Pornography Shop." *Modern Fiction Studies* 43.2 (1997): 319–48.

Index

Ackroyd, Peter, 101, 205
Arac, Jonathan, 206
Ariès, Philippe, 201
Armstrong, Frances, 205
Armstrong, Nancy, 183
Auerbach, Erich, 202
Auerbach, Nina, 125, 211
Austen, Jane, 1, 18–20, 27–28, 63, 64, 169, 187
    Emma, 41, 56, 183, 188, 192
    Letters, 191
    Mansfield Park, 55, 189, 192, 194
    Northanger Abbey, 44
    Persuasion, 18–19, 22, 28, 42–57
    Pride and Prejudice, 18–19, 28–42, 50, 187
    Sense and Sensibility, 196
autobiography, 164, 218

Babb, Howard S., 195, 197
Bachelard, Gaston, 185
Bakhtin, Mikhail, 33, 181, 189
    chronotope, concept of, 16
    on "dialogue," 190
    on the novel, 3, 4, 180, 189
    on "situatedness," 17, 197
Balée, Susan, 207, 210, 212
Balzac, Honoré de, 1, 20–22, 57, 58–65, 67, 71–73, 104, 171, 174
    Le Colonel Chabert, 204
    La comédie humaine, 6, 22
    Eugénie Grandet, 63, 220
    La fille aux yeux d'or, 220
    Lettres, 200
    La maison Nucingen, 6
    Les parents pauvres, 15, 62, 72–73, 83–85, 95, 98
        La Cousine Bette, 21, 67, 71, 72, 85–94, 96
        Le Cousin Pons, 21, 94–100
    Le Père Goriot, 21, 62, 71, 73–83, 96
    Sarrasine, 32, 187
    Splendeurs et misères des courtisanes, 83
Barickman, Richard, 207, 210

Baron, Anne-Marie, 201, 203
Barthes, Roland, 26–28, 32, 39, 42, 125, 183, 215, 217, 218
Beaumarchais, Pierre-Augustin Caron de, 3
Beizer, Janet, 203
Bell, David, 203
Benjamin, Walter, 12, 182, 191
Bentham, Jeremy, 127
Bersani, Leo, 213, 215, 216
boundaries, *see* walls
Bowen, Peter, 183
Bowie, Malcolm, 216
Braddon, Mary Elizabeth, 136
Brantlinger, Patrick, 184
Brée, Germaine, 215
Brennan, Teresa, 179
Brontë, Charlotte, 27–28, 115, 137
    Jane Eyre, 13, 130, 183
Brontë, Emily, 27
    Wuthering Heights, 10–13, 26, 27, 137
Brooks, Peter, 22, 180, 182, 200, 214, 216
Brown, Julia Prewitt, 195, 196
Brown, Lloyd W., 189, 193
Browne, Hablot, 107
Bryson, Norman, 179
Burney, Frances, 4, 29
    Cecilia, 29
    Evelina, 29–30, 40
Butler, Judith, 217
Butler, Marilyn, 188, 195
Butor, Michel, 9

Carlson, Thomas B., 184
Castle, Terry, 212
Cavell, Stanley, 37, 38
Cervantes, Miguel de, 180–181
Chandler, Alice, 195
Chandler, Marilyn R., 199
Chase, Karen, 60, 181, 198, 200, 201, 202
Clark, Herbert H., 184
Clarke, William M., 212

Collins, Wilkie, 1, 215
  Armadale, 135
  The Law and the Lady, 135–136
  The Moonstone, 12
  No Name, 135, 137
  The Woman in White, 22–24, 63, 111–138, 174
communication, 28, 31, 37, 39, 43
Compagnon, Antoine, 214, 216, 218
concierge, *see portière*
confession, 133
Conrad, Joseph, 167–176
  The Secret Agent, 167–176
  Under Western Eyes, 220
conversation, 10, 31, 170
  in Jane Austen's novels, 19, 37–38, 40, 45, 52–54
  and Bakhtin's concept of "dialogue," 190
  see also Milton, John
Crary, Jonathan, 200, 201
Crémieux, Benjamin, 214
Cruikshank, George, 63
Culler, Jonathan, 183
curiosity, 5, 7–8, 22, 25, 34, 79, 83, 138, 147–148, 153–154
Cvetkovich, Ann, 207

Daguerre, Louis-Jacques-Mandé, 200
Dante Alighieri, 214
Deaucourt, Jean-Louis, 205
Debarre-Blanchard, Anne, 202
Deleuze, Gilles, 218
de Man, Paul, 215
desire, 24, 142, 144, 152, 155–156, 164
  epistemological, *see* epistemophilia
  narrative, 23, 129, 138, 140–141, 162
  and reading, 150–151, 162–163
  sexual, 138, 146, 162
Dickens, Charles, 1, 7, 13, 20–22, 57–65, 73, 169
  Bleak House, 12, 102, 219–220
  Great Expectations, 102, 158
  Dombey and Son, 7, 12, 13, 21–22, 54, 60, 62, 71, 100–111, 168–169
  Letters, 212
  Little Dorrit, 60
  Oliver Twist, 6, 63
  Our Mutual Friend, 169
Dickinson, Linzy Erika, 201
Diderot, Denis, 3
domestic architecture, 61, 156
  history of, 20, 65–73
domestic ideology, 15, 58–59, 62, 99, 172
  see also home, concept of
Donaghy, Mary, 209, 211

Donzelot, Jacques, 199
Doubrovsky, Serge, 216
drama, *see* theater
Duby, Georges, 201
Duckworth, Alistair, 192, 195, 196
Dupuis, Danielle, 200

eavesdropping
  definitions of, 2, 22, 101, 106
  in other languages, 2–3, 101
  set-up, 12, 19, 24, 49–51, 159–160, 164, 180, 181, 184
  theory of, 7–18
Eleb-Vidal, Monique, 202
Eliot, George, 115, 137
  Adam Bede, 115
  Middlemarch, 14, 64, 184
epistemophilia, 7–8, 23, 24, 34, 150–153, 162, 177
  definition of, 140, 182
epistolary fiction, 66
Erickson, Joyce Quiring, 197
espionage, 18, 167
Evans, Robin, 73, 201

Fanger, Donald, 200
Farrant, Tim, 199–200
Farrell, Thomas J., 193
Farrer, Reginald, 28
Finch, Casey, 183
Flaubert, Gustave, 220
Ford, Ford Maddox, 221
Forster, E. M., 214
Fortin, Nina E., 212
Foucault, Michel, 11, 127, 183–184, 186, 199
Frank, Ellen, 199
Freud, Sigmund, 151–152, 216
  primal scene, 151
Fuentes, Carlos, 180

Garrett, Peter K., 185
Garrod, H. W., 197
Gaskell, Elizabeth, 137
Gasson, Andrew, 207
gender, 23, 42, 43, 47, 51–52, 57
  and domestic space, 69–70
  and narrative agency, 51, 52, 112, 115–138
  see also women
Genette, Gérard, 14, 182, 218
Gide, André, 4, 163
Gilbert, Sandra, 195, 196, 197, 212
Gillis, Christina Marsden, 199, 201
Girouard, Mark, 201, 202
Goffman, Erving, 16–17, 200
Gordon, Jan B., 183

gossip, 32–33, 48, 64, 75, 107–108, 183, 189
Gray, Margaret E., 213, 218
Greene, Donald, 197
Greimas, A. J., 185
Grosz, Elizabeth, 185
Gubar Susan, 195, 196, 197, 212

Habermas, Jürgen, 9, 54, 58, 181
Hall, Catherine, 198, 201
Hamon, Philippe, 61, 202
Haraway, Donna, 17
Harding, D. W., 188, 191, 194
Hardy, Barbara, 43, 192, 194, 195
Hart, Francis B., 197
Hayman, Ronald, 213, 218
Heller, Tamar, 115, 136, 207, 208
Helsinger, Elizabeth, 211, 212
Hennedy, Hugh, 192, 194
Hennelly, Mark, Jr., 188, 189, 210
Holly, Michael Ann, 179
Holquist, J. Michael, 17
home, concept of, 18, 21–22, 52–53, 57, 100–111, 175, 196
  see also domestic ideology
homosexuality, 121–122, 152–153, 163–164, 217
Honan, Park, 191
Hughes, Winifred, 207, 210
Hunt, Lynn, 198

identity, 146, 150, 164, 168, 174–176
  fashioning of, 10–12, 18, 112, 184
  and gender, 5, 22, 113–138
  sexual, 24, 123, 138, 140, 152–153, 159
information society, 4
information technology, 5, 14, 24–25, 60, 64
interpretation, 9, 27
Irigaray, Luce, 214
irony, 125

James, Henry, 185, 201, 221
Jay, Martin, 179, 214
Jenks, Chris, 179
Johnson, Claudia, 188, 193, 195
Johnson, Samuel, 190
judgment, 28–29, 31, 32, 35, 36, 121

Kaplan, Deborah, 195
Kendrick, Walter M., 208, 211, 212
Kermode, Frank, 185, 204
Kerr, Robert, 68
Kettle, Arnold, 197
Kirkham, Margaret, 195
Knoepflmacher, U. C., 208, 209, 210, 212
Kohon, Gregorio, 214

Kozloff, Sarah, 180
Kucich, John, 181, 184

Lacan, Jacques, 179, 184
La Fayette, Marie-Madeleine Pioche de La Vergne, comtesse de, 180–181
Lang, Andrew, 208
Langbauer, Laurie, 210
Lanser, Susan Snaider, 185, 192, 193
Lascelles, Mary, 194
law, 23, 37–38, 88, 117–118, 121, 127, 190
Lefebvre, Henri, 198
Leicht, Thomas M., 219
Lesage, Alain-René, 13
  Le diable boiteux, 13, 185
Levenson, Michael, 60, 181, 185, 198, 200, 201, 202
Levine, George, 186
liminality, 2, 122–123, 125–126, 152
Litvak, Joseph, 180, 215, 217, 218, 219
Litz, A. Walton, 188, 194
Loesberg, Jonathan, 207, 210
Lonoff, Sue, 207
Lorant, André, 204
Loyer, François, 199, 202

MacDonald, Susan, 207, 210
Mack, Arien, 198
madness, 119–122
Mansart, François, 69
Marcus, Sharon, 61, 98, 186, 201, 203, 204, 205
Marivaux, Pierre Carlet de Chamblain de, 3
Markus, Thomas A., 199
Maudsley, Henry, 210
May, Leila Silvana, 209
McCuskey, Brian, 181, 185, 202
McGregor, Graham, 9, 27, 182
McGuire, James, 205
McLaughlin, Kevin, 200
melodrama, 4, 180, 200, 214
Metz, Christian, 185
Meyersohn, Marylea, 191, 192
Mill, John Stuart, 180
Miller, D. A., 26–27, 187
  on *The Woman in White*, 121–122, 123, 208, 209, 211
Miller, J. Hillis, 185
Miller, Nancy K., 180
Milner, Max, 199
Milton, John, 37–38
Miner, Earl, 193
Mitchell, W. J. T., 179
Moler, Kenneth, 188, 189
Molière (Jean-Baptiste Poquelin), 3
Monaghan, David, 190, 195, 196

Moretti, Franco, 31, 36, 189, 209, 221
Morris, Robert, 201
Moss, Howard, 213, 214, 217
Moxley, Keith, 179
Mudrick, Marvin, 194

narrative
　agency, 7, 20, 22, 43–45, 51, *see also* gender
　closure, 7, 10, 40–43, 122
　voice, 12–14, 185
　　first-person, 12, 13, 160–161, 163, 218
　　third-person, 12–15, 84, 98, 106, 161
Neefs, Jacques, 200
Nesci, Catherine, 201
Neuman, Robert, 202
Newman, Karen, 192, 195, 197

O'Connor, Frank, 191
O'Farrell, Mary Ann, 184
Ong, Walter J., 184
O'Neill, Philip, 209, 210
Orange, Michael, 192

paranoia, 22, 59, 176
parlor, 16, 19, 56, 169–170
Perec, Georges, 201
performance, 39–40, 89, 142–145, 159
　see also theatricality
Perkins, Pamela, 209, 211
Perrot, Michelle, 81, 181, 198, 201, 202
Peters, Catherine, 212
Poovey, Mary, 180, 193, 194, 195, 196
Porter, Roy, 202
portière, 21, 83–84, 94–98
police, 81, 92, 167, 176
Preiss, Nathalie, 200
Prendergast, Christopher, 60
Proust, Marcel, 1, 8, 171, 176
　Correspondance, 215, 218
　"Journées de lecture," 219
　À la recherche du temps perdu, 8, 23–24, 138–166, 167
　　Du côté de chez Swann, 24, 141–146, 150, 182
　　Sodome et Gomorrhe, 24, 141, 146–153
　　Le temps retrouvé, 24, 140, 141, 153–156, 158, 164–166
publicity, 4–5, 18, 59, 111

realism, 60, 62, 138, 161
Richard, Jean-Pierre, 199, 214, 216
Richardson, Samuel, 4, 30
Rivière, Jacques, 218
Robb, Graham, 84

Ruskin, John, 139, 198, 219
Rybczynski, Witold, 66, 102, 198, 201

Sand, George, 150
scopophilia, 151
secrecy, secrets, 9, 12, 53, 76, 169, 175, 187
Sedgwick, Eve Kosofsky, 187, 214, 216, 217, 218
separate spheres, ideology of, 5, 18, 20, 70, 111
　denial of, 23, 59–62, 100–101, 167, 168
Sennett, Richard, 58, 181, 201
servants, 7, 62, 64, 67–69, 72, 108, 172–173
Shakespeare, William, 3, 10
Shattuck, Roger, 213, 215
Sheets, Robin Lauterbach, 211, 212
Sheridan, Richard Brinsley, 3
Showalter, Elaine, 209
Shuttleworth, Sally, 207
Sicher, Efraim, 200
Silverman, Kaja, 179, 184, 185, 216, 218
Simmel, Georg, 179, 182
Simpson, Richard, 191
Smollett, Tobias, 4
Spacks, Patricia Meyer, 181, 182, 183, 206
Stallybrass, Peter, 186
Stark, Myra, 207, 210
Stone, Lawrence, 190
Stout, Janice P., 193, 194, 195
Strachey, James, 216
subjectivity, 1, 176, 177, 179, 183–184
surveillance, 25, 71, 172, 176
suspicion, 31–32, 176
Sutherland, John, 209
Swanson, Janice Bowman, 194
Symons, Julian, 210

Talon, Henri, 206
Tanner, Tony, 28, 43, 189, 194
Tave, Stuart, 43, 192
Taylor, Jenny Bourne, 209, 210
Terrasse-Riou, Florence, 203
Thackeray, William, 5–6
theater, 3–4, 65, 180
theatricality, 91, 143–145, 180, 217
　see also performance
Thomas, Ronald R., 207, 219
Thompson, James, 195
Thoms, Peter, 115
Tillotson, Kathleen, 206
threshold, 16, 83, 165
Todd, Janet, 189
transgression, 7, 16, 23, 25, 43, 113–138, 140, 156
trespass, 2, 37, 118, 152
Trilling, Lionel, 190
Tristram, Philippa, 199, 206

Trodd, Anthea, 202
Tuchman, Gaye, 212
Tucker, Herbert F., 180

Vanoncini, André, 199
Varey, Simon, 199
Veeder, William, 211, 212
Vernon, John, 181
Voyeurism, 15, 39, 140, 152, 179, 186

Walker, Frederick, 113
walls, 61–62, 74, 162–163, 170
    social role of, 16–17, 20, 56, 71, 158, 174–175
Watt, Ian, 181, 189
Weis, Elizabeth, 179
Welsh, Alexander, 181
Wharton, Edith, 188, 201, 220

Whately, Richard, 191
White, Allon, 186
White, Burton L., 216
Williams, Raymond, 54, 198
Willis, Lesley H., 189, 190
Wollstonecraft, Mary, 128
women, 56
    and agency, 19, 42, 45, 48–51, 176, 194
    see also gender
Wood, Mrs. Henry (Ellen), 136
Wyler, William, 26

Yates, Edmund, 211

Zimring, Rishona, 220
Zola, Emile
    Nana, 69
    Pot-bouille, 23

CAMBRIDGE STUDIES IN NINETEENTH-CENTURY
LITERATURE AND CULTURE

General editor
Gillian Beer, *University of Cambridge*

Titles published

1. The Sickroom in Victorian Fiction
The Art of Being Ill
by Miriam Bailin, *Washington University*

2. Muscular Christianity
Embodying the Victorian Age
edited by Donald E. Hall, *California State University, Northridge*

3. Victorian Masculinities: Manhood and Masculine Poetics in Early
Victorian Literature and Art
by Herbert Sussman, *Northeastern University, Boston*

4. Byron and the Victorians
by Andrew Elfenbein, *University of Minnesota*

5. Literature in the Marketplace
Nineteenth-Century British Publishing and the Circulation of Books
edited by John O. Jordan, *University of California, Santa Cruz*
and Robert L. Patten, *Rice University, Houston*

6. Victorian Photography, Painting and Poetry
by Lindsay Smith, *University of Sussex*

7. Charlotte Brontë and Victorian Psychology
by Sally Shuttleworth, *University of Sheffield*

8. The Gothic Body
Sexuality, Materialism, and Degeneration at the Fin de Siècle
by Kelly Hurley, *University of Colorado at Boulder*

9. Rereading Walter Pater
by William F. Shuter, *Eastern Michigan University*

10. Remaking Queen Victoria
edited by Margaret Homans, *Yale University*
and Adrienne Munich, *State University of New York, Stony Brook*

11. Disease, Desire, and the Body in Victorian Women's Popular Novels
by Pamela K. Gilbert, *University of Florida*

12. Realism, Representation, and the Arts in Nineteenth-Century Literature
by Alison Byerly, *Middlebury College, Vermont*

13. Literary Culture and the Pacific
by Vanessa Smith, *University of Sydney*

14. Professional Domesticity in the Victorian Novel
Women, Work, and Home
by Monica F. Cohen

15. Victorian Renovations of the Novel
Narrative Annexes and the Boundaries of Representation
by Suzanne Keen, *Washington and Lee University, Virginia*

16. Actresses on the Victorian Stage
Feminine Performance and the Galatea Myth
by Gail Marshall, *University of Leeds*

17. Death and the Mother from Dickens to Freud
Victorian Fiction and the Anxiety of Origin
by Carolyn Dever, *Vanderbilt University, Tennessee*

18. Ancestry and Narrative in Nineteenth-Century British Literature
Blood Relations from Edgeworth to Hardy
by Sophie Gilmartin, *Royal Holloway College, University of London*

19. Dickens, Novel Reading, and the Victorian Popular Theatre
by Deborah Vlock

20. After Dickens
Reading, Adaptation, and Performance
by John Glavin, *Georgetown University, Washington DC*

21. Victorian Women Writers and the Woman Question
by Nicola Diane Thompson, *Kingston University, London*

22. Rhythm and Will in Victorian Poetry
by Matthew Campbell, *University of Sheffield*

23. Gender, Race, and the Writing of Empire
Public Discourse and the Boer War
by Paula M. Krebs, *Wheaton College, Massachusetts*

24. Ruskin's God
by Michael Wheeler

25. Dickens and the Daughter of the House
by Hilary M. Schor, *University of Southern California*

26. Detective Fiction and the Rise of Forensic Science
by Ronald R. Thomas, *Trinity College, Hartford, Connecticut*

27. Testimony and Advocacy in Victorian Law, Literature, and Theology
by Jan-Melissa Schramm, *Trinity Hall, Cambridge*

28. Victorian Writing about Risk
Imagining a Safe England in a Dangerous World
by Elaine Freedgood, *University of Pennsylvania*

29. Physiognomy and the Meaning of Expression in
Nineteenth-Century Culture
by Lucy Hartley, *University of Southampton*

30. The Victorian Parlour
A Cultural Study
by Thad Logan, *Rice University, Houston*

31. Aestheticism and Sexual Parody 1840–1940
by Dennis Denisoff, *Ryerson University, Toronto*

32. Literature, Technology, and Magical Thinking 1880–1920
by Pamela Thurschwell, *University College, London*

33. Fairies in Nineteenth-Century Art and Literature
by Nicola Bown, *Birkbeck College, London*

34. George Eliot and the British Empire
by Nancy Henry, *The State University of New York, Binghamton*

35. Women's Poetry and Religion in Victorian England
Jewish Identity and Christian Culture
by Cynthia Scheinberg, *Mills College, California*

36. Victorian Literature and the Anorexic Body
by Anna Krugovoy Silver, *Mercer University, Georgia*

37. Eavesdropping in the Novel from Austen to Proust
by Ann Gaylin, *Yale University, Connecticut*

OHIO UNIVERSITY LIBRARY

Please return this book as soon as you have finished with it. In order to avoid a fine it must be returned by the latest date stamped below. All books are subject to recall after two weeks or immediately if needed for reserve.

JUN 1 7 2003

MAY 2 4 2004

CF